The Solar Greenhouse Book

The Solar Greenhouse Book

Edited by James C. McCullagh

Assistant Editor: Jack Ruttle
Technical Consultant: Herb Wade
Illustrated by: Roy H. McCullagh

With Contributions from:
David J. MacKinnon
James B. DeKorne
Leandre Poisson
John White
Conrad Heeschen

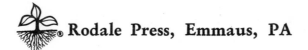 Rodale Press, Emmaus, PA

Printed in the United States of America on recycled paper

Library of Congress Cataloging in Publication Data
Main entry under title:

The Solar greenhouse book.

    Bibliography: p.
    Includes index.
      1. Solar greenhouses—Design and construction.
2. Greenhouse gardening. 3. Vegetable gardening.
I. McCullagh, James C.
SB416.S64   631.5′4   77-17028
ISBN 0-87857-198-1 hardcover
ISBN 0-87857-222-8 paperback

            8 10 9   hardcover
            8 10 9 7 paperback

Raise High the Solar Greenhouse, Carpenter

Place your hand in the sun
like an oak length of beam,
turn your wrist until the roots
of the pulp deliver muscle
and sap to the garden roof.
Walk the property line
like a child, swaggering and sure,
marking with your toe the axis
which is as flush as equator heat.
Raise your arms overhead
like a sextant
bringing down the heavens in an arc
making an A with your hands
and imagine what green will sprout
from that blessed plot.

James C. McCullagh

Table of Contents

Acknowledgments

The Solar Greenhouse Book represents the work of many people, both in America and Canada, who see the greenhouse as an appropriate technology device which can furnish both food and heat. This book would not have been completed without them.

My special thanks to the contributors, to Jack Ruttle for his editorial assistance, and to Herb Wade for his technical advice.

I am grateful to the many solar greenhouse operators throughout the country who generously shared their experiences and their findings with us, to W. Doug Davis who prepared "Some Regional Considerations Concerning Glazing Materials" (in Chapter Four) and Appendix I, to David Kruschke, Karen Funk, George and Pamela de Alth, and Dan Knapp who supplied information for Chapter Fourteen, to Diane Matthews and Bob Flower who recorded the Maxatawny, Pennsylvania, greenhouse experience, to ACCESS Projects (University of Wisconsin School of Architecture) for information on solar greenhouse developments in Milwaukee, to Greg Mackie for his insights concerning greenhouse construction in the Southwest and to T. L. Gettings and John Hamil of the Rodale Photo Lab. And my thanks to Melvin Goldberg of Practical Solar Heat for use of a multipoint recording thermometer in the Maxatawny greenhouse.

Quoted material has been reproduced, by special permission of MIT Press, Cambridge, Massachusetts, from *The Glass House* by John Hix, 1974.

James C. McCullagh

Introduction

The solar greenhouse occupies a point where high and low technology intersect; where formal research has applications to low-technology living.

The solar greenhouse is an appropriate-technology tool which can be geared to the needs of people in rural, urban, and suburban areas.

The solar greenhouse is an exciting "growth chamber" which offers more than hope for extending the growing season; it offers the real possibility of year-round growth.

And the attached greenhouse, which is surely one of the least-costly and most-efficient solar collectors "on the market" today, can supply approximately 50 percent of a home's heat requirement—and more if nighttime shutters are installed.

The interest in solar greenhouses comes at a time when the energy used in food production—approximately 16 percent—is increasing faster than energy used in other sections of the economy. According to David Pimentel of Cornell University, the one-pound can of sweet corn is a good example of how energy-intensive our food production has become. "The one-pound can contains about 375 kilocalories of food energy. But its production requires about 450 kilocalories of fossil energy for planting, cultivating, fertilizing, and harvesting, and an additional

1,760 kilocalories to can it, and about 800 kilocalories to bring it home, via the family car, to the consumer."

The interest in solar greenhouses comes at a time when the nation is experiencing the vagaries of climate: severe winters in the Northeast and Midwest; prolonged dry spells in the West and Southwest. And the effects of severe winter weather are borne by the commercial houses and, in turn, by the consumer.

And the interest in the solar greenhouse comes at a time when 60 percent of the fresh vegetables consumed in the country are grown in California and Florida.

It has been in this "climate" that *The Solar Greenhouse Book* has been written.

The Solar Greenhouse Book is a modest attempt to marry the fine work of formal researchers with the fine work of many informal, "backyard" researchers. And there is a surprising convergence of ideas. For example, it is not unusual for a "backyard" researcher to arrive at the same solar-greenhouse design principles as a formal researcher but by a different route.

The reader will note a "proliferation of I's" in the text, representing the various contributors who have been actively engaged in some phase of solar greenhouse or solar cold-frame work. Thus, the contributors (as well as the other voices you will hear throughout the text), speak out of their personal experiences.

The first part of the book explores all essential design features of the solar greenhouse, including the collector, insulation, storage, glazing, and weather. This part concludes with recommendations for minimum design criteria for glazing, night curtains, perimeter insulation, R-value of interior insulation, and water storage for all sections of the country.

But the first part is the background music against which the rest of the book is played. The chapters on freestanding greenhouses, attached greenhouses, pit greenhouses, and solar cold frames, not only provide construction details, but also provide numerous examples of structures from diverse regions of the country with emphasis on significant design detail. For example, on a "porch" greenhouse in Milwaukee, perhaps the night shutters are of interest. Or, in a greenhouse in Occidental, California, perhaps the sauna attachment to the greenhouse is noteworthy.

However, the book moves throughout towards the essence of the solar greenhouse: plant production. The subject is treated generously in Part II within the context of specific greenhouses. In Part III vegetable production in the solar greenhouse is explored in detail with special attention to CO_2, humidity, and composting methods. Furthermore, this part includes firsthand reports from gardeners in various sections of the country who report their growing experiences in the solar greenhouse.

Interestingly, many of the greenhouses featured in *The Solar Greenhouse Book* successfully grew plants during one of the severest winters in memory, providing convincing evidence that the solar greenhouse does indeed work.

A major theme of this work is that there is a solar greenhouse for every home, for every climate, for every need. For the open field, the garden, the center-city rooftop; attached to the house, a garage, a toolshed, a barn, a porch; at schools, hospitals, retirement homes. . . .

Part I

Designing the Solar Greenhouse

Chapter One

Climate Control

David J. MacKinnon

Climate control refers to actions which change and/or maintain the climate at a state different from its natural (uncontrolled) state. The methods for achieving climate control depend on the results desired and the resources and technology available. Indeed, climate control is at the very heart of man's struggle for survival.

Climate controls the bounty of the plant world, which in turn, controls the migration, behavior, and population regimes of the animal world. Primitive man largely adapted and flourished according to these same patterns. Eventually, a more refined application of fire, shelter, and of food production and storage began to reduce man's nomadic dependences. With the domestication of stock and the development of field agriculture, generations could be born and buried on the same ground. Yet, man was not freed from the vagaries of climatic change: drought and flood, heat and cold, often created severe hardships on an otherwise tolerable existence.

Modern man has coupled energy and technology to provide small-scale climate control. A central-air heating system has replaced the simple wood fire; a refrigerator-freezer now serves as a year-round snowbank. In spite of all these great achievements in personal comfort, relatively few advances have been realized in climate control for field agriculture. The reason is simple: field agriculture is just too extensive. The great grain, fruit, and vegetable fields which collect the sun's energy and fuel the organic engines of land-based mammals are still at the mercy of the climate.

Fertilizers, pesticides, and mechanization have dramatically increased field-crop productivity. Yet, world populations have increased almost in proportion to the productivity, thus limiting food reserves. Furthermore, evidence shows the energy-intensive countries are now nearing the limit of field-crop production within the constraints of the natural climate. Small wonder that experts feel climate is the single greatest factor determining world agricultural productivity. Population, climate, and now, the energy crisis, have placed man in triple jeopardy, a Pandora's box which can remain closed only by change.

Signs of change are beginning to surface at many levels. Alternative sources of energy and energy conservation have become a national concern. Climate control for shelter and food production, requiring low energy and resource input, is catching the interest of modern societies, not *now* so much as a means for a new life-style, but as a hedge against economic bankruptcy. Early indications are that the nonrenewable energy needs for shelter can be significantly reduced by solar and energy conservation technology. Unfortunately, outside of large-scale weather control (a very distant reality whose side effects cannot even be imagined), open-field agriculture appears headed for little change. On the smaller scale, however, many climate-control techniques, both old and new, indicate that man will be able to grow food year-round at the community and individual level throughout diverse climatic regimes.

Climate Control Techniques

It is almost impossible to specify just what is and what is not climate control. For example, one might expect irrigation to be used only for a plant's water and nutrient needs. Yet, irrigation has been successfully used for many years on otherwise well-watered plants to provide frost control during the spring and fall, and cooling during the summer. So it is that almost anything, including the growth of plants themselves, can modify the plant environment, and if the modification is beneficial, it is often called, as if by magic, climate control.

The distinction between a natural or an artificial control generally will refer to whether natural or man-made technologies and materials are used to achieve the results. Such distinctions are sometimes academic: a row of trees versus a fence for a windbreak. Nevertheless, this distinction is useful for showing that most artificial controls are just more elaborate energy and resource consumptive forms of their natural counterparts.

Natural Climate Control

A. Orientation

Proper location and orientation of homes and fields are not so much a climatic control as an adaptation.

The ancient Indian communities of the southwestern United States adapted themselves quite well to climatic extremes. Only recently have scientists come to appreciate the superior design of the Indian cliff dwellings. Even though the cliff dwelling is suspected to be primarily defensive, the prevalence of southerly oriented locations indicates the ancients appreciated solar energy. Many of these dwellings not only received direct sun during the winter, but also were shaded in the summer by the rock overhangs under which they were built. These principles alone essentially dictate the design criteria for modern solar greenhouses and other simplified solar technologies.

Since water was (and still is) severely restricted in the Southwest, the Indians usually planted in or near natural drainages where subsurface water supplied the crop. In addition, those localities which were open to the spring and fall sun, next to cliff walls to the north, and perhaps slightly up on the slope out of the natural water channel, seemed to remain frost free longer than other localities. These zones, perhaps discovered through trial and error, became favored planting localities. These favored zones incorporate a number of very important climatic factors.

First, localities open to the spring and fall sun can support a longer active growth season if temperatures remain sufficiently high. Second, localities next to south-facing cliff walls receive additional heating during the day and experience reduced heat losses at night compared to more open localities. Third, cooling air on a sloping surface flows away like water from the plant site along the actual water drainages, collecting in the valleys below. The cold air from the plant site is continually replaced by warmer air above. The result is often spectacularly warm temperatures on the sloping plant site with frosts in the flats and valleys.

The modern-day ancestors of these ancients (Hopi, Zuni, to name a few) still practice planting in favored zones. Furthermore, the principles underlying these ancient climate controls (adaptions) are used in modern agriculture: orchards are planted on hillsides above drainages; large orchard fans mix cooling air near the ground with warm air above; plants next to south-facing walls remain frost free longer than plants on open sites. Indeed, most of the modern climate-control techniques are just modifications or improvements of principles discovered long ago.

South-facing slopes are not always ideally matched to the crop. Recent research near Morgantown, West Virginia, has shown that Kentucky bluegrass yields from north-facing slopes are more than twice that from south-facing slopes. The lower soil temperature and higher soil moisture on the north-facing slopes are so optimum for growth that fertilization made no difference. With this knowledge a grower could improve his crop productivity. First, he could maintain a sustained yield of bluegrass without fertilization on the north slopes, and second, he could plant a different crop, more adaptable to heat and dryness, on the south slopes. Examples similar to this indicate a careful matching of the small-scale climate with plant needs is very important for open-field agriculture.

B. Windbreaks

The windbreak is frequently used in the Midwest where dry winds reduce crop productivity. Rows of trees, slat fences, walls, and tall grasses can often be seen separating fields. While benefits range from insignificant to spectacular, the majority of reports show positive results. One report has shown that two rows of corn windbreaks spaced at 45 feet protected an irrigated sugar beet crop at Scottsbluff, Nebraska. The results indicated a 25-percent increase during years when yields from unprotected fields were low, but no difference during high-yield years.

C. Mulches

Soil coverings such as ashes, straw, and other plant fibers have been used by many different cultures to improve the climate near the plant. Mulches are often more effective for achieving higher production during the normal growing season than extending the growing season by frost protection. Yet mulch piled over garden plants before a frost epoch can be very effective. There is evidence that the ancient Indians near Flagstaff, Arizona, used naturally occurring volcanic ash to help maintain soil moisture in cornfields.

D. Shade

Many crops in tropical climates are grown under the shade of a tree canopy (e.g., coffee under banana trees); in the United States tobacco is grown under shade cloth. Shade not only reduces plant temperatures but also improves humidity levels. This simple and inexpensive climate control has shown productivity improvements in soybeans, mustard, lettuce, radishes, potatoes, and cotton.

Artificial Climate Control

In his efforts to prolong the growing season, modern man has resorted to a variety of climate-control techniques, including: Tunnels and mulches, fog and smoke, foam blankets, and so on. But perhaps the most well-known and intensely studied man-made climate-control system is the greenhouse.

A perfect plant-growing environment can be maintained year-round in a greenhouse, and all it costs is sufficient labor and energy. It is these last two factors, labor and energy, that have recently cast a shadow on commercial-greenhouse development, but may very well pave the way for greenhouse enterprise at the small community and individual level.

A. Commercial Greenhouses

Productivity from commercial greenhouses can be spectacular. Hydroculture of Phoenix, Arizona, using methods piloted by the Environmental Research Laboratory in Tucson, Arizona, claims the following:

1. tomato production of 120 tons per acre annually
2. lettuce production per acre 30 times greater than field crops
3. 11,700 gallons of water to produce 1 ton of greenhouse tomatoes compared to 162,500 gallons for 1 ton of field tomatoes
4. a stacked-tray growth chamber requiring only 1.3 square feet of floor space to produce each ton of "sprouted" livestock feed annually, requiring only 1 percent of the water needed for full-field plant growth.

Even less elaborately run greenhouses show similar productivity. The field and greenhouse tomato yields per acre for New York in 1973 were 9.8 and 96 tons, respectively. Nonetheless, the phenomenal difference between greenhouse and field productivity is not achieved without a price. The energy used to maintain environmental control and the labor required for planting, maintenance, and harvesting in a greenhouse is staggering. In 1973, New York greenhouses required 100 times more fuel oil to produce a ton of tomatoes than field crops. It can be shown that this energy use in production adds only $\frac{1}{5}$¢ per pound to field tomatoes, but may add from 5 to 10¢ or more per pound to greenhouse tomatoes. Such differences as these make greenhouse produce competitive only on the off-season when high prices can be charged.

Both field and greenhouse agriculture generate high labor costs. (Field agriculture is slightly lower.) The average Ohio greenhouse grower in 1972 spent 30 percent of his operating costs on hired labor. Over 40 percent of Hydroculture of Arizona's operating cost is labor.

So it is that commercial greenhouses are riding on the thin edge of bankruptcy. Labor and energy demands have forced greenhouses either out of business or to a more profitable crop such as flowers.

The Energy Research and Development Agency in Washington, D.C., and other agencies are developing more economical systems for existing greenhouses. These include design modifications, extra insulation, solar heating of various elaborate types, and so on . . . all with alternative-energy sources and energy conservation in mind. Machines and new labor techniques are being developed to increase labor productivity as well. For example, a new method for supporting plants in greenhouses has reduced labor for this activity by 66 percent. Whether commercial-greenhouse vegetable production survives, even with massive energy and labor reduction, remains to be seen.

B. Home Greenhouses and Cold Frames

The climate-control techniques previously described have application primarily on the commercial scale. Undoubtedly, research efforts in this area are meant to ensure that the patterns of large-scale agribusiness remains unchanged. The vegetables will still be purchased at the store, subject to unkown quality control, high transportation costs, seasonal availability, and ever-increasing costs. Certain levels of society are concerned about these prospects and are beginning to develop partial solutions.

Numerous individuals and research groups throughout the United States are showing that environmental control using simple technologies can be implemented by homeowners and communities. Among these are the so-called solar greenhouse and similar devices, such as solar cold frames.

What Is a Solar Greenhouse?

The term solar greenhouse generally refers to greenhouses whose heating and light requirements are largely provided by the sun. Certainly all greenhouses receive most of their light from the sun, but, until recently, not many were designed to use the sun for heating as well. In this connection, most solar greenhouses collect and store solar energy for heating, and are insulated to retain this heat for use at night and during periods of cloudy days. It is perhaps these last characteristics that separate the solar greenhouse from the conventional glasshouse. In light of these distinctions a more appropriate term for the solar greenhouse might be "solar-heated, energy-conserving" greenhouse in order to focus first on the change from conventional to solar heating, and second, to emphasize the conservation of the available energy.

Solar greenhouses can be designed to collect and store solar energy in many ways, and perhaps these design features become the prime distinction among types of solar greenhouses. The type of solar collection-storage system used depends on many factors: climate, orientation, greenhouse size, economics, and whether the structure exists or is planned. For example, the southwestern United States has sufficient sunlight so that the interior of a properly designed solar greenhouse alone can collect and store sufficient solar energy for its heating needs. On the other hand, the northeastern United States may require supplements of externally collected solar heat or conventional heating.

Using the current terminology, solar collection-storage systems can be divided into two main types: passive and active. *A passive system collects energy at one point, transports and stores it at another, and delivers it for use at again another, but requires no conventional energy to transport the solar energy from collector to storage and from storage to point of need.* Such systems typically used in a solar greenhouse include rock walls, water containers, water pools open to direct-sun heating. These systems collect, store, and deliver solar heat directly, and the collector, storage, and delivery system are one and the same.

Another form of passive system uses solar collectors external to and below the greenhouse structure. Heat is provided from the collector to storage or directly to the interior by natural circulation. (Heated air or water from the collector tends to rise naturally from the collector into the greenhouse or storage.) *If at any point in the collection, storage, and delivery system supplementary energy (electric fan or water pump) is used for solar-energy transport, then that portion of the system becomes active.* There are many combinations of active and passive systems which can be used together or independently, not to mention the integration of supplementary conventional heating, to meet heating needs. These features will be discussed in more detail in later chapters.

In addition to the combination of active/passive systems, there are even more variations of greenhouse design. No attempt will be made to classify greenhouses according to design.

One type of solar greenhouse should be mentioned separately. Instead of standing by itself in a field or yard (freestanding) a solar greenhouse can be built onto a house (house-attached). Vents can also be provided in a common wall, or the greenhouse may be built over existing doorways or windows, so that the house and greenhouse freely exchange air. This rather unique relationship between house and greenhouse reduces the need for the greenhouse to store its own heat. A well-designed, house-attached greenhouse can deliver more heat to the house during the day than the house returns at night.

The most immediate and obvious advantage provided by a solar greenhouse is the extended or year-round growing season at a much lower operating cost than conventional units. Depending on the climate, solar greenhouses can operate without conventional energy supplements, or when conventional energy is needed, amounts used will be far less than required by standard glasshouses. In every other respect, the advantages of the solar greenhouse are simliar to the conventional greenhouse.

The solar greenhouse on the small community or homeowner level has additional advantages. They are relatively easy to build, requiring simple technology, and low-cost materials. Each owner or community can decide what they want to grow and how much, and can be more certain of the quality of the food at all stages of production. Markup costs from the farmer to the warehouse to the store, added costs from crop failures, spoilage, and processing, can all be reduced or eliminated by year-round home gardening.

A solar greenhouse whether integrated into the home environment or detached and surrounded by skyscrapers can also significantly improve the physical and mental environment, something that cannot be stamped with a dollar sign, but something that is coming to mean more and more in this crowded, confused world.

Perhaps one neglected and potentially valuable advantage is that on the community level the solar greenhouse can provide work and incomes for the unemployed, indigent, and retired.

The solar greenhouse is a classic example of what modern technology should be doing for man: bringing him closer to his environment instead of separating him from it. The solar greenhouse is an encapsulated version of the life processes on this planet, and perhaps from this point of view man can learn to accept the earth as his solar greenhouse and become more concerned with the quality of life about him.

Chapter Two

The Greenhouse as a Solar Collector

Conrad Heeschen

There is, *on the average,* enough solar energy in the winter to adequately heat a greenhouse in most locations in the United States and Canada, providing the greenhouse is properly designed and built. On a clear day in late January, about the coldest time of the year, the intensity of direct solar radiation is about 290 Btu's per square foot per hour at noon (at 40° north latitude).

The Btu

The Btu, or British thermal unit, is a commonly used measure of heat. Technically it is the amount of heat required to raise the temperature of one pound of water one degree Fahrenheit, specifically from 59°F. to 60°F. Heat losses, and capacities of furnaces are described in terms of Btu's per hour. The heat output of baseboard radiators is given in Btu's per foot per hour. Solar energy is measured in Btu's per square foot per hour. The heat content of different fuels can be expressed in Btu's. For example, one gallon of oil, if burned at 70-percent efficiency, will deliver about 100,000 Btu, while one kilowatt-hour is the equivalent of 3,412 Btu. In comparison, the maximum intensity of sunlight, at 40° N latitude, is 306 Btu per square foot per hour.

Box 2-1: *The Btu.*

At that intensity enough energy would pass through three square feet of a properly oriented 12' x 16' greenhouse in just one hour to heat the air inside from 40° up to 70°F. The most intense light comes during the middle of the day but there is some energy available whenever the sun is shining. Certainly, on a clear day a well-designed solar greenhouse would receive much more heat than it needs to maintain proper growing temperatures.

To design your greenhouse you really only need to know two more things. This chapter will explain how to determine the amount of solar radiation available where you live and how to design your greenhouse to capture most of it. Later chapters will tell you how to design to keep the heat in for those cold nights and cloudy days, and how long you can expect to keep it in.

Solar Radiation

Solar radiation is the driving force of the greenhouse; it supplies not only the light necessary for plant growth, but also the heat necessary to maintain a growing environment. Solar energy enters the greenhouse as shortwave radiation, or light, but when it is absorbed by the plants and other surfaces inside the greenhouse, the light is

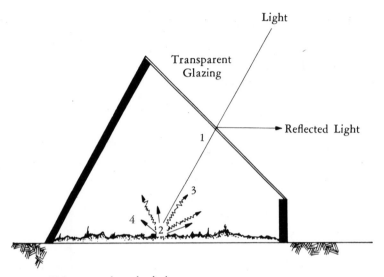

1. Light passes through glazing.

2. Light is absorbed by plants and is changed to heat.

3. Heat is radiated from plants as long-wave thermal
   radiation.

4. Some green light is reflected.

Figure 2-1: *How greenhouse absorbs heat.*

changed to thermal energy, or heat.

Radiation is the process by which heat is transferred from one object to another. You feel radiated energy when you stand in front of a campfire, even if a cold wind is blowing the fire away from you. In this case, you know the air between you and the fire is not warmed. In fact, all objects are constantly radiating energy in all directions, no matter what their temperature. The hotter an object is, the more radiation it emits.

Also, the hotter an object the shorter the wavelength of the energy that it emits. Thus, the sun, which is the hottest body in our solar system, emits radiation at short wavelengths (light) to which our eyes are sensitive, as well as even shorter radiation (ultraviolet), some of which our skins are sensitive to. On the other hand, a hot-water bottle, which is quite cool compared to the sun, emits much longer wavelengths of radiation, which we call *infrared,* or *thermal radiation.*

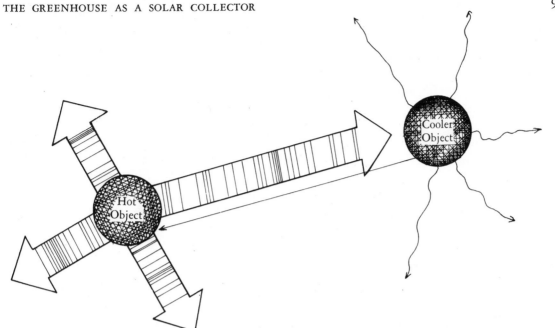

Figure 2-2: *Radiative heat transfer.*

The heat contributed by the sun is a large part of the total heat requirements of any greenhouse, and for a properly designed solar greenhouse, it is all the heat necessary. The light is also very important for plant growth, however.

You must balance light requirements against heat requirements in your greenhouse. But the problem is complicated by the fact that the daily cycle of light and darkness does not coincide with the continual need for heat. And akin to

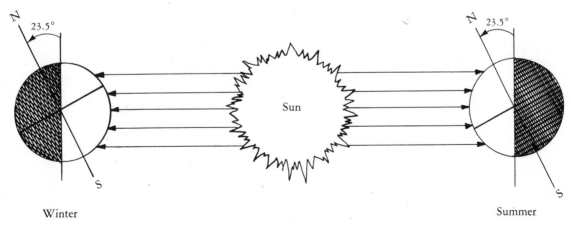

Winter

Summer

Figure 2-3: *Seasonal variation in sun's altitude and in radiation received.*

the daily cycle, wintertime is the dusk of the year. Annually, the long days and high sun angles of the summer progress to short days and low sun angles in the winter. We owe these changes and our distinct seasons to the earth's rotation and to the fact that the earth's axis is tilted 23½° from the plane of its orbit.

Even though the sun does not get very high in the sky during the winter in the Northern Hemisphere, the radiation reaching the earth on a clear day at that time is actually more intense than during the summer. This happens because the atmosphere is generally less dense at that time of the year and because the earth is slightly closer to the sun in midwinter. That explains in part why enough energy is available from the sun to heat a greenhouse in winter and why steady, though slow, plant growth is possible.

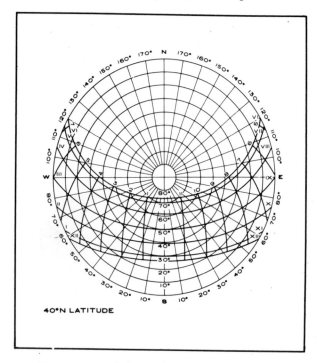

Figure 2-4: *Solar angles: 40°N latitude.*

Sun Path Diagrams

A sun path diagram, which shows you the sun's position in graphic form, can help you to understand how both the annual and daily cycles of the sun influence the design of a greenhouse. Figure 2-4 illustrates one type of sun path diagram. (Just the diagram for 40° north latitude is shown here.) This chart shows you how low the sun will get in December, and where and when it rises and sets at any time of the year. You can see how long the day will be and how high the sun will be at any time of year as well. It will be useful to you, as you will see, in determining the proper shape and orientation of your greenhouse. Charts for other latitudes are available in Appendix V.

The Sky Dome

Of course, it is not absolutely necessary for you to know the precise position of the sun in order to do a good job of designing your greenhouse. There is a wide range of angles of roof slopes and orientations you could give the greenhouse which will result in substantially equivalent performance. All you need is a good understanding of the general nature and direction of the radiation available in order to make reasonable choices among the range of possible angles.

In order to understand the type and amount of radiation the greenhouse will receive, it is useful to think of the sky as a hemispherical dome with the greenhouse at the center of the flat side. Solar radiation is either direct or diffuse (scattered) (see Figure 2-5). Direct solar radiation is that which comes directly from the sun and which casts a distinct shadow. On the other hand, diffuse radiation has been scattered by the

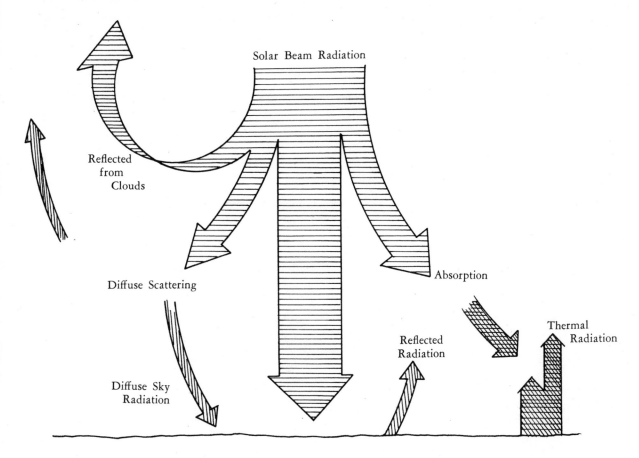

Figure 2-5: *Daytime radiation balance.*

earth's atmosphere or by clouds or the ground before it reaches the greenhouse. Even on the clearest day, some of the light will be diffuse. On very cloudy days, however, only diffuse light will reach the ground.

To get a better idea of how important these two types of light are to solar greenhouse design, consider that on a clear day, the light intensity in direct sunlight can be as great as 8,000–10,000 foot-candles, or ft-c (see Box 2-2), while the diffuse radiation which reaches the greenhouse from the blue sky is only about 500

ft-c in intensity, or only about $\frac{1}{20}$ as great as the direct radiation. On a very clear day the direct light comes from a very small portion of the total sky dome, the sun's disk, while the diffuse light comes more or less evenly from all parts of the sky (see Figure 2-6, The Sky Dome).

A day which is heavily overcast has no component of direct radiation and all the light is scattered. This light is usually of low intensity, typically in the range of 500–1,000 ft-c, and is contributed equally from all parts of the sky.

The Footcandle (ft-c)

The footcandle, abbreviated ft-c, is simply a measure of illumination. It is the intensity of light produced by one candle at a distance of one foot. The numbers here are used simply to allow you to make comparisons between the intensities of light in different weather conditions. The measurement of illumination using the footcandle is designed specifically to fit the needs of the human eye. It is not a reliable indicator of either solar energy or energy available for photosynthesis.

Just to give you an idea of how intense outdoor levels of lighting are, consider the fact that many offices are illuminated only to 100 ft-c. There are lighting experts, however, who believe that a level of 30–50 ft-c is more than adequate for all except the most demanding of tasks. Of course, you cannot grow most plants very well at those intensities.

Box 2-2

Clear Day

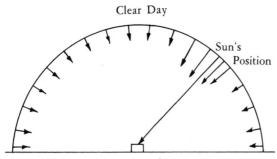

Total Light Intensity at Ground—8,000–10,000 Ft-C
Direct Radiation 85–90%
Scattered Radiation 5–15%

Heavy Overcast Day

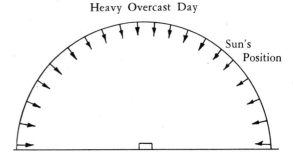

Total Light Intensity at Ground 500–1,000 Ft-C
No Direct Radiation
Scattered—100%

Bright Overcast Day

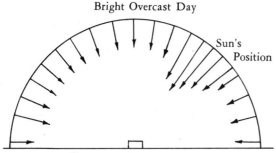

Total Light Intensity at Ground 2,000–5,000 Ft-C
Direct Radiation 0–25%
Scattered 75–100%
(As the Total Intensity Increases, a Greater
Percentage Comes From the Region of the Sun.)

Partly Cloudy Day—Clear Sky

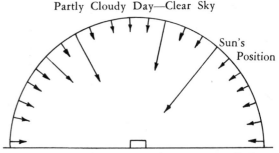

Total Light Intensity at Ground 10,000–15,000 Ft-C
Direct 60–100%
Scattered 0–40%
(Mostly Reflected from Clouds)

Figure 2-6: *The sky dome.*

Between these extremes are bright overcast and hazy days, and clear but partly cloudy days.

On bright overcast days, with total light intensities ranging from 2,000 to 5,000 ft-c, the light will be fairly evenly distributed over the entire sky at the lower end of the range of intensities. On the brightest days, much of the total radiation will come from the general region of the sun, although a significant contribution is made from the rest of the sky as well.

Clear, partly cloudy days are the hardest to quantify, because the white clouds can reflect a large amount of sunlight to the greenhouse, supplementing the direct radiation. The intensity of the light received can vary from relatively low levels (around 1,000 ft-c) in full shade, to 10,000 to 14,000 ft-c in sunlight. The intensity of the light can change very rapidly on such days.

For clear days, a general rule is that the lower the sun is in the sky, the greater the percentage of the total radiation that is scattered, since the light must penetrate a greater distance of atmosphere. This rule cannot be used to compare the amount of diffuse radiation at different times of the year, since the atmosphere in some regions of the country is much clearer in the winter and this counteracts the effect of the lower solar altitudes. For most places in North America, except for the far west, there is probably a greater proportion of diffuse radiation in the summer than in the winter. Humid and industrial areas will also have a greater proportion of diffuse light at any time of year, and the total intensities will be lower than the average clear day at the same latitude, but in a clearer area.

The reason it is important to understand the distinctions between the different types of light and where it comes from in the sky is because most plants you would wish to grow in your greenhouse require a light intensity of at least 2,000 ft-c to make decent growth. Even greater peak intensities are necessary if the light is not available for a long enough period of time. Since you will probably want to grow plants that would like the 13 to 15 hours of light they would get in the summer, but in days that are only 8 to 10 hours long, it is clear that your greenhouse needs to get as much as possible. Chapters Twelve, Thirteen, and Fourteen will give you an idea of the light requirements of the plants you may wish to grow.

Shape of the Greenhouse

It is extremely interesting to study traditional greenhouse designs to see just how well they capture light for heat and plant growth. The roof of a standard-frame greenhouse is divided into two parts, usually of equal, and shallow low slopes (see Figure 2-7). Researchers at the Brace Research Institute in Montreal say that this form developed in the Low Countries of northern Europe as a response to the low levels of predominantly diffuse light prevalent in the region in the wintertime. This design was brought to this continent with little consideration of the differences in climate and latitude encountered here. Until recently, little research has been done on more suitable shapes for other types of climates.

The traditional greenhouse loses more heat than it gains from the sun during the winter, no matter what its orientation. But I have analyzed the angles of the roofs and the incoming solar energy, and found that just changing the direction of the greenhouse can make a significant difference. If the axis of the roof is running east-west, the greenhouse will gain 25-percent

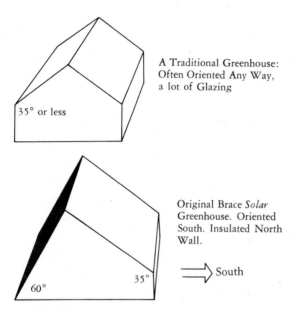

A Traditional Greenhouse: Often Oriented Any Way, a lot of Glazing

35° or less

Original Brace *Solar* Greenhouse. Oriented South. Insulated North Wall.

⟹ South

60°　　35°

Note: The International Greenhouse Standard for roof slopes is 26.5°; in most of my calculations I have used 30° or 35°. For convenience, this would mean that a standard greenhouse would get even less solar energy than I had calculated.

Figure 2-7: *Greenhouse orientations.*

more solar radiation (on January 21, at 40° north latitude) through the roof than if the roof axis runs north-south. This gain is despite the fact that the north side of the roof on an east-west orientation receives no direct radiation at all on that day, and both sides of the north-south oriented roof receive a little. Since many greenhouses run north-south so as to get the sun on all sides of the plants, this represents an enormous sacrifice of solar energy in this country. J. Seeman, in the World Meteorological publication, *Climate under Glass,* reports that studies in the vicinity of London show that light incidence in a greenhouse with an east-west orientation may be up to 12 percent higher than for a greenhouse with a north-south orientation.

North-Facing Roofs

It is easy to see why the north-facing roof contributes so little to the heating of the greenhouse. From a sun path diagram or from tables of the sun's positions you can see that at 40° north latitude the maximum solar altitude at noon on January 21 is only 30°. Figure 2-8b shows that at this angle the north roof would be in shadow. Even in March, maximum solar altitude is only 50°, and only a relatively small amount of radiation will strike a 35° north slope (Figure 2-8a). You don't even need to calculate radiation to see that the north-sloping roof contributes little to the heating of the greenhouse during the winter.

If you are designing your greenhouse to maximize the amount of solar energy received, with the least possible energy lost, you should make north walls and roofs solid and insulate them well. The only reason the north wall might be glazed is for light, but on clear days the intensity of north light is only $\frac{1}{10}$ to $\frac{1}{20}$ as great as direct sunlight. Since it plays such a small role in plant growth at these intensities, we can safely make the north side opaque without sacrificing any solar radiation; altogether, this is what makes a solar-heated greenhouse possible.

The Importance of the Angle of Incidence

If your compare the amount of radiation received on the north- and the south-facing roofs of the greenhouse in Figures 2-8a and 2-8b, you can see one reason why the angle of the roof is important in capturing the most solar radiation. Only when a surface is perpendicular to the sun's rays will it intercept an area of radiation equal to its own

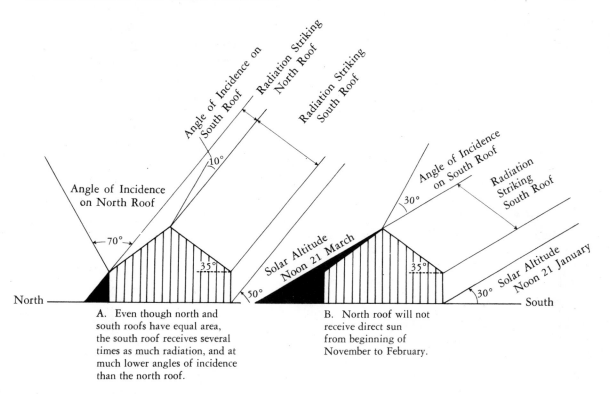

A. Even though north and south roofs have equal area, the south roof receives several times as much radiation, and at much lower angles of incidence than the north roof.

B. North roof will not receive direct sun from beginning of November to February.

Figure 2-8a: *Direct solar radiation on north-facing roofs (40°N latitude).*
Figure 2-8b: *Direct solar radiation on north-facing roofs (40°N latitude).*

area (see also Figure 2.9). If a surface is turned away from the sun's rays, it will present less area and receive less radiation.

The angle the sun's rays make with a line perpendicular to the surface is called the angle of incidence. Besides determining how much radiation the surface will intercept, the angle of incidence also determines how much of that radiation is reflected, and in the case of transparent materials, how much is transmitted (see Figure 2-10a). The maximum amount of radiation is transmitted when the radiation is perpendicular to the surface. If radiation strikes the surface away from the perpendicular, more is reflected and less is transmitted. The relation-

ships between the angle of incidence and the percentage of radiation transmitted, and between the angle of incidence and the amount of radiation intercepted are shown in Figure 2-10b.

The reason for choosing an "optimum" orientation and shape for your greenhouse is to try to find an angle for the south face which is close to the ideal angle of incidence, for as long a period each day as possible and for as much of your chosen season as possible. It is important to do this for the middle of the day when the radiation is most intense and for the specific season when you will be using the greenhouse. You know that almost all of the solar energy that will enter your greenhouse will be through the south roof; you are now ready to determine the best angle for that roof.

The South-Facing Roof

The slope of the south-facing glazing should maximize the amount of solar radiation passing through it during the period of the year when you actually use the greenhouse. If you intend to use your greenhouse all winter long, you might at first think that the best slope would maximize transmission for December, the time of the lowest solar altitudes. This would result in the steepest possible slope at any latitude (64° at 40°N latitude). This is generally *not* advisable, however, because the period of greatest *underheating,* the time when the combined effect of temperature and reduced solar radiation is most severe, occurs in January and February. The angle of the south slope should usually be determined for this period.

The number of hours of light and its intensity are both greater in January and February than in December. Even though a greenhouse optimized for January might not transmit quite as much in December as one designed solely for that month,

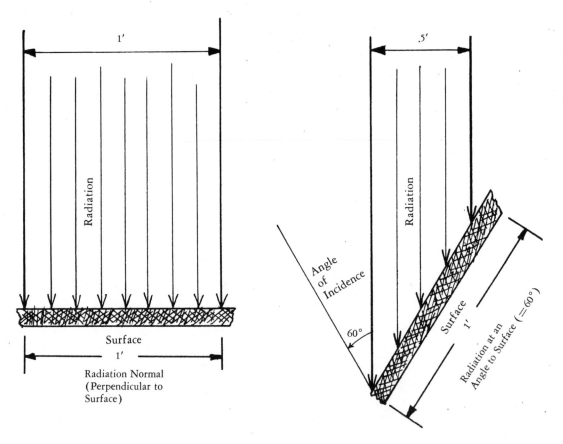

Figure 2-9: *Angle of incidence.*

it has a better performance on the average over the entire winter. It is better to optimize the greenhouse for a range of months than for one extreme.

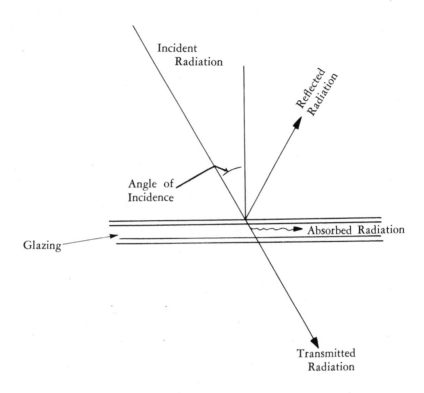

Glazing Losses: When radiation strikes a surface, some of the radiation is reflected, some is absorbed, and some may be transmitted (depending on the type of radiation and properties of glazing material).

Figure 2-10a: *Glazing losses.*

The South-Facing Roof: Finding the Best Slope

Rather than going to all the trouble of calculating angles of incidence and intensities of the radiation striking your greenhouse—a long and tedious process—you can use relatively simple rules of thumb or radiation tables to determine the angle of the south roof. You can simply add 20° to your latitude to get the desired slope. Or

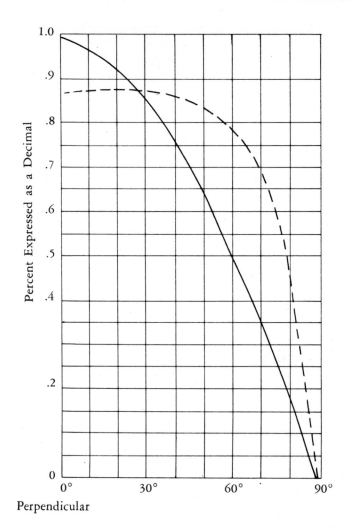

Perpendicular

- - - - - Transmittance through single layer
of glass (*ASHRAE Handbook*, p. 395)

——— Ratio of intercepted area of
radiation on tilted surface to
actual surface area

$$A_o/A_s = cos\theta \quad (\theta \text{ Angle of Incidence})$$

This graph shows that the angle of incidence (θ, theta) has little effect on transmittance through single glass for angles up to 45°. The area presented to the sun by a surface at that angle to the sun's rays is only 70% as great as straight on.

Figure 2-10b:

you can look up on a sun path diagram what altitude the sun is at noon on January 21 and make your initial choice of roof slope the angle perpendicular to that solar altitude. At 40° north latitude the solar altitude at noon on January 21 is 30°, so your first choice would be 60°. Now you should consider the type of sunshine you usually receive in your area. If you have nearly all clear

days and few cloudy days you could leave it at this angle. However, if you have a lot of bright overcast days and relatively few really clear days, you should make that angle a little less steep so that the inside of the greenhouse at the plant level can see a greater part of the sky dome.

Alternatively you could use the tables to find the slope which would receive the greatest

Date	Solar Time		Solar Position		Btu. Sq. Ft. Total Insolation on Surfaces						
	AM	PM	Alt.	Azm.			South—Facing Surface Angle with Horiz.				
					Normal	Horiz.	30	40	50	60	90
Jan 21	8	4	8.1	55.3	142	28	65	74	81	85	84
	9	3	16.8	44.0	239	83	155	171	182	187	171
	10	2	23.8	30.9	274	127	218	237	249	254	223
	11	1	28.4	16.0	289	154	257	277	290	293	253
		12	30.0	0.0	294	164	270	291	303	306	263
	Surface Daily Totals				2,812	948	1,660	1,810	1,906	1,944	1,726

Date	Solar Time		Solar Position		Btu. Sq. Ft. Total Insolation on Surfaces						
	AM	PM	Alt.	Azm.			South—Facing Surface Angle with Horiz.				
					Normal	Horiz.	30	40	50	60	90
Feb 21	7	5	4.8	72.7	69	10	19	21	23	24	22
	8	4	15.4	62.2	224	73	114	122	126	127	107
	9	3	25.0	50.2	274	132	195	205	209	208	167
	10	2	32.8	35.9	295	178	256	267	271	267	210
	11	1	38.1	18.9	305	206	293	306	310	304	236
		12	40.0	0.0	308	216	306	319	323	317	245
	Surface Daily Totals				2,640	1,414	2,060	2,162	2,202	2,176	1,730

Date	Solar Time		Solar Position		Btu. Sq. Ft. Total Insolation on Surfaces						
	AM	PM	Alt.	Azm.			South—Facing Surface Angle with Horiz.				
					Normal	Horiz.	30	40	50	60	90
Mar 21	7	5	11.4	80.2	171	46	55	55	54	51	35
	8	4	22.5	69.6	250	114	140	141	138	131	89
	9	3	32.8	57.3	282	173	215	217	213	202	138
	10	2	41.6	41.9	297	218	273	276	271	258	176
	11	1	47.7	22.6	305	247	310	313	307	293	200
		12	50.0	0.0	307	257	322	326	320	305	208
	Surface Daily Totals				2,916	1,852	2,308	2,330	2,284	2,174	1,484

Date	Solar Time		Solar Position		Btu. Sq. Ft. Total Insolation on Surfaces						
	AM	PM	Alt.	Azm.			South—Facing Surface Angle with Horiz.				
					Normal	Horiz.	30	40	50	60	90
Apr 21	6	6	7.4	98.9	89	20	11	8	7	7	4
	7	5	18.9	89.5	206	87	77	70	61	50	12
	8	4	30.3	79.3	252	152	153	145	133	117	53
	9	3	41.3	67.2	274	207	221	213	199	179	93
	10	2	51.2	51.4	286	250	275	267	522	229	126
	11	1	58.7	29.2	292	277	308	301	285	260	147
		12	61.6	0.0	293	287	320	313	296	271	154
	Surface Daily Totals				3,092	2,274	2,412	2,320	2,168	1,956	1,022

Date	Solar Time		Solar Position		Btu. Sq. Ft. Total Insolation on Surfaces						
	AM	PM	Alt.	Azm.			South—Facing Surface Angle with Horiz.				
					Normal	Horiz.	30	40	50	60	90
Dec	8	4	5.5	53.0	89	14	39	45	50	54	56
	9	3	14.0	41.9	217	65	135	152	164	171	163
	10	2	20.7	29.4	261	107	200	221	235	242	221
	11	1	25.0	15.2	280	134	239	262	276	283	252
		12	26.6	0.0	285	143	253	275	290	296	263
	Surface Daily Totals				1,978	782	1,480	1,634	1,740	1,796	1,646

Figure 2-11: *Solar position and insolation, 40° N latitude.*

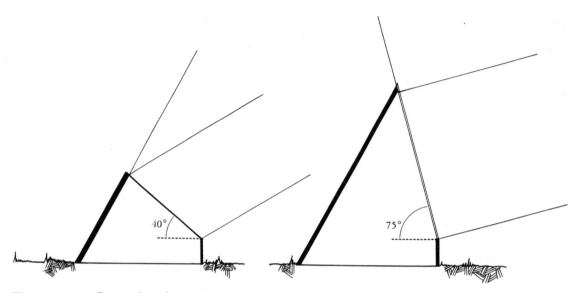

Figure 2-12: *Range of south-glazing angles proposed by Brace.*

amount of solar energy (Btu's) at your location on average clear days (see Figure 2-11). Again let us assume you are at 40° north (anywhere in a line from New Jersey to northern California); if you look at the figures for total radiation received on different slopes (see Figure 2-9), you will see that angles of 50° and 60° receive nearly the same amount of radiation. In fact they are within two percent of each other. These tables include both direct and diffuse radiation for average clear days. Since the percentage of diffuse radiation on a clear day is only about five to ten percent of the total, you would still need to go to a slightly lower angle if you don't get mostly clear days. If you use the tables you will get a better idea of the range of angles which will give nearly the same performance.

Just to give you an idea of the wide range of angles possible, the Brace Research Institute used a computer program and found that anywhere from a 40° to 70° slope for the south roof would allow near-optimum performance for their latitude of 44° north (Montreal). Moreover, when it came right down to building their experimental greenhouse, they used a slope of 35°. The reason they chose this angle, which they claimed would not make their greenhouse perform much worse than their optimum range, was because they are limited by the length of the materials they could get to build the greenhouse. This factor might influence your decision to make a lower than "ideal" angle. You might also be limited to shallower angles if you are attaching it to a low wall of the home. Also, if your greenhouse is at all large you will find that steep roof slopes result in very high greenhouses, which have more surface area to lose heat and which tend to collect warm air at the top. If you want to make your greenhouse roof slope lower for practical reasons, you will be in good company.

There are many reasons for doing it, and generally it makes the greenhouse slightly more efficient in spring and fall months. However, lowering the slope may cause overheating problems at other times of the year.

Optimizing the South Slope for Other Seasons

Suppose you won't be using your greenhouse in the winter, but only in the fall to extend the season or in the early spring. You need not worry about the fall so much, because outside temperatures are still fair then, but March, even though the sun is getting higher in the sky, can still get quite cold at night. Since the beginning of March is not given in the table (Figure 2-11) you could add the values of radiation given for both February and March to see which angle gives the best overall performance. Adding the two months we find a 30° slope receives a total of 4,368 Btu's, 40°—4,492, 50°—4,486, and 60°—4,350. The most energy falls on a 40° to 50° slope and there is only three-percent difference in energy between the two angles. Since there is so little difference you can be confident in choosing whatever angle in that range is easiest to build. If a large proportion of the solar radiation in your area is diffuse, you should choose an angle from the lower end of the range.

Regional Clearness Factors

Since the values in these tables are for *average* clear days, they may not be representative of your area. The southern Rocky Mountain area usually has from five- to ten-percent greater intensities of sunshine because of the elevation, and the far northern part of the United States and southern Canada may have about five-percent greater intensities. South of Tennessee and North Carolina, however, the intensity of the radiation may only be from 90 to 95 percent of the values in the tables, while industrial areas and cities may have even lower intensities.

Slope of the Rear Wall

Once the slope of the front wall is chosen, you are ready to design the rest of your greenhouse. The next thing to consider is the insulated rear roof. Is there any special slope it should have? The Brace Research Institute examined this question too, and found that the proper slope, with a reflective surface on the inside would let the sunlight reach the back of the greenhouse during the winter and would distribute the light to the plants evenly. In tests they found that the light reflected from the rear wall/roof in their greenhouse produced earlier crops than could be grown in an adjacent conventional greenhouse.

They suggest that the slope should be about equal to the solar altitude at noon on June 21, but their computer optimization showed a range of from 60° to 75° would give about equivalent performance for Montreal's latitude (44° north). This is a good range to work with anywhere in the northern part of the United States and Canada, except perhaps in areas where there is an extremely high proportion of bright, cloudy days and a relatively mild climate. In that type of climate, a large part of the available radiation would be diffuse radiation scattered over the entire sky, and you might wish to open up the inside of the greenhouse to a greater part of the sky dome.

Shallow slopes, on the other hand, would tend to limit the amount of light plants near the back

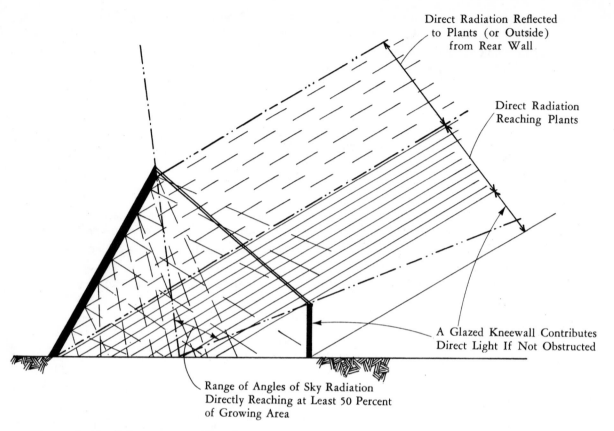

Figure 2-13: *Solar energy reaching plants.*

of the greenhouse would receive. The extreme case is a horizontal ceiling; a greenhouse with an insulated horizontal north roof would be little better than a room with south-facing picture windows. The only region where you might wish to consider rear/north slopes much less than 60° or so is where overheating is a serious problem, as in parts of the South and Southwest.

No matter what your location or the slope of your north greenhouse wall, you should make the inside surfaces reflective. Experiments done on plant growth with reflectors indicate that vege-table production is enhanced to a greater extent with diffusing white reflectors rather than specular reflectors, like aluminum foil, or non-reflectors, like black walls. These experiments have been reported in *Organic Gardening and Farming*® in April 1976, and in R. Geiger's *The Climate Near the Ground*. While both types of reflectors improve yields, only black walls tend to increase plant growth.

Despite this, some solar-greenhouse designers have turned their rear walls into solar collectors by making them black to absorb solar radiation.

If you are interested in fruit or root crops, rather than greens or foliage growth, you would be far better off to allow as much as possible of the sun's energy to reach the plants as light, and to remove any excess heat, which they reradiate, from the air. Unless you live in an area with extremely intense sunlight, like the high altitudes of the Southwest, you should use reflectors on the rear wall instead of absorbers.

White paint is usually less expensive and easier to renew than foil reflectors, whose reflecting ability will decrease over a period of time no matter how expensive they are. Another reason for choosing white paint over foils is that you could inadvertently create "hot spots" with foils, which could dry out or cook plants in those areas. You can also give the plants a better environment of diffuse light by using a diffusing material for the greenhouse glazing. If you use a diffusing glazing, the exact angle of the north wall is a little less critical since you will not have to depend on it to distribute all the light in the greenhouse.

Extreme Roof Slopes: Problems

If you use very steep slopes you could end up with a high greenhouse. Besides increased heat losses from the extra surface area, especially from the glazing, a pocket of warmer air will form at the very top. Heat losses through this part of the greenhouse would be even greater because of the increased temperature difference between inside and outside, and you would have to use fans just to get the warmth down to the plants. It will also cost you more to build since more materials are necessary.

There are also problems with using very low slopes for either the south or north walls, besides the increased angles of incidence. In snowy climates, the roof must be able to support the expected snow load; this is particularly difficult to achieve with glass surfaces without a lot of heavy structure and small pieces of glazing. Also, unless you will always be around to clear snow off when necessary (although snow on the roof on a cloudy day would add some insulation), the slope should be steep enough to allow it to slide off. In the event that your solar greenhouse employs multiple layers of glazing and movable insulation, the glazing will not be as warm as in an uninsulated, single-glazed greenhouse and the snow will not melt or slide off as readily.

A low roof angle may also affect the utilization of all the space in your greenhouse, particularly if you wish to use benches rather than to plant directly in beds on the ground. You could end up with unusable and unreachable nooks where the roof rises from the ground, unless you provide a kneewall. A kneewall on the south side would actually be a good idea in snowy regions, as it would provide a place for the snow to accumulate when it slid off the roof. If a bench were used along the south wall, it would tend to block any light coming through a kneewall.

Orientation of the Greenhouse

A solar greenhouse should obviously be oriented with the majority of the glazing facing in a southerly direction. The question most people ask (with good reason, since few sites allow alignment directly south), is how far from true south can the greenhouse be oriented? Fortunately there is little need for you to be locked into due-south orientation, at least for greenhouses with sloping glazing. (Identical green-

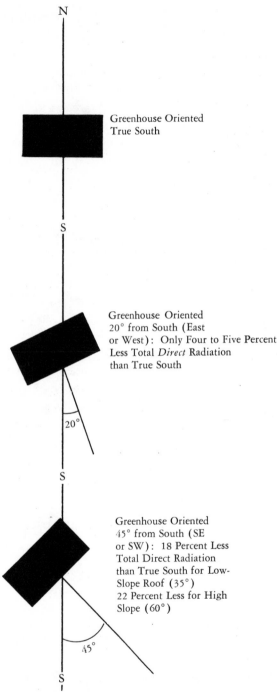

Greenhouse Oriented
True South

Greenhouse Oriented
20° from South (East
or West): Only Four to Five Percent
Less Total *Direct* Radiation
than True South

Greenhouse Oriented
45° from South (SE
or SW): 18 Percent Less
Total Direct Radiation
than True South for Low-
Slope Roof (35°)
22 Percent Less for High
Slope (60°)

Figure 2-14: *Effects of greenhouse orientation.*

houses with roof slopes of 35° to 60° at orientations as much as 20° off true south will receive only four- to five-percent less total daily radiation through the glazing than a greenhouse oriented true south.) Even as much as 45° off south will result in a decrease of only 18 percent for a 35° slope and 20 percent for a 60° slope.

If scattered or diffuse radiation makes up a large part of the total radiation, the differences for angles off due south would be even less, no more than two percent at 30° off true south. Additionally, when you orient your greenhouse off true south you can make the northerly end wall of the greenhouse totally opaque and insulated, with little loss in total radiation transmitted and a significant decrease in heat losses, while the end wall which is shifted towards the south will have improved solar radiation during the winter months and can be glazed.

Ideal conditions rarely prevail; the site you have available may be partially obstructed by hills, trees, or buildings, or for other reasons you may wish to orient the building on some other axis than east-west. In this case it is convenient to plot your site's horizon on a sun path diagram in order to evaluate the effect of the obstructions (see Box 2-3 with Figures 4-15a and 4-15b).

Another factor you should consider before deciding on the orientation of your greenhouse is the local weather pattern. The incoming radiation figures quoted in the preceding examples were for days which were uniformly clear through the entire day. This kind of day may occur only rarely in some regions. For instance, parts of New England seem to experience clear mornings with increasing cloudiness leading to complete overcast later in the day. On the other hand, the San Joaquin Valley in California is often foggy in the morning with clearing later

Using Sun Path Diagrams to Evaluate
Site Obstructions

It is very helpful to plot the horizon line and any nearby buildings or trees on a sun path diagram in order to see where most of the sun will actually come from at your site. You can make a tracing from the circular sun path diagrams given in the Appendix, or you could plot the altitudes and azimuths on a rectangular grid. This method gives you a plot which is more like your site actually appears when you are standing on it facing south and may be easier to work with.

In the Figures 2-15a and 2-15b I have plotted the same site. At this location there are three types of obstructions: the true horizon consists of ground and distant hills. There is also a distinct line formed by the tops of the trees in the middle distance. If you tried to do anything to reduce their effect on the site, it would take substantial cutting. Possible but highly unlikely. The major obstructions are half-a-dozen nearby trees, which shade the site during the brightest hours, all of which could be cut without any difficulty or visual damage to the site. All in all, a southern orientation would work well at this site, since both east and west obstructions are fairly evenly balanced.

Suppose, however, that the trees at A in Figure 2-15b were on another property or were particularly valuable specimens. If they were heavily branched, the sun would drop behind them in midwinter by 1:30 or 2:00 P.M. Since the amount of sun in the morning and afternoon is no longer about equal, you should orient the greenhouse more toward the east, say 10° or 15° to improve the angle of incidence in the mornings when you have the most sun.

You can treat local climatic features in the same way as physical obstructions. If you know you have, for example, morning fogs which rarely lift before 10:00 A.M., you should shade out everything below 10:00. A slightly western orientation might be appropriate in this instance.

Box 2-3: *Using sun path diagrams to evaluate site obstructions.*

in the day. Either pattern should influence your choice of orientation and you can indicate periods of cloudiness on the sun path diagram as well as physical site obstructions. An orientation off-south which takes weather patterns into account captures a gerater proportion of the total daily radiation actually available than would a true-south orientation.

It will be necessary for you to know your local weather, which may involve several years of observation, or to have available long-term records which record cloudiness on an hourly basis in order for you to be certain that what you observe is consistent behavior, rather than one year's aberration. Some major weather stations, airports, or air bases make records of cloudiness on an hourly basis, and if you live nearby, they would probably be accurate enough for you to use in evaluating your site.

Independent of all other considerations, there is a good argument for orienting the greenhouse somewhat to the east of south, even for consistently clear weather. An easterly orientation, while sacrificing a small fraction of the total

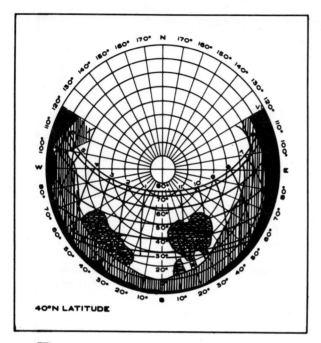

40°N LATITUDE

◼ Horizon, ground, or immovable objects, like buildings

▥ Tree line: impractical to remove (too many)

▦ Nearby trees should be removed

Figure 2-15a: *Evaluating site.*

daily radiation, would allow the greenhouse to warm up slightly earlier in the morning. Since mornings are generally somewhat colder than afternoons, and since the supply of heat from the previous day may be at its lowest ebb just as day begins, perhaps only sufficient to keep everything from freezing, if the greenhouse warmed up earlier it would allow the plants to have the warmth they need to take advantage of the available light and continue growing. This orientation would also help to minimize some of the

overheating that would occur in the afternoons of sunny spring or fall days.

End-Wall Glazing

One of the first things you learn when you look at the solar performance of a greenhouse is that the north roof plays little part in the heating of the greenhouse, and that a large amount of energy enters through the south roof. What about other orientations, for instances, the east and west end walls? It is obvious that these orientations, if they are vertical surfaces, will not receive as much total daily radiation during the winter as a south-facing surface, since the sun only strikes them for half the day and never gets around to striking them full face until March 21. In fact, on January 21, one square foot of vertical east or west glazing receives less than one third the radiation of a vertical south-facing surface. The question is: How much are the losses compared to the gains for a given orientation?

End-wall glazing in short (east-west) greenhouses is usually counterproductive because much of the sunlight passes into the greenhouse from the south wall and passes right on through the east-west walls. If these walls are reflective or contain absorptive storage mass, this energy is available within the greenhouse.

A general rule of thumb for vertical glazing at different orientations is as follows: For the climate of Washington, D.C., you would break even, on the average, with single-glazing on a south wall and double-glazing on east or west walls. You would have a net gain through a south wall if you double-glazed, but you would lose through a north wall in any case. For the climate of Boston, on the other hand, double-glazing on a south wall and triple-glazing on east

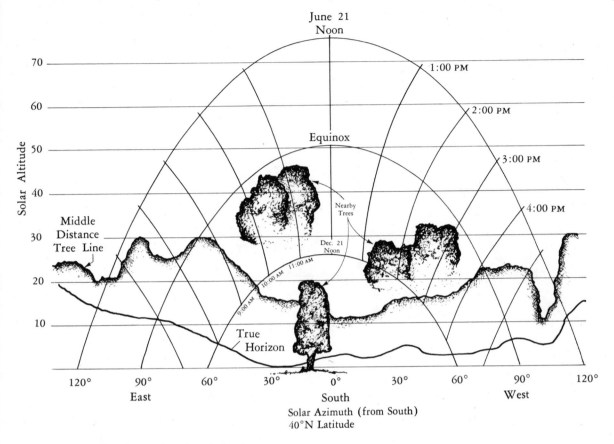

Figure 2-15b: *Evaluating site obstructions.*

or west walls would be required to break even. Of course, if an east-facing or west-facing wall was shaded in the morning or afternoon, respectively, it would be a net loser no matter how many layers you had. Consistent morning or afternoon cloudiness would have the same effect. Actually, these rules of thumb apply only to glazing without movable insulation. If you used movable insulation, which you should, you could have net gains for almost any orientation except northerly, although the more southerly orientations would still gain the most.

Your decision whether or not to glaze the end walls of your greenhouse will be influenced by most of the same considerations that you give to orientation. In general, the smaller your greenhouse, the more important it would be to glaze the end walls. If you used solid end walls, they might shade the inside of the greenhouse too much compared to the amount of light available through the southern glazing. Southeast or southwest end walls almost always should be glazed, as they could make a substantial contribution to heating.

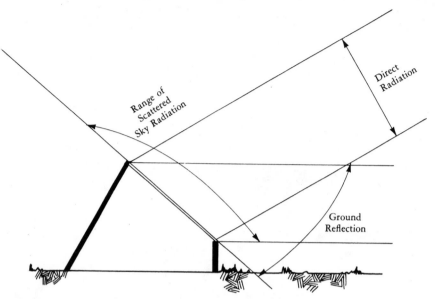

Figure 2-16: *Radiation reaching greenhouse surface.*

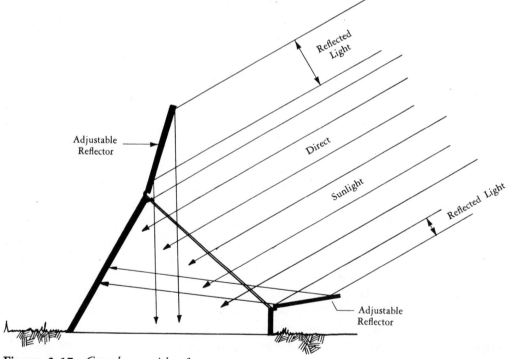

Figure 2-17: *Greenhouse with reflectors.*

External Reflection

The amount of light striking the outside of the greenhouse and the glazing can be increased by external reflectors, either natural or artificial. You could build large panels which you would attach to the outside of the greenhouse. These would either be made of a reflective material like aluminum or of plywood or Masonite with foil or reflectorized plastic applied. Such panels can contribute a large amount of solar energy, mostly on clear days, and they can also be used to provide nighttime insulation for the greenhouse. On the other hand, they could cause some problems for you in some parts of the country. If you live in a snowy climate, you might find that the snow makes it difficult to operate them. Even on clear days snow could drift onto the reflectors, and high winds could tear large, light panels right off your greenhouse or slam them into the glazing unless they were very securely fastened. The surface of even the best reflector will deteriorate with time and exposure to the elements, so you should not count on long-term reflectivity of greater than about 75 percent.

Natural reflectors include snow, light dry soil, and water between the greenhouse and the direction of the sun. You cannot control these materials like you can panels, nor are they as reflective in most cases, but they are free. Snow is the most effective, reflecting between 40 and 95 percent of the light striking it, depending on its freshness. It is a diffuse reflector, however, and would not make a great contribution to the greenhouse unless the greenhouse faced out across a large expanse of snowy ground. Water is not very reflective if the solar altitude is greater than 40°, so its greatest effect will come shortly after sunrise and before sunset. If your site were suitable it could be helpful in getting the greenhouse to warm up a little earlier in the day. Dry, sandy earth can reflect between 15 and 45 percent of the light striking it. This may only be a significant factor in certain western locations where sandy expanses sometimes occur.

Effect of Greenhouse Thermal Improvements on Solar Radiation Received

Many of the things that you could do to decrease the heat losses of your greenhouse would have

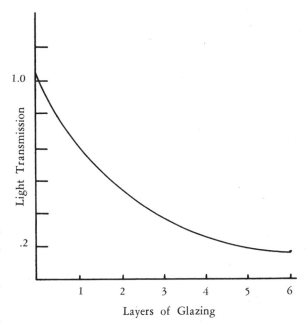

Theoretical U-Value, Illustrating Law of Diminishing Returns for Number of Layers of Glazing Installed

Figure 2-18: *Graph showing law of diminishing returns for number of layers of glazing.*

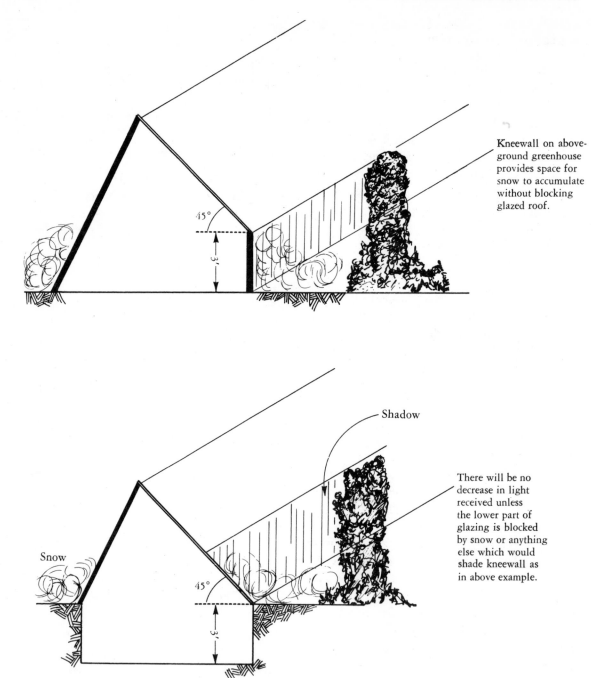

Kneewall on above-ground greenhouse provides space for snow to accumulate without blocking glazed roof.

45°

3'

Shadow

There will be no decrease in light received unless the lower part of glazing is blocked by snow or anything else which would shade kneewall as in above example.

Snow

45°

3'

Figure 2-19: *Effect of pit greenhouse on light received.*

little or no effect on the amount of radiation the greenhouse receives. Multiple glazing, one of the first things you should consider to reduce greenhouse heat losses (since most of the heat loss occurs through the glazing) does reduce the amount of light transmitted. Each additional layer of glass used will reduce the transmission through the glazing by about 13 percent, but the reduction of heat losses is less with each additional layer. The optimum number of layers to use depends on the material used, the severity of the climate, and the cost of the material, and will be discussed more fully in Chapter Four.

Thermal shutters, or movable nighttime insulation, another design feature you should incorporate in your greenhouse, should have little effect on the amount of radiation received in the greenhouse, provided they can be moved or collapsed when necessary. There may be some losses if you use permanently installed shutters just inside the glazing, but if they are reflective, the

losses will be small. Insulation which can be removed completely during the daytime will not decrease the amount of light received, unless you don't remove it early in the morning. On particularly cloudy days it may be worthwhile to leave them up to save heat and to supplement sunlight with artificial light, or if it is too cool to make any growth anyway, not to bother with light.

Many pit greenhouses have glazing which comes right down to the ground, since the space inside could get unmanageably high otherwise. Unless snow accumulation at the foot of the glazing is removed, there will be reduced amount of light getting into the greenhouse.

Attached Greenhouses

Attached greenhouses have the greatest reduction of solar radiation from April to September. They also suffer the most of any of the designs

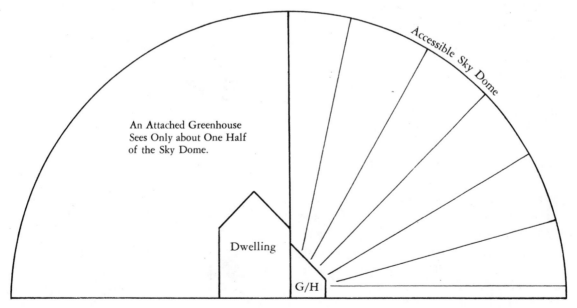

Figure 2-20: *Sky dome of an attached greenhouse.*

discussed so far under overcast conditions, since if a small greenhouse is attached to the two-story house, the roof of the greenhouse is exposed to little more than one half of the entire sky at any time. This is not a problem for clear days in the winter, but it will diminish the total light in the greenhouse when the sky is uniformly bright by about 50 percent, depending on the height of the wall above it. The wall above, if painted a light color, can reflect some light into the greenhouse, although it would be most effective for higher sun angles and direct radiation as the angle of incidence of the reflected radiation with the roof surface would be fairly high otherwise.

Since attached greenhouses have so many thermal advantages, many of you will wish to take advantage of them and sacrifice a little solar energy. If you are going to build an attached greenhouse on your home, you should place it on the south side. If your house is not exactly on a north-south axis, you should put the greenhouse on the southeast face, if that face is no greater than 45° off south and there are no obstructions. If it is more than that, the greenhouse should go on the southwesterly face, since it will be more to the south. If the house is truly north-south, the greenhouse could go just about anywhere on the south side, but if it is possible to put it in front of a one-story wall instead of a higher wall, it would improve the light in the greenhouse under cloudy sky conditions.

If the house is not exactly north-south, put the greenhouse on the southerly corner and be sure to glaze the southerly end wall. If the optimum location on your house would send tons of snow down on the greenhouse, you are going to have to find another place or build a separate greenhouse. One further word of caution which applies equally well no matter where you are going to put your greenhouse (but is particularly

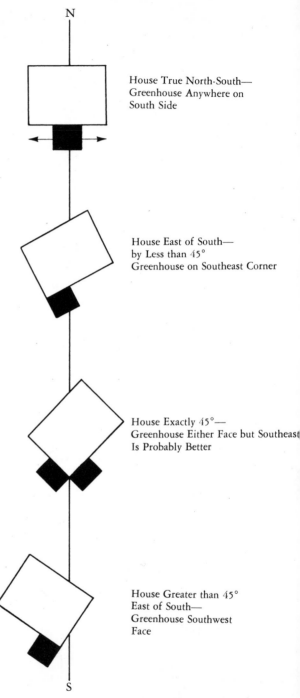

House True North-South—
Greenhouse Anywhere on South Side

House East of South—
by Less than 45°
Greenhouse on Southeast Corner

House Exactly 45°—
Greenhouse Either Face but Southeast Is Probably Better

House Greater than 45° East of South—
Greenhouse Southwest Face

Figure 2-21: *Locations of attached greenhouse.*

Figure 2-22: *Snow load.*

important for attached greenhouses), is that you should make sure that you are working with true north and south, rather than magnetic north and south.

Summarized Greenhouse Design Process for Solar Energy

All this information should enable you to choose a form and orientation for your greenhouse which will work quite well. The first thing you must do is to decide what the purpose of your greenhouse is; the type of plants you wish to grow and their light and heat preferences will have an impact on the greenhouse design. You must also determine just when you will use the greenhouse, whether it is only to be a season extender, or for year-round vegetable or flower production. With these ideas in mind you can find the positions of the sun during the period you will use the greenhouse, and using a sun path diagram and weather data you can analyze your

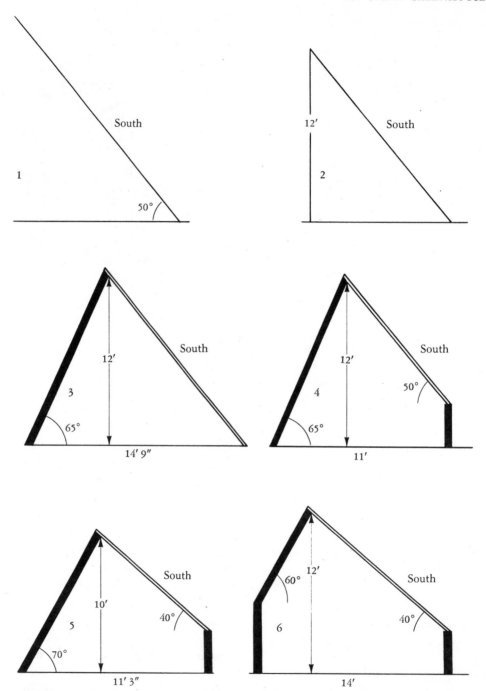

Figure 2-23: *Planning size and shape of greenhouse.*

site to determine the most effective orientation for your greenhouse. You will consider the relative amounts of sunshine and cloudiness, and the type of cloudiness.

You can use the following steps to help you plan the actual size and shape of your greenhouse:

1. Determine the angle/slope of the glazed south face of the greenhouse from the guidelines given earlier. Draw this slope on a piece of graph paper;

2. Decide about how high the top of your greenhouse should be. As you start out you might try to keep the height somewhere from nine to twelve feet for a family-size greenhouse. Draw a vertical line that height from ground level to intersect the south slope; this will mark the peak of the greenhouse;

3. For most of the United States, a rear slope between 60° and 75° is acceptable. From the peak, draw this line down to the ground level on your graph paper;

4. You can now measure the width of the greenhouse created by this combination of front and back slopes. You can experiment with slightly different angle and height combinations to get a growing area suited to your needs;

5. Since you have determined the angles of these slopes to get the most energy in your greenhouse, make your greenhouse longer to get the floor area you need, instead of changing the angles;

6. You can also use kneewalls to compromise between your "ideal" angles and such practical considerations as material lengths, width of greenhouse you need, and headroom. Feel free to use them to come up with a design that is solar efficient, easy to build, convenient to maintain, and meets your growing needs.

In most instances, if you use this procedure to interpret the range of possible angles and orientations in light of the trends of weather and your particular site restrictions, you will come up with a greenhouse design which will give you as good a performance as any precisely calculated design.

Chapter Three

Keeping the Heat in the Greenhouse

Conrad Heeschen

It won't do you much good to design your greenhouse to maximize the input of solar radiation if you don't know how to keep the heat in. Any heat saved is that much less heat you will have to supply. If there was a continuous natural input of solar energy 24 hours a day, there would be no need to be concerned with heat lost since the sun's radiation is nearly always greater than the greenhouse losses. Only the intermittent nature of this energy source makes it necessary

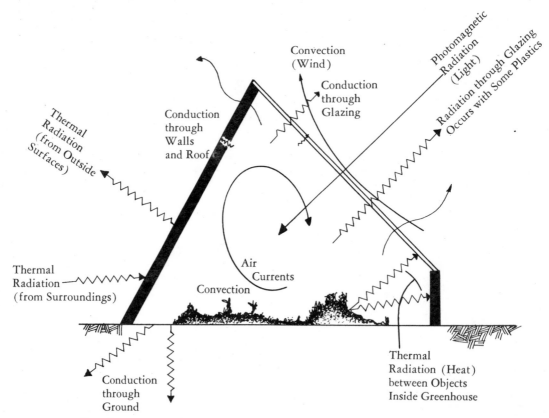

Figure 3-1: *Greenhouse energy flows.*

to store and retain as much heat as possible for use during the colder, underheated periods. Heat can be lost from the greenhouse in several ways: radiation, convection, and conduction; all are involved in heat loss from the greenhouse.

Heat transfer by radiation was described in the last chapter, since solar radiation is the major source of heat for the greenhouse (see Figure 2-2, Chapter Two). Most of the heat losses in the greenhouse will be from conduction through the walls and roof, and from air leakage out of and into the greenhouse through cracks. Thermal conduction is the process of heat transfer through a material where there is no material flow. The energy is transferred by the vibration of molecular particles and is always transferred in the direction of decreasing temperature.

Thermal convection is heat transfer by the movement of materials in liquids and gases, again from a warmer to a cooler region. This movement occurs because, as a liquid or gas is warmed, it expands and becomes less dense. It then rises, while the cooler, denser liquid or gas falls.

A greenhouse will occasionally gain heat by conduction or air leaks into the greenhouse, primarily during the summer when the air temperature outside is greater than the greenhouse temperature. There will be few such gains in the winter.

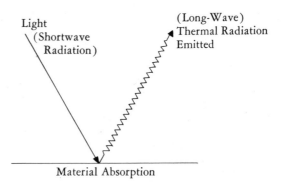

Figure 3-3a: *Absorption by opaque materials.*

Heat Losses through the Glazing

When the shortwave energy of sunlight is absorbed by plants or materials inside the green-

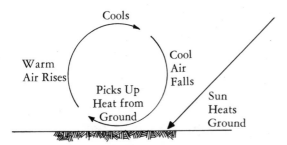

Figure 3-2: *Convection.*

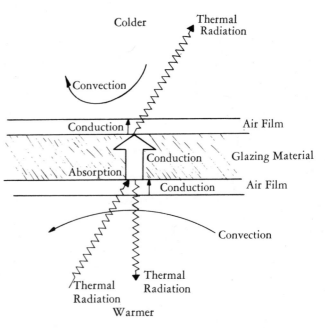

Figure 3-3b: *Heat loss through one glazing layer.*

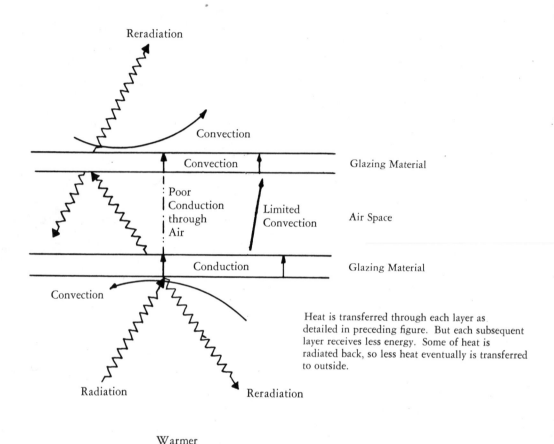

Figure 3-4: *Heat loss through multiple glazing.*

house, part of it is reradiated as long-wave or thermal energy. Some plastic glazing materials are transparent to long-wave radiation as well as light; in a greenhouse, using those material radiation losses may play an important role. Glass, fiberglass, and acrylics are opaque to long-wave radiation, but are good conductors of heat. In the thicknesses commonly used, the material resistance to heat transfer is virtually negligible.

Air films on each surface of the glazing provide most of the resistance to heat transfer, so multiple layers are used to maximize this type of resistance. Chapter Four describes the properties of different glazing materials.

The "Greenhouse Effect"

Were it not for the glazing, heat losses from con-

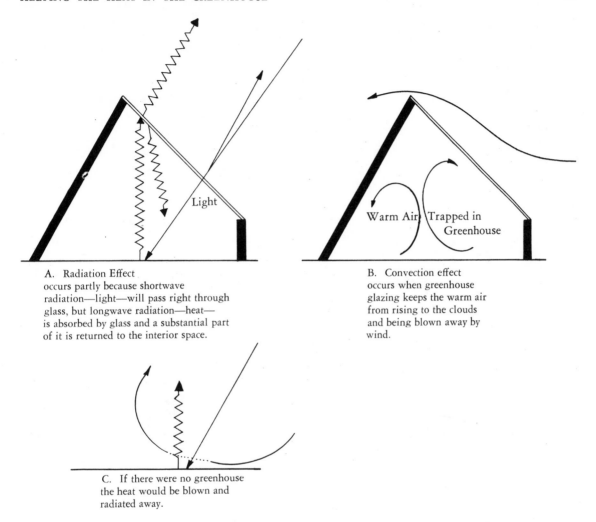

A. Radiation Effect
occurs partly because shortwave
radiation—light—will pass right through
glass, but longwave radiation—heat—
is absorbed by glass and a substantial part
of it is returned to the interior space.

B. Convection effect
occurs when greenhouse
glazing keeps the warm air
from rising to the clouds
and being blown away by
wind.

C. If there were no greenhouse
the heat would be blown and
radiated away.

Figure 3-5: *The greenhouse effect.*

vection would make it impossible to grow anything. The "greenhouse effect," commonly
attributed to the fact that glass is opaque to
long-wave radiation but transparent to light or
shortwave radiation, comes about primarily because a layer of glazing suppresses air convection
from the soil to the atmosphere. You can demonstrate this by making an enclosure of polyethylene, known to be quite transparent to long-wave
radiation; this enclosure will warm up just like a
glass enclosure.

Convection and Infiltration

Within the greenhouse convection contributes
indirectly to loss of heat from the greenhouse by

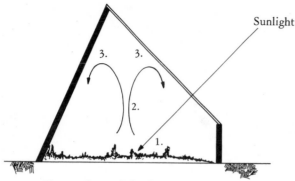

Sunlight

1. Plants and ground absorb light and warm up

2. Air picks up heat and rises

3. Air transfers heat to cooler surfaces, particularly glazing, and falls.

Figure 3-6: *Convection in greenhouse in daytime.*

transferring heat from warmer to cooler places; for instance, from the soil and plants warmed by the sun to the cooler glazing. The glazing then conducts the heat to the outside and also reradiates it both to the inside and outside. A stratification of air can occur in the greenhouse with a pool of warmer air forming near the peak,

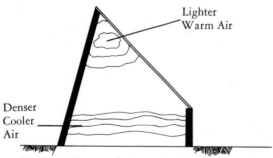

Lighter
Warm Air

Denser
Cooler
Air

Simple case here usually occurs at night when there is no heat input. During period of extreme overheating stratification may be combined with convection. This has benefit of removing excessive heat from plants.

Figure 3-7: *Air stratification in greenhouse.*

leaving the lower regions relatively cool (see Figure 3-6). This occurs because warm air is less dense, being lighter than cold air. It may be desirable to set up a forced convection by means of fans, to distribute the warm air more evenly where it is needed. More heat is lost outside the greenhouse by convection to the atmosphere on a windy day than a still day. Since outside air is rarely still, this differentiation is not very critical, but there are other reasons why you should place your greenhouse in sheltered locations.

When the wind blows around a building it creates high pressure on the windward side and low pressure on the sheltered side (Figure 3-8). Because there is a pressure difference between the two sides of the building, air is sucked out through cracks wherever there are low pressures outside. Since a lower pressure is created inside the greenhouse if air is sucked out, outside air is sucked into the greenhouse through cracks wherever there are high pressures on the outside. This inward air leakage is called infiltration. Because the pressure difference between inside and outside is greater the harder the wind blows, there is much more infiltration when the greenhouse is exposed to high winds.

Moving air can also carry water vapor and this can contribute to the loss of heat from the greenhouse. It takes about 1,000 times as much energy to evaporate a given amount of water as it does to warm it up one degree Fahrenheit. If water is evaporated from plant or soil surfaces and the vapor is carried to a cooler region, say the glazing, it may condense and give off much of that heat to the glazing, which in turn will conduct and radiate the heat away. Thus, condensation on the glazing, besides decreasing the ability of the glazing to transmit light, also contributes to heat losses from the greenhouse. The same measures taken to decrease conductive and radi-

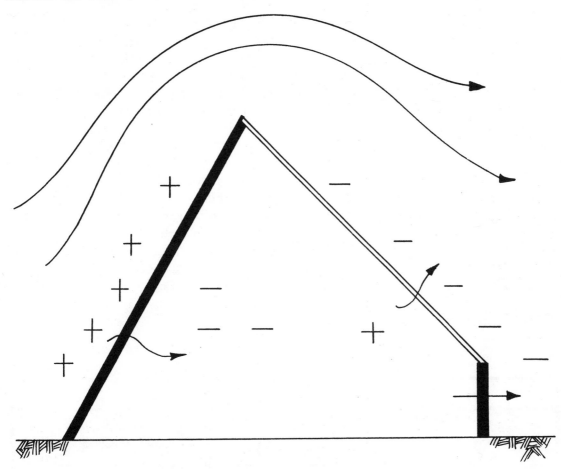

Figure 3-8: *Infiltration caused by difference in air pressure.*

ative heat losses through glazing should serve to reduce the incidence of condensation, since the inner layer of glazing generally will be warmer. The addition of a second glazing layer not only reduces heat loss due to its additional insulative properties but greatly reduces condensation and resultant losses.

Heat Losses through Opaque Surfaces

Conduction of heat from warmer to cooler regions takes place through every surface in the greenhouse. Most of the losses will be through the glazing, even if measures are taken to reduce these losses. The rate of heat transfer by conduction depends on the resistance of the material to heat transfer, as well as on the difference in temperature between the inside and the outside. If both temperatures are the same there will be no heat transferred by conduction, but this is hardly the case in the winter when you are trying to maintain a warm environment for your plants against the chill outside. Because heat losses depend on the temperature difference between inside and outside, heat losses from a greenhouse may be considerably greater in the upper part if the warmer air is simply allowed to collect there. Heat is lost before the plants are able to benefit from it, but if the air could be circulated through the greenhouse, the plants would benefit, even though the overall heat loss may be about the same.

Heat Loss to the Ground

There are heat losses through the ground as well as through the walls of the greenhouses. Nearly all the losses are from the edge and heat losses through the interior of a slab can be ignored for all but very small floor areas. This is natural,

since the edges are much closer to cold soil than the interior. The temperature of the ground is relatively constant at depths greater than 16 feet for the severest climates. But there is also a well-established frost line. The ground usually does not freeze below this line even though it is exposed to below freezing temperatures at the surface. This is partly because of the supply of continuous, although low (45° to 50°F.), temperature heat from deeper in the ground and partly because there is a delay before the cold temperatures can penetrate and make their effect felt at a given depth. This accounts for the lag between the usual time of lowest air temperatures in January and the lowest ground temperatures. Average ground temperatures at different depths throughout the year are shown in accompanying illustrations.

Relative Economics of Some Common Insulation Materials				
Type of Insulation	Assumed Density	R/in.	cost/bd. ft.	Thermal Resistance per $ Spent (10 20 30 40 50 60 70 80 90 100)
Fiberglass batts	—	3.2	3.7¢	
Vermiculite	5.0	2.2	9.3¢	
Cellular glass board	9.0	2.5	25¢	
Extruded polystyrene (Styrofoam)	1.8	4.0	20¢	
Expanded polystyrene (beadboard, cellofoam)	1.0	3.5	12.5¢	
Extruded urethane board	1.5	6.2	28¢	
Isocyanurate foam board (technifoam)	—	9.0	30.5¢	
Macerated paper or pulp products	2.5	3.7	5¢	
Wood (log-cabin walls)	32	1.3	15¢	

Density (lbs./ft.³): Many of these generic types of insulation are available in a range of densities. For a given type, lower densities usually have greater insulating value.

R/in.: Thermal resistance per inch thickness, hr. °F. Ft.²/Btu. The higher the R, the greater the insulating value. R values are average values taken from the *ASHRAE Handbook of Fundamentals*, 1974.

Cost/bd.ft.: Material cost only for a section of insulation one foot square and one inch thick. Costs are retail prices, 1976.

Thermal resistance/dollar spent: R/in. divided by $ cost/bd.ft. The larger the number, the better the buy.

Table 3-1: *Relative Economics of Some Common Insulation Materials*

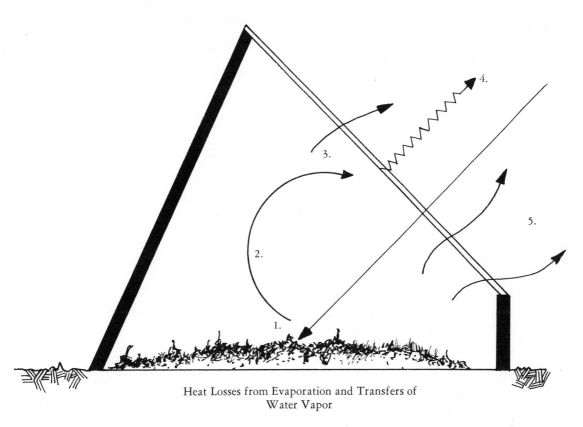

Heat Losses from Evaporation and Transfers of
Water Vapor

1. Part of sun's energy goes toward evaporating water
   from plants or soil. (One-thousand times as much
   energy as that required to warm up the water one
   Fahrenheit degree.)

2. Water vapor carried by air convection currents.

3. Condensation occurs on cooler surfaces, particularly
   glazing. When condensation occurs, the heat of
   vaporization is given off and surface becomes warmer.

4. Warmer surface conducts and radiates more heat to
   outside.

5. If greenhouse is not sealed well, moist air escapes and
   heat is directly lost to the outside. This can be a
   serious source of heat loss in humid, poorly constructed
   greenhouses.

Figure 3-9: *Evaporative heat loss.*

When a heated building is placed over a piece of ground, the temperature of the ground under the building never freezes at any depth, except at the edges, because the building loses a small amount of heat to it and the ground is not directly exposed to the outside temperatures. A zone of warm earth also develops as heat is slowly lost from the inside (groundwater can carry this heat away). Thus after a long enough period of time the temperature in the ground below the greenhouse approaches an average of the inside temperature of the greenhouse and deep ground temperature.

Proper insulation of the edges of a building overcomes most of the heat losses and allows you to take advantage of the moderating effect of the earth's temperature. This is where most greenhouses, particularly the prefabricated models you find advertised everywhere, fail. Besides being totally glazed, even on the north side, they pay little or no attention to heat losses through the ground. In fact, some designs are so small that the floor area can be considered all edge from the point of view of heat losses and the ground will provide no contribution to heating. Greenhouses which are set on concrete slabs or concrete-footing edges may be even worse, unless insulated, since heat is conducted through concrete more rapidly than through soil (see Chapter Five).

Reducing Greenhouse Heat Losses through Glazing

The most obvious way to reduce greenhouse losses through the glazing is to reduce the amount of glazing area. In the previous chapter we have seen to what extent this approach can be followed, and here we will concentrate on

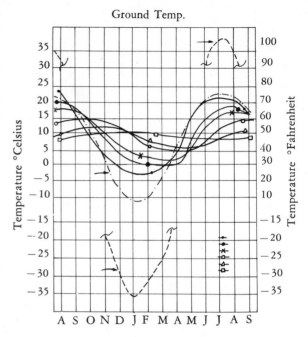

Figure 3-10: *Average monthly temperature variation with soil depth (E. Bowers, University of Minnesota).*

how to make the necessary glazing a more effective heat retainer.

Radiation losses alone are not usually an important factor in heat losses except if polyethylene is used, but the effect of the conduction and reradiation of heat from glazing once it has absorbed heat from convection or radiation can be minimized in several ways. Multiple layers of glazing reduce the amount of heat ultimately transmitted through the layers to a minimum, because the trapped air spaces and air films on the surfaces inhibit both conductive and convective losses while radiation from each layer to the next outside layer decreases with decreasing temperature of the glazing layers. The use of layers

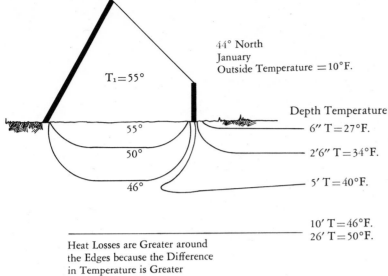

44° North
January
Outside Temperature = 10°F.

$T_1 = 55°$

Depth Temperature

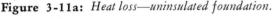

55°

6" T = 27°F.

50°

2'6" T = 34°F.

46°

5' T = 40°F.

10' T = 46°F.
26' T = 50°F.

Heat Losses are Greater around
the Edges because the Difference
in Temperature is Greater

Figure 3-11a: *Heat loss—uninsulated foundation.*

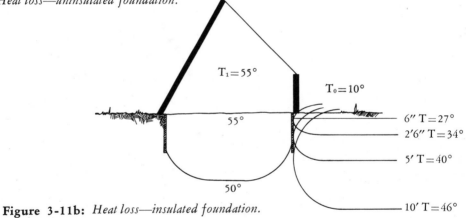

$T_1 = 55°$

$T_0 = 10°$

55°

6" T = 27°
2'6" T = 34°

5' T = 40°

50°

10' T = 46°

Figure 3-11b: *Heat loss—insulated foundation.*

reduces heat losses through glazing to about one half the losses through a single layer. In all but

R-Value

Insulation works to decrease the flow of heat through a material, such as the greenhouse wall. The measure of how much resistance a material has is called its R-value. The higher the R-value, the more resistance a material has.

Box 3-1: *R-Value*

the mildest climates you should use at least two layers of glazing in your greenhouse.

The only reason to have a glazed surface is to admit sunlight into your greenhouse. Do you get any sun at night? Of course not; the only thing glazing does for you at night is lose heat, and it's very good at that. The most effective method of reducing glazing heat losses, and overall greenhouse heat losses is to use some type of movable insulation, during the nighttime or even during periods of extremely low temperatures and low light intensities.

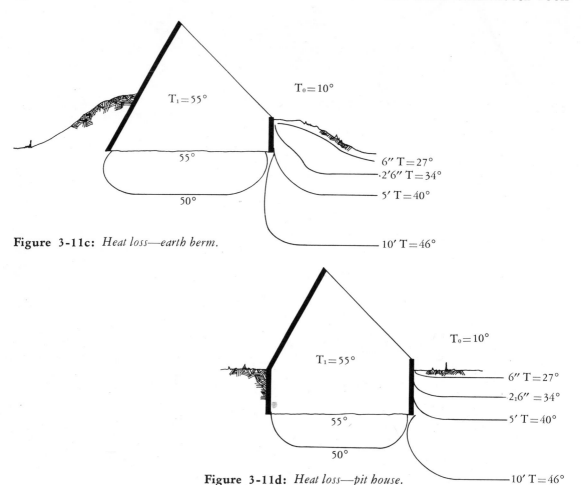

Figure 3-11c: *Heat loss—earth berm.*

Figure 3-11d: *Heat loss—pit house.*

You can cut total daily heat losses through double-glazing by a minimum of one half if you use nighttime movable insulation equivalent to 3 inches of fiberglass or 1½ inches of Styrofoam for 14 hours each night. You could use it for even longer periods in December in most northern locations. If your local weather requires you to use more glazing because of a high proportion of cloudy days, or if the average outdoor winter temperature is less than about 30° to 35°F., it is usually necessary to use movable insulation, even if you have two layers of glazing, so that the glazing will be a net producer rather than a net loser of energy. (For an in-depth discussion of glazing see Chapter Four.)

Movable Nighttime Insulation

Taylor and Gregg describe rather simple methods of nighttime insulation using rolls of canvas-covered insulation unrolled down on the greenhouse at night and rolled up again in the morning. These must be made secure against wind, and if it snows at night, they may be diffi-

Photo 3-1: *"Bamboo" snow curtain. Eugene, Oregon.*

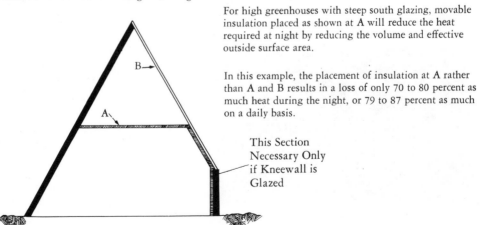

For high greenhouses with steep south glazing, movable insulation placed as shown at **A** will reduce the heat required at night by reducing the volume and effective outside surface area.

In this example, the placement of insulation at **A** rather than **A** and **B** results in a loss of only 70 to 80 percent as much heat during the night, or 79 to 87 percent as much on a daily basis.

This Section Necessary Only if Kneewall is Glazed

Figure 3-12: *Location of movable insulation.*

Photo 3-2: *Styrofoam insulating panels: attached pit. Milwaukee, Wisconsin.*

Photo 3-3: *Movable curtain in commercial green-house. Pennsylvania State University.*

cult to roll up again. Locating the insulation on the inside, while avoiding these problems, does present some new ones. (Accumulations of snow during the night will slide off the roof when it begins to warm up after the insulation is removed, and in the meantime, the snow does transmit some light.) The insulation must be held up in place, rather than being draped, and if removable, whether panels, batts, or rolls, must be stored somewhere. Tight-fitting insulation is preferable to drapes since drapes do not do a very good job of combatting convective losses. If movable or adjustable shutters or louvers are used there must be sufficient clear-

Photo 3-4: *Beads filling air space between glazings.*

ance for them to operate, as well as mechanical means for adjustment and locking them in place.

Although it makes use of rather sophisticated technology, there is one recent breakthrough in greenhouse design which deserves mention here. This is the Beadwall system of nighttime insulation. Developed by Zomeworks in Albuquer-

Photo 3-5: *Beads in place.*

que, New Mexico, the Beadwell method uses the dead-air space between the two layers of glazing as a nighttime storage area for thousands of tiny plastic "beads." Used by the plastics industry as the basic "building block" for such products as disposable coffee cups, the beads are normally forced together under heat and pressure to form the product concerned. Zomeworks uses these beads in another way. A powerful electric motor which can be used as either a vacuum or blower is connected to the air space between the glazing via a length of ductwork and a storage container. At night, when insulation is desired, the motor blows thousands of the tiny beads into the air space until it is completely filled. In the morning, the motor reverses itself, becoming a vacuum which sucks the beads out from between the glazing and back to the storage cannister. While very effective, this tends to be a rather expensive system.

Removable interior insulation can be fairly inexpensive if it consists simply of panels that can be clipped into place at night and easily removed come morning. The panels could be made of Styrofoam or other rigid insulation, possibly backed with Masonite or plywood. Storage of the panels might be a problem in a small greenhouse.

An advantage of permanent insulating shutters or louvers is that they also offer a means of sun control in the hotter months. Removable panels are basically an on or off proposition, whereas louvers could be adjusted or installed to cut off direct sunlight while still allowing a good deal of direct light. For sun-control purposes alone, venetian blinds would be an excellent device, and are readily available, but would have to be used in conjunction with some other method to achieve any insulating value.

Many greenhouses are made with aluminum frames; since aluminum conducts 250 times as much heat at the same thickness of glass for the same period of time, the amount of heat lost through the aluminum frame of a glazed surface can be as great as the amount lost through the glazing itself. For this reason, wood frames are preferable to metal. If you must use metal, or wish to improve a metal-frame greenhouse you already have, you should insulate the glazing bars so that they don't serve as "thermal bridges." (See Chapters Seven, Eight, and Ten for additional details on night curtains and shutters.)

Reducing Conduction Heat Losses through Opaque Surfaces

Heat losses by conduction through the surface outside of the greenhouse can be reduced with insulation. In fact, insulation serves to decrease the flow of heat, which is expressed in R-value (Box 3-1). There are several different types of insulation available today, and each has its appropriate use. The least expensive insulation per unit of insulating value is fiberglass, either batts or loose fill. Rock wool and cellulose-fill insulations are nearly as cheap per unit of thermal performance. The board-foam insulations, although the most effective per inch of thickness, are also the most expensive per unit of insulating value; they do possess properties which make their use superior to fiberglass or other insulations in certain circumstances. Anywhere above ground, not in contact with moisture, and where space is no limitation, fiberglass batt or fill-type insulations are suitable and should be used.

In contact with ground, where moisture may be a problem, where pressure may crush insulation, or where space is a critical limitation,

you need a strong water-resistant insulation. The foam boards obviously find their place here, despite their expense. It is reported that some types of foam are eaten by carpenter ants, so appropriate metal flashing should be used to protect it. The different types of foam insulation are expanded polystyrene (commonly known as beadboard), a low-density board composed of small white Styrofoam pellets molded together; extruded polystyrene, a solid, usually blue, foam board, and extruded polyurethane, similar to extruded polystyrene but of a finer texture. There are also foams which can be applied on site from a mixture of chemicals; these are usually installed by dealers only.

The major disadvantage of the board foams, besides their cost, is that they are either flammable or give off toxic fumes when heated; the only truly safe place to use them is where they cannot burn or be exposed to high heat, underground, as foundation insulation, for instance. Fiberglass does not burn; although the paper or foil backing is flammable, it would not contribute much to a fire already underway. Cellulose fibers are usually treated with a fire retardant.

Earth as Insulation

The earth itself, *if not wet,* can also be an effective insulator. Although not as effective per inch of thickness as artificial insulations (it takes about 24 inches of dry loam to equal the performance of 1 inch of fiberglass), earth is often a convenient and inexpensive insulator, provided it can be kept dry. If there is much groundwater or a high water table, the movement of cool underground water could remove large amounts of heat from an uninsulated structure, and render the earth as having no insulating value.

Proper building drainage and diversion of run-off from the roofs can minimize wetting of the earth to a limited extent, but if the water table is high, you would be wise not to count on the earth for insulation. The use of earth berms does not by itself allow the greenhouse to benefit from ground heat, but the berms simply act as insulation against outside temperatures beyond (see Figure 3-11c).

Reducing the Temperature Difference between Inside and Outside

Another way to reduce the amount of heat lost by conduction is to reduce the difference in temperature between the inside of the greenhouse and the outside. To do this you could consider maintaining your greenhouse at lower average temperatures and then grow plants that respond to this environment. Also, by setting the greenhouse deep in the ground, you could place part of the greenhouse adjacent to a "warmer" outside temperature, thus reducing the rate of heat loss. Of course, if you attach your greenhouse to your house or other heated buildings you will achieve the same results.

Since the air inside a greenhouse may easily overheat during the day, often excess heat must be ventilated to the outside (or to the house, in the case of an attached greenhouse), and the heat losses through conduction are higher than usual because of the greater difference between outside and inside temperatures. High ventilation rates greatly increase water losses, which is a factor in dry climates. While daytime conduction losses during overheated periods do not have an immediate deleterious effect on the greenhouse environment, if heat will be required later at night it would be preferable to keep as much of it as possible. The heat *must* be removed from the air to storage if conduction losses during these periods are to be minimized.

Reducing Infiltration and Ventilation Heat Losses

Greenhouses have traditionally been constructed rather loosely because of the need to provide adequate ventilation by natural means. By providing enough cracks there would usually be enough air exchanged, but a solar greenhouse requires control over air flows in order to take full advantage of the heat the greenhouse receives.

The first thing to do to reduce losses from convection is to control air infiltration. All joints where air can get into the greenhouse, including glazing, sills, door frames, corners, etc., should be carefully caulked and weather-stripped, and a continuous vapor barrier of four- or six-mil polyethylene should be installed; use as large a sheet as possible to avoid joints and cut out openings for doors, etc., after installing it. The use of large pieces of acrylic, fiberglass, or plastic for the glazing rather than glass (which for purposes of strength must be installed in relatively small pieces), would help to reduce considerably the amount of caulking that must be done.

You can also reduce the amount of infiltration your greenhouse experiences by reducing the surface area exposed to the outside. A pit greenhouse, an attached greenhouse, or a greenhouse with earth berms will do this. Since houses are usually heated, an attached greenhouse would have the added benefit of being able to tap the warm air in the house in an emergency.

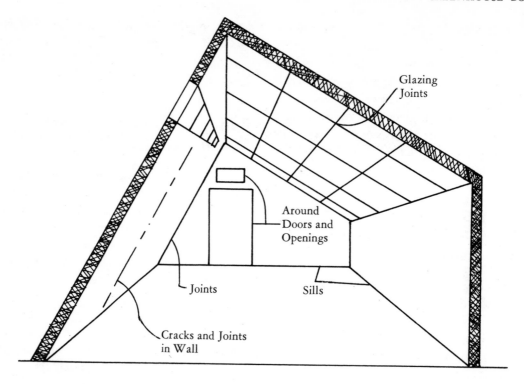

Glazing
Joints

Around
Doors and
Openings

Joints   Sills

Cracks and Joints
in Wall

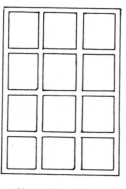

Glass—Too Many
Potential Air Leaks

Large Sheets of
Plastic including
Fiberglass, Acrylic—
only Edges Are
Potential Leaks

Figure 3-13: *Infiltration.*

You can also reduce the need for ventilation. There are two major reasons to ventilate a greenhouse. The most wasteful is to eliminate heat buildup in the greenhouse, since most greenhouses have no provision for storing excess heat. You should definitely provide some means for removing the heat from the air without venting it to the atmosphere, in order to store it for future use (see Chapter Five). The second reason for ventilation is to assure an adequate supply of carbon dioxide to the growing plants. Of course, an attached greenhouse shares a natural venting relationship with the house.

I can't say how much ventilation the plants in your greenhouse will require, since carbon dioxide requirements depend on the rate of growth and on the heat available and the plant species. During periods of low temperatures, such as at night or on cold cloudy days in an unheated greenhouse, the requirement for carbon dioxide will probably be fairly low. Carbon dioxide requirements are directly tied to light levels since photosynthesis uses both. At night, carbon dioxide is given off by the plants and if respiration exceeds photosynthesis due to low light levels, carbon dioxide may be released as well. It has been suggested that attaching a greenhouse to your home would set up a symbiotic relationship between plants as oxygen producers and people as carbon dioxide producers, but people do not provide quite enough carbon dioxide for a roomful of rapidly growing plants.

The New Alchemy Institute claims that some of their greenhouses are absolutely airtight and that because they never sterilize their soil, and in fact, encourage many microorganisms and animals such as frogs to live in the greenhouse, there is always an adequate supply of carbon dioxide to the plants.

Rabbits, fish tanks, and burning candles all have been demonstrated to increase carbon dioxide levels enough to be significant. The inclusion of a compost pile within the greenhouse has also been suggested as a means to provide carbon dioxide as well as heat. The subject is complex and poorly researched to date. (See Chapters Thirteen and Fourteen for further discussion.) It is complicated by the fact that plants use carbon dioxide only during photosynthesis, and produce carbon dioxide and use oxygen during the night, so the plants themselves may produce some of their own carbon dioxide. The chapters on plant physiology will give you a better understanding of the carbon dioxide, light, and heat requirements of your plants.

Some air movement is desirable in the greenhouse, to avoid humidity buildup around the plants and to break up the resistance of the boundary layer of air on plant leaf surfaces, which inhibits the transfer of carbon dioxide and water vapor. Air movement can be generated within the greenhouse, and may be associated with the removal of heat from storage.

Air Lock

An air lock at the entrance can also reduce the amount of cold air introduced directly into the greenhouse. If you can't provide an air lock you should at least place the entrance on the leeward side of the building. A small antechamber will prevent strong gusts of cold air from reaching the plants, and will reduce the overall amount of air infiltration around the door. It also provides a handy place to keep tools. An attached greenhouse can be entered directly from your house.

After all measures have been taken and you still need to provide additional ventilation, a heat exchanger could be used. There are sophisticated and expensive heat exchangers on the market, but it would probably work just as well to provide a two-chamber rock box, through one half of which the air is exhausted for a period of time, while air is drawn in through the other half. After a certain period (only experience and local conditions/temperature will determine its length) the exhaust half will become relatively saturated with heat and the direction of flow is reversed. The incoming air now picks up the heat from the warmed rocks, while the warmer air heats up the now-cool side. It must be borne in mind that the efficiency of this heat ex-changer is probably not high, and that it will only be effective if all other infiltration and air leaks are controlled.

Surface to Volume Ratios

A small, freestanding greenhouse will lose more heat per unit volume than a larger greenhouse. This is because the smaller the greenhouse is, the larger the ratio of its exposed surface area to its volume. For example, a box, 5 feet on each side, sitting on the ground has a surface area exposed to the air of 125 square feet and a volume of 125 cubic feet, for a ratio of 1 square foot of

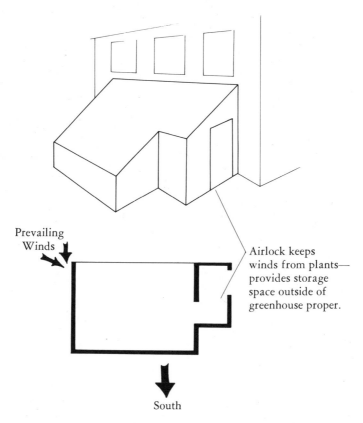

Prevailing
Winds

Airlock keeps
winds from plants—
provides storage
space outside of
greenhouse proper.

South

Figure 3-14: *Air lock.*

surface to 1 cubic foot of volume. On the other hand, a box 10 feet on each side has 500 square feet of exposed surface area and 1,000 cubic feet of volume, for a surface volume ratio of 1 square foot per 2 cubic feet of volume.

Larger structures not only have lower surface to volume ratios, but in addition, the air temperature inside is less affected when the door is opened, since the amount of air that is changed, in proportion to the entire volume, is much less. It is easier to maintain a relatively constant temperature with the larger volume of air. If at all possible, smaller greenhouses should be built attached to heated buildings in order to offset the disadvantage of size. A shared community-sized greenhouse, if built freestanding, would have a definite thermal advantage over several independent freestanding greenhouses.

The cost per square foot of growing area would also tend to decrease with a larger greenhouse, since the surface area to volume ratio is lower. This is partly offset, however, by the larger structural members necessary in large greenhouses.

Summary

The most important thing to do in your greenhouse is to reduce the heat losses through the glazing, since that is where most losses will occur in a well-constructed building. We have already learned (in Chapter Two) how we can design the greenhouse for the optimum amount of glazing and what shape to make it. Even in a greenhouse of the proper shape and the right amount of glazing, over 60 percent of conduction losses will be through the glazing. It is also important to insulate the opaque walls as well, and to keep a balance between the insulation used for the different parts of the greenhouse. But the glazing should be tackled first.

Using the basic rules of thumb found in Chapter Two, we have developed a greenhouse "model," which is presented in Appendix Three, to illustrate the effects of insulation alternatives. A specific application of that procedure follows.

If we start with an uninsulated structure, single-glazed, we can cut conduction heat losses 34 percent by installing a second layer of glazing. On the other hand, we would cut heat losses by only 28 percent by using $3\frac{1}{2}$ inches of fiberglass on the north wall. Ideally we should do both, thereby reducing the total conduction heat losses by 62 percent.

Now if we compare the relative losses through the different surfaces, we find that the glazing is about 77 percent of the reduced total, so what we do to improve the performance of the glazing will have a significant effect. We have several options to further reduce losses; we can build an attached or pit greenhouse, which reduces the amount of surface exposed to outside air, or we could add insulation to the opaque walls. We could also devise and use some type of nighttime insulation on the glazing. We could do any one or any combination of these, but let's look at the relative benefits of each.

The first $3\frac{1}{2}$ inches of insulation improves the thermal performance of uninsulated walls by a factor of 4; the next $3\frac{1}{2}$ inches brings about a further improvement of only a factor of two. For an example, the greenhouse with $3\frac{1}{2}$ inches of fiberglass lost only about 30 Btu/hr./°F. through the walls; with 7 inches it would save an additional 15 Btu/hr./°F.

If we attached the greenhouse to our house we would effectively eliminate heat losses through approximately one half of the total opaque wall area. (There may be gains through this wall, but

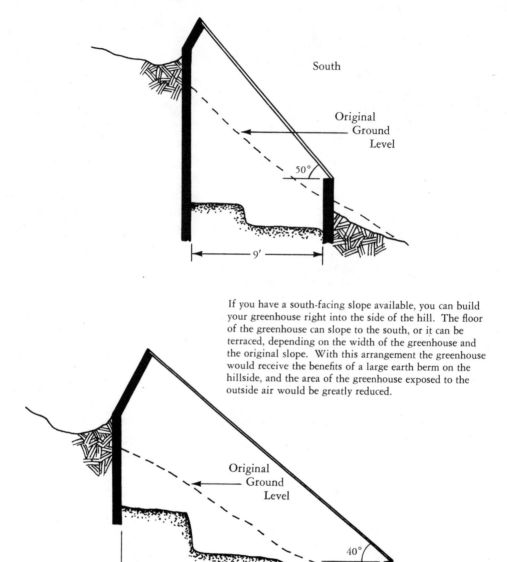

If you have a south-facing slope available, you can build
your greenhouse right into the side of the hill. The floor
of the greenhouse can slope to the south, or it can be
terraced, depending on the width of the greenhouse and
the original slope. With this arrangement the greenhouse
would receive the benefits of a large earth berm on the
hillside, and the area of the greenhouse exposed to the
outside air would be greatly reduced.

Figure 3-15: *Sloping sites.*

for the time being we will ignore them.) This will also result in a savings of about 15 Btu/hr./°F.

Our third option is to provide nighttime insulation over the glazing. If it is used for 14 hours each night during the winter, it can save over 45 Btu/hr./°F. on the average, or three times what either additional insulation or attaching the greenhouse can do.

Of course, there are other considerations involved in making these choices. Adding insulation requires that you have the space available, but its cost would be low. An attached greenhouse, although saving heat, may also cut down on the amount of sunlight received by the greenhouse. On the other hand, it can provide very convenient and reliable heat storage in the house. The nighttime insulation (while clearly making a significant contribution to the reduction of heat losses), is also the most significant contribution to the reduction of heat losses, and is the most expensive option. Remember, however, that it is almost always easier and cheaper to do something during initial construction than to add it later. The labor required for insulation, in particular, is no greater for 6 inches than for 3½ inches.

At a minimum, the greenhouse should be insulated with the equivalent of 3½ inches of fiberglass, and up to about 6 inches in the cooler regions. For house construction, up to 6 inches of insulation in walls and 9 inches in ceilings will pay for itself in, at most, two to three years. Greenhouses would probably not exhibit quite as good payback periods because the temperatures are lower, but six inches is still a good amount to use. The foundation, down to frost line, must also be insulated with 1 or 2 inches of foam if you expect to make effective use of the ground for heat storage.

Any location with a climate cooler than about Washington D.C.'s should use double-glazing, whether or not some form of nighttime insulation is used. I would also highly recommend the use of the nighttime insulation if your area is cooler than Washington D.C., or if you are in a warmer area, and only using single-glazing.

From the standpoint of greenhouse performance alone, small greenhouses would be much better if attached to a heated building. By small I mean something smaller than 100 to 200 square feet, depending on the climate. Of course, the larger an attached greenhouse is, the more heat it can contribute to the house.

Chapter Four

Glazing

Leandre Poisson
David J. MacKinnon

The most important and complex element in a solar greenhouse is the glazed wall. Many solar greenhouses and other collectors have failed because the glazing system was ill-conceived or otherwise inadequate.

The glazed wall is multifunctional. It permits solar energy to pass through the structure to energize the plants through the process of photosynthesis. Photosynthesis uses less than five percent of the available energy. The remaining energy not reflected out of the greenhouse is converted, by absorption and reradiation within the greenhouse, into long-wave (infrared) heat radiation and heated air.

As shown in Chapter Three, the primary purpose of a glazing is to pass solar energy and prevent heat from leaving. For this purpose the ideal glazing maximizes the transmission of shortwave solar radiation and minimizes the transmission of both long-wave infrared radiation and energy from the heated air. Secondary desirable properties for a glazing are: good weatherability, resistance to stress (fracture and tear) and abrasion, low cost, easy installation, and low maintenance.

This chapter will evaluate the primary and secondary desirable characteristics for glazings commonly available to you for both single and multiple layers.

Single Layers

A. Maximization of Solar Transmission

Reflection of solar light from the glazed surface contributes to low solar transmission. All common glazings, glasses, and plastics, reflect roughly two to four percent of the solar light at each surface. Since each glazing has two surfaces, the total reflectance (which refers to the fraction of light reflected) amounts to about four to eight percent when light perpendicularly strikes the surfaces. As the light strikes the surface more and more away from the perpendicular, the percentage of reflection increases slowly. But beyond about 45° from the perpendicular, the reflection increases rapidly until at 90°, the percent reflection is 100 percent. For most clear glazings used in solar applications, reflection constitutes the greatest loss to light transmission. Usually greenhouses should be designed so that most of the sun's light strikes the glazed surfaces at less than 45° (see Chapter Two). Without special, expensive coatings, the inherent reflection cannot be avoided.

A relatively new, but very expensive glazing, Teflon, has an extremely low reflectance, while Mylar has a relatively high reflectance. The rest of the common materials discussed in this chapter have reflectances between these two materials.

Impurities within a glazing material can absorb solar light causing additional reduction in transmittance. Generally, glazings have very low absorptance (which refers to the fraction of light absorbed) when new, but some (plastics, in particular) can and do acquire high absorptances as they deteriorate in the sun and weather elements.

In glasses the absorption occurs primarily from iron impurities. Glass which "looks" green on edge has many iron impurities; glass which "looks" blue on edge has few iron impurities. The latter is commonly called water-white glass and has the lowest solar-light absorption. When glass is used, many solar aficionados prefer water-white glass, but cost and availability usually convince most of us that we don't need it. Generally, common window glass has a sufficiently low absorption to constitute an effective glazing.

For plastics, the absorption occurs not from foreign impurities per se but from plastic molecules which have changed their structure with respect to their neighbors. Whereas the length of solar exposure does not affect the absorption properties of glass, light (ultraviolet in particular) and ozone will increase the number of "destructured" molecules in the plastic leading to increased light absorption and deterioration of strength.

Some plastics are more sensitive than others. The polyethylenes, acetates, mylars, and vinyls are sensitive to ultraviolet degradation. On the other hand, Teflon and Tedlar are much less sensitive. The fiberglass and acrylics also are less sensitive (primarily because they have been weatherized or protected at the factory).

In summary, you should choose materials which have low reflectance and absorptance, or conversely, high transmittance. (In rating the materials to follow, the effects of reflectance and absorptance are combined into the measure of transmittance.) The transmittance for new materials will be rated in Table 4-1, column A. The weatherability of the material will be separately rated in Table 4-1, column D.

B. Minimization of Infrared Radiation Transmission

Infrared radiation can be transmitted, absorbed, and reflected when it strikes a surface. Of course for the purpose of keeping heat in the greenhouse, the worst materials transmit the infrared radiation and the best reflect it. Unfortunately, there are no common materials which transmit both solar and reflect infrared. Work performed at Massachusetts Institute of Technology shows that coatings, such as tin oxide, transmit solar and reflect infrared, but they are very difficult, and therefore probably expensive, to apply to substrates such as glass and plastics. Therefore, we are left with the next best material property: absorption of infrared radiation. When infrared radiation is absorbed by a thin material, the material heats up and reradiates that energy (in the infrared) in the forward and backward direction as shown in Figure 4-1. The result is that roughly half of the incoming infrared radiation is prevented from passing through the material.

For all the common glasses and plastics (uncoated), their interaction with infrared radiation lies somewhere between the worst and better conditions shown in Figure 4-1.

In normal thicknesses glass absorbs 100 percent of the infrared, while thin plastic sheets transmit a great deal of it. Polyethylene in four-mil sheets (one mil equals one-thousandth of an inch) transmits over 70 percent (absorbs 30 percent) of the infrared which strikes it. Acetate (four mil), on the other hand, transmits only 8

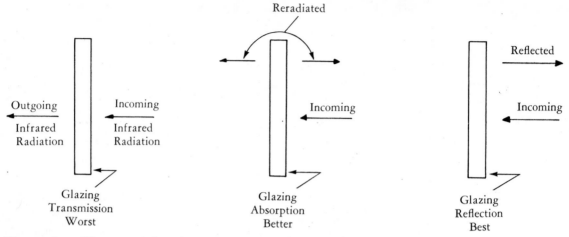

Figure 4-1: *Three ways infrared radiation interacts with a glazing.*

percent (absorbs 92 percent), making it very attractive from this standpoint. All the other thin plastics rated in Table 4-1 lie between these two extremes.

Thick plastics on the other hand (40-mil or greater) absorb almost all the infrared radiation. In this respect, then, thick acrylics, polycarbonates (Lexan), and fiberglasses are equivalent to glass.

C. Minimization of Energy Transmitted from the Heated Air

As shown in Chapter Two, energy from the heated air within the greenhouse is transmitted by convection to the inner glazing surface and passed by conduction to the outer glazing surface where it is lost again by convection. Since glazings are usually quite thin, the effect of the material on the rate of conduction is virtually negligible. It is the dead-air film next to the surfaces which gives some resistance to the heat flow, and *this has nothing to do with material properties.* This is true for the thicker glazings such as glass, acrylics, and fiberglass as well. So

when you hear that a thin material significantly reduces heat flow, be wary.

Actually, it is the creation of large dead-air spaces with multiple layers of glazing that gives transparent walls significant resistance to the conduction of heat.

D. Weatherability

In many respects, glass is virtually inert to the sun and the elements, hail and birds being some of the exceptions. Plastics will deteriorate with exposure overtime both in solar transmittance and strength. Thick plastics will remain strong longer, however.

Weatherized versions of all the plastics are available, and for economic and environmental reasons they should be used. Some have guarantees; make sure you read and understand them.

E. Resistance to Stress (Fracture and Tear) and Abrasion

Glass has a low resistance to fracture, but good abrasion resistance. The thick acrylics, polycarbonates, and fiberglass have good resistance to stress and a generally low resistance to abrasion. But in this connection, very few environmental conditions (dust storms) will lead to significant abrasion.

For the semirigid materials, more effort must be taken to prevent wind flap which could lead to tearing and pulling loose from supports.

The thin flexible films are particularly subject to fracture and tear. Therefore, they should not be exposed to environments of undue stress. Nevertheless, some of the thin plastics are very strong: Mylar, Tedlar, and vinyl. Polyethylene and Teflon will not tear easily but will permanently deform under stretching. Acetate is brittle and tears easily. This material should be used only under special conditions, such as a second inner glazing protected by a rigid outer glazing. (The specific greenhouse case studies cited in Part II will explore a range of glazing materials used in many regions of the country.)

The strength of the material will indicate the best way to attach it to a support: nailed, stapled, or glued. For example, acetate is so brittle that you should glue it to a wood frame which in turn can be nailed to a rigid support. This method was used in the Flagstaff greenhouse (see Chapter Eight). The fiberglass sheet is sufficiently strong enough to be nailed to its support; care should be taken to predrill slightly oversized holes in the fiberglass before final nailing. It appears, however, that screws will work better than nails to permanently secure the outer glazings. A neoprene gasket should be placed between the screw (or nail) so that the fiberglass is not shattered upon securing with a screwdriver or hammer. Some plastics, such as polyethylene, can be stapled directly to a support if used as an interior glazing. Generally, it is better to provide a wider surface of support by clamping and nailing with strips of wood or metal.

Finally, you should choose the securing system that seals easily and one that is permanent.

F. Low Cost

The least expensive glazing may not be the best when you consider the material's weatherability. Certainly, polyethylene is the best buy of any glazing, but if you have to replace it every six months (if used as an outer glazing), the total cost(your labor included) can be very high over the long term.

Of the rigid materials, polycarbonates (Lexan) are by far the most expensive ($2.50 per square foot) followed by acrylics and glass. On the other hand, the semirigid materials are not inexpensive. The semirigid fiberglasses specifically made for greenhouse exterior glazing run from 40¢ to over a dollar per square foot depending on quality.

There are usually various grades offered by any one manufacturer. The grades refer to the guaranteed solar transmittance for a period of time. A typical manufacturer's guarantee might read: "Our A grade is guaranteed to have 92-percent solar transmittance and not to drop below 95-percent of the new value at the end of 15 years." There might also be a rider which says something like, "Length of transmittance guarantee is reduced to 10 years in the southwestern United States, specifically, Arizona, New Mexico. . . ." and so on. Make sure you understand the limitations and consider them in the overall cost.

You can purchase a very-good quality, semirigid glazing for about 50¢ per square foot.

The thin flexible films vary considerably in cost from a few cents per square foot for polyethylene to over 40¢ per square foot for Teflon. You should choose the least costly with the highest infrared absorptance and install it as an inner glazing.

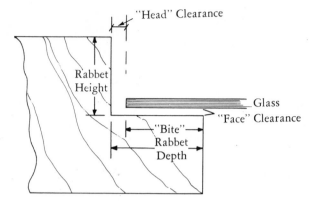

Figure 4-2: *Definitions.*

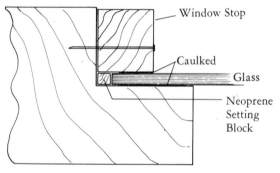

Figure 4-3: *Glazing (glass) with window stop.*

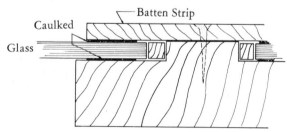

Figure 4-4: *Glazing (glass) with batten strip.*

G. Ease of Installation and Low Maintenance

Glass can be very difficult to install and seal in an inexpensive greenhouse. Large sheets of glass will be subject to breakage as the supports move with changing humidity and temperature. Except for breakage, rigid plastics have problems similar to glass.

Most rigid materials, such as glass and thick acrylics, have limited structural usefulness; the bulk of the structural load will be passed on to the main members, such as the studs. If the span between the structural members is increased, then the thickness of the rigid glazing will have to be increased. Usually the manufacturer will give recommended loadings and span criteria to help you with your construction.

Glass, though quite beautiful when clean, is a difficult material for the owner/builder to handle successfully. The best configuration for glass is in a vertical position, where it is easy to seal and where it provides the most structural benefits.

In optically clear overhead situations, such as in a skylight, the rigid acrylics (clear) are more advisable. These can be fastened (screwed) to the structural members and caulked or gasketed to assure a weathertight seal. The rigid acrylics are about five times lighter than glass and won't break as easily. Accordingly, this material might have usefulness in situations where people, for aesthetic reasons, want to see out of their greenhouses and at the same time desire a more impact-resistant material than glass.

Of more significance to the owner/builder are the semirigid glazing materials, of which fiberglass-reinforced plastic (reinforced fiberglass) is recommended. The flat sheets of reinforced fiberglass are preferable to the corrugated variety because they offer at least 10-percent less

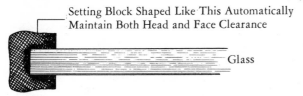

Figure 4-5: *Glazing for thermopane.*

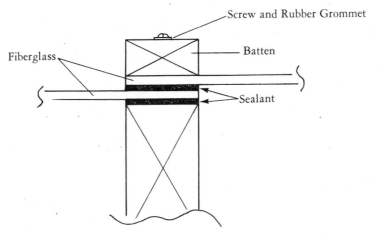

Figure 4-6: *Fiberglass—single-glazing.*

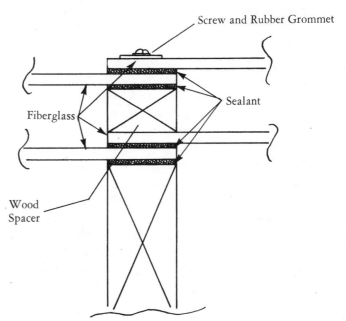

Figure 4-7: *Fiberglass—double-glazing.*

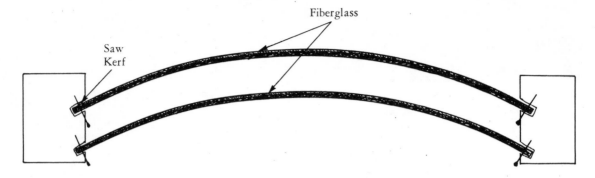

Figure 4-8: *Fiberglass—double-glazed, alternate method.*

surface through which the heat can escape. This flat material is lightweight and comes in four- or five-foot widths and a standard length of 50 feet. Reinforced fiberglass can be utilized in a flat rigid sheet and in certain situations can be "distorted" like a membrane film. This type of material has the best impact-resistance record and won't shatter. Ideally, it can have the same lifetime as the structure, which should be at least 20 to 30 years.

For the owner/builder, this glazing material offers many advantages: design possibilities, permanence, low cost, ease of fabrication and maintenance. Importantly, reinforced fiberglass is a very easy material to work with. Unlike glass, reinforced fiberglass eliminates "hot-spot" problems in the greenhouse by diffusing the light, which makes the light more readily available to plants in the greenhouse environment.

Reinforced fiberglass can be cut with a pair of metal shears and can be secured with a hammer or screwdriver. Sealing can be achieved with proper caulking, gasketing, or both. Ideally, the skins should be fastened with neoprene-gasketed screws (or nails) or by use of a clamping strip.

There are a number of manufacturers of reinforced fiberglass (Filon, Lascolite, and Kalwall). In general, those fiberglasses which diffuse the light most seem to be best for the plants. You should make sure you choose a fiberglass designed for greenhouse use. Don't just buy fiberglass from the local hardware store without checking.

The third category of glazing material is the flexible film or the membrane type of glazing. While polyethylene is used extensively both by commercial and "backyard" greenhouse operators, primarily because it is relatively inexpensive and easy to work with, readers interested in materials with a long life might consider other alternatives for the outer glazing.

Strictly speaking, polyethylene is very uneconomical; it is produced by energy-intensive methods and, when exposed to sunlight, has a life expectancy of approximately six months.

If you want to use polyethylene or other films, the proper place to use them is out of direct sunlight, such as under a cement slab or inside an insulated exterior wall where they function as a vapor barrier. In these situations polyethylene

Photo 4-1: *Alternate fiberglass glazing method, installed (New Alchemy Institute).*

spans are somewhat longer than polyethylene. Their inability to survive the elements for any appreciable time makes them a poor choice for someone who wants to construct his own greenhouse and not replace the glazing every six months. Again, as a second, inner glazing, they will do well.

Rating of Glazings

The glazings commonly available to you will be rated in terms of the various categories previously discussed. The rating will be on a one to five scale for *single*-layered materials exposed to the sun and weather; the results are presented in Table 4-1.

The total that appears in Table 4-1, denoted as column T_1, accumulates all the positive aspects of a glazing. Generally, T_1 evaluates the material's potential as an outer glazing. Clearly, the reinforced fiberglass is recommended, followed by thin acrylics and glass. The second total, denoted as column T_2, evaluates the material's potential as an inner glazing (eliminating categories D and E from the total). Of the thin materials vinyl, Mylar, and acetate are recommended followed by polyethylene.

has an almost unlimited life span. Also, these light-sensitive plastics will do well as a second glazing below a rigid outer glazing. The outer glazing usually will absorb most of the ultraviolet light before it reaches the inner glazing. Some companies have developed "weatherized" versions of the light-sensitive plastics and these will last even longer as an inner glazing.

The vinyl and Mylar membranes are equally energy-intensive materials, though their life

Multiple Layers

The use of multiple layers is specifically meant to increase the resistance to heat flow through the glazed walls. The more layers you add, the greater the resistance, but also the smaller the transmittance of solar light. To add more than two layers does not increase the resistance to heat flow significantly. For example, two layers reduce the conductive heat loss to 50 percent of the single-layer rate; three layers to 33 percent; four

Rating of Single-Layer Glazing Materials		A	B	C	D	E	F	G	T_1	T_2
Rigid 125-mil	Glass	4	5	1	5	4	2	3	24	15
	Thick Acrylic	4	5	1	4	4	2	3	23	15
	Polycarbonates	4	5	1	4	5	1	3	23	14
Semirigid 25 to 40-mil	Reinforced Fiberglass	4	5	1	4	5	3	5	27	18
	Thin Acrylic	4	4	1	4	4	3	5	25	17
	Vinyl Sheets	4	4	1	3	4	3	4	23	16
Flexible Film 4-mil	Polyethylene	3'	1	1	1	2	5	5	18	15
	Vinyl	4	3	1	2	3	4	5	22	17
	Mylar	4	4	1	3	3	3	5	23	17
	Acetate	4	5	1	1	2	4	3	20	17
	Tedlar	5	3	1	3	3	2	3	20	14
	Teflon	5	3	1	3	3	1	3	19	13

1 Bad	A	Solar Transmittance
2 Poor	B	Infrared Absorption
3 Good	C	Reduction of Heat Flow
4 Very Good	D	Weatherability (UV, O Zone)
5 Excellent	E	Resistance to Tear, Fracture and Scratching
	F	Low Cost
	G	Installation and Maintenance
	T_1	Total of A through G. Evaluate materials as an outer glazing.
	T_2	Total of T_1 minus D and E. Evaluates material as an inner glazing.

Table 4-1: *Rating of glazing materials.*

layers to 25 percent. Thus, the effect of each additional layer beyond the first becomes progressively smaller. Furthermore, the expense and effort to attach more than two layers may be unrealistic.

The separation between layers can be from ¾ inch to 4 inches without significantly changing the resistance value of the enclosed air layer.

This is convenient if your glazing supports are 2 x 4 wood studs; the separation between glazings would be 3½ inches when secured to the narrow dimension of the studs.

Frames can be made by cutting ¾-inch-thick wood boards into ¾-inch-wide strips, and securing the strips with corner fasteners. The glazings can be secured to the frame by staples or glue and then nailed to the main supports. Such framing will be necessary when installing more than one inner glazing to the greenhouse.

For most geographic areas, it is essential that the solar greenhouse have at least two airtight layers of glazing material (see Chapter Seven, "Minimum Design Criteria for Solar Greenhouses") for daytime operation. During nights and sunless days it is imperative that for northern climates, the glazed wall be well integrated with an effective thermal-shuttering system.

You might consider a rather unique material some people have found to provide an effective and virtually work-free inner glazing. They have used the "bubble pak" sheets which protect delicate articles for mailing. The flat side of the "bubble pak" sheet adheres to the underside of the outer glazing by water cohesion. If your greenhouse is dry, you may find it difficult to stick the "bubble pak" to the glazing. The sheet should be cut to cover the glazing completely. No information was available at this writing to determine its effect on the solar transmittance and infrared absorptance.

Don Shanks of Flagstaff, Arizona, has developed another unique form of double-glazing. The entire glazing wall is constructed of cleaned-out fluorescent tubes placed side by side and sealed with caulk.

Researchers are experimenting with many new glazing materials. For example, some glazings become opaque when the temperature rises above or humidity drops below a certain threshold indicating an application for hot-weather greenhouses. Nevertheless, their new glazing materials are not yet competitive with "available" materials in terms of cost, availability, and weatherability.

Some Regional Considerations Concerning Glazing Materials

A. Hail Damage

In areas of the United States where hailstorms are common, tempered glass should be used for roofing greenhouses instead of regular double-strength glass (if a glass skin has been decided upon). Untempered glass is not that safe in the overhead position whether it is exposed to hail or not.

Hail rarely causes problems with the thicker plastic greenhouse-skin materials, but an extremely bad storm could scratch your Plexiglas and dimple your Lexan.

One-eighth-inch-thick tempered glass has been used effectively against hailstone impact.

B. Ultraviolet Degradation

In parts of the United States suffering an intense, ultraviolet solar-radiation component (high altitudes and the Southwest, etc.), you should carefully consider the effects upon plastic greenhouse "skinning" materials. Plastic and glass both absorb ultraviolet light. Only the plastic group suffers molecular degradation from ultraviolet. The lifetime characteristics of plastics in sunny parts of the United States are often very disappointing. Plexiglas and polycarbonate are the best performers and polyethylene the worst.

One common effect upon plastics is discoloration of the material, often a yellowing "ultraviolet bloom." Another effect often observed is embrittlement of the material. As the thin films become brittle, their resistance to bending fatigue is reduced considerably. They normally fail soon after embrittlement due to wind-loading upon the material.

A considerable amount of time and money has

recently been invested by manufacturers trying to find ways to improve the resistance of plastics to UV degradation. "Stabilized" forms have been produced which contain small amounts of complex hydrocarbons.

Monsanto 602, or "stabilized polyethylene," has found widespread application to greenhouses, being commonly used to form the inner glazing of double-walled greenhouses. Its use in exterior applications has still proved disappointing to some Arizona researchers who found that the material failed after one year due to wind-loading. The plastic film broke around the edges next to the frame.

In cloudy coastal climates, with atmospheric filtration of ultraviolet light, you may get much better results using plastic greenhouse cover materials.

C. Thermal Cycling through Temperature Extremes

Some climates are obviously much more severe than others. In mild climates like the San Diego area or in the South, daily and yearly temperatures may not vary much more than 60 Fahrenheit degrees. Move to the Midwest and one may experience yearly extremes of as much as 180 Fahrenheit degrees.

Winters can be severe trials for the greenhouse glazing. The greenhouse skin can experience a nightly temperature of $-40°F.$ and get up to the high 80s (especially near the peak of the structure) on a bright winter day.

The major problem caused by thermal "load-ing" your greenhouse is alternate expansion and contraction of the cover material, causing considerable movement and stress where the material is attached to the frame. Be sure to give both plastics and glass room to move—especially plastics! Don't ever butt two pieces of glass together. Many amateur builders often make their frames too tight when they are framing for glass. (The glass could break if the frame moves even slightly.) If you are putting screws through Plexiglas, be sure to use oversize holes or the material can buckle. A four-foot-wide piece of Plexiglas will move just under a third of an inch in a 150 Fahrenheit degree thermal cycle.

Thermal cycling in many of the thinner film plastics will also cause an alternate, sagging condition in the daytime and a drum-tight skin at night. The sagging plastic is usually easily destroyed by wind whipping it back and forth. A tight-drum skin during cold weather can become brittle and very susceptible to breaking upon impact.

Some solar greenhouse builders in Colorado have tried to support large spans of polyethylene with chicken wire to keep the wind from flapping it back and forth. Others have placed blowers between two pieces of polyethylene in order to maintain an insulating air space and to meet a wind front with at least an air-pressure-supported film.

Finally, readers living in particularly windy regions of the country should remember that wind uplift can be a serious problem. Therefore, wind uplift in glazing must be considered and the appropriate attachment method employed.

Chapter Five

Heat Storage

David J. MacKinnon

Introduction

No matter how well insulated a greenhouse may be, heating is required when outside temperatures are below proper growing levels. How to best provide this heat is the subject of this chapter.

On a clear day a well-designed solar greenhouse receives far more energy than it needs to maintain proper growing temperatures. Invariably, even when the outside temperature is zero the vents of my greenhouse open to prevent overheating.* Unfortunately, a solar greenhouse which vents out hot air under these conditions might not be storing as much heat as it could for the inevitable cloudy days and cold nights. Squandering of heat might be allowed in the Southwest and Florida where there is an abundance of light, but should be avoided in the rest of the country.

The sunlight that passes into the greenhouse strikes the wall, plants, and open soil. A part of the sunlight is reflected back out of the greenhouse, but only a small amount for the properly designed greenhouse.

* My vents operate on a "heat motor." The heat motors look like bicycle pumps, containing a liquid which expands and contracts with temperature changes, thus opening by themselves when it's hot and closing when it's cold.

The sunlight is converted into other forms of energy. With the plants and ground warm, water is evaporated, some energy is conducted into the ground and stored, and some energy transfers to the air by conduction and convection from the hot plants and the ground. All of this energy eventually finds its way out of the greenhouse, through the walls and vents. Plants use only a few percent of the sun's energy for growth, the heat just keeps them alive to grow.

The solar greenhouse reduces the outflow of heat energy by storing some in the greenhouse and by damping its flow through the walls.

In addition to conduction and convection, another important mechanism of heat flow not often discussed is heat radiation. Heat radiation as it is called (also referred to as infrared or long-wave radiation) is emitted from all material objects. A hot object surrounded by cool objects will cool and a cool object surrounded by hot objects will warm, strictly by exchanging heat radiation. Thus any object can cool or warm at a distance, depending on whether it loses more heat radiation that it receives in return from surrounding objects. The presence of air among the objects complicates matters somewhat, because not all the energy a hot object loses is by heat radiation; some is lost by conduction and convection to the air. The air does not absorb heat radiation, but is heated by contact with a warm object.

Heat radiation cannot be seen by the human because the color range is beyond that sensed by the eye. However, heat radiation can be sensed as a warming of the skin, if the heat radiation is strong enough. Alternate shading and exposing the face to a hot, open fire will bring a sense of alternate heating and cooling, caused by the heat radiation. Unlike the human, the rattlesnake is particularly sensitive to heat radiation and can discriminate (in total darkness) between two adjacent objects whose temperatures differ by as little as one-hundreth of a degree Fahrenheit, just by sensing minute differences in their heat-radiation intensity. The warmer a body becomes the higher intensity of heat radiation it emits.

The heat radiation generated in a greenhouse is one of the strongest forms of heat transfer. Even though this form of radiation is relatively weak compared to fire it is present nonetheless. The heat radiation that leaves the plants and soil is absorbed by other objects in the greenhouse (other plants, walls, and so on). These heat up in turn and emit heat radiation. The heat radiation, passing through the air without effect, is absorbed and reemitted from all objects in the greenhouse at all times; cool objects become warm and warm objects become cool.

When stored in the greenhouse solar heat can be delivered as hot air to the plants or transmitted through the air naturally without assistance by heat radiation. Hot air delivery works best naturally if the plants are above the heat-storing area. Plants below hot air do not receive its heating effects. However, heat radiation is transmitted up, down, sideways, in any direction. You can put heat storage above the plant-growing area and the plants will still receive heat.

All these forms of heat delivery are used in solar greenhouses in some very innovative and unique ways. All of them work in their respective areas, and no single one seems best.

Because plants occupy most of the area in the greenhouse, only a few areas are left for placement of heat storage. Furthermore, because plants have little heat capacity, they have no capacity to store solar heat themselves. Most of the sunlight that does strike them goes to heating and humidifying the air, whose energy is difficult to store. This heat causes most of the greenhouse's overheating problems.

The simplest way to collect and store solar energy in the greenhouse is by direct absorption in massive materials. The collector and storage volume are one and the same. These massive materials almost invariably are rock, earth, and water, because they are cheap, found everywhere, and very effective. Large quantities of these materials create a strong thermal "flywheel," storing energy when the greenhouse is hot and releasing energy when it's cold. This interaction between the storage and the greenhouse is called passive, symbolizing the absence of "active" machinery to collect, store, and deliver the energy.

Any area, not blocking direct solar illumination of the plants, is a potential location for heat storage: the bare ground, walkways, and walls for example. These are primary areas. All heat storage does not require direct illumination by the sun to be effective. Secondary areas, such as the ground under the foliage, or shaded walls, receive indirect and slower heating. Over a longer term these areas can store significant heat and may rescue your greenhouse (and your plants) during an extremely cold, cloudy period.

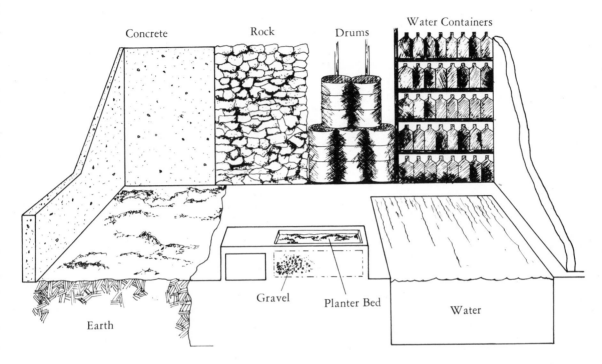

Figure 5-1: *Common locations of passive heat-storing materials.*

Figure 5-1 shows the place where passive heat-storing materials are commonly placed in the greenhouse to receive direct illumination.

Heat Storage in the Ground and Water Pools

Ground exposed to the sun's rays on a daily and yearly basis, acts as a very complicated heat-storage medium. The amount of heat stored depends on the types of minerals, amounts of air, water, and organic matter in the soil, the soil color and covering, and the local climate. Most bare soils are such that the daily cycle of heat penetrates from 8 to 32 inches, accumulating 30 to 50 percent of the solar heat striking it. However, most of this heat is lost at night by heat radiation and convection. During the summer months the daytime heat gain is greater than the night losses. The excess forms the annual heat cycle which penetrates to depths of from 15 to 60 feet. The amount of heat gained and lost during the annual cycle passing at the three- to four-foot level is usually negligible. Below this level the heat generated from the earth's interior becomes more important.

Bare ground within the greenhouse is not exposed to the open sky and elements. The presence of the greenhouse over the soil creates greater heat gains during the day and lower heat

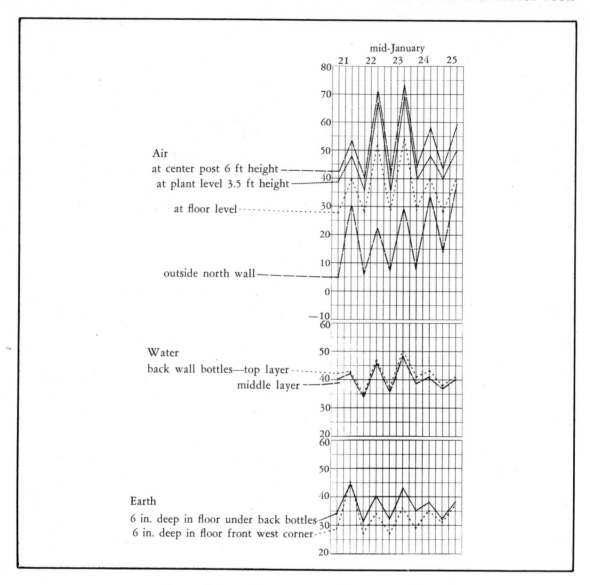

Figure 5-2a: *Air, water, earth temperatures. Maxatawny, Pennsylvania.*

losses at night. This form of heat storage is still not ideal because the extra 50 to 70 percent of the solar heat not stored goes to heat the air and evaporate water, contributing to overheating. Even though the daily collection and storage of heat in the ground is small, the amount collected over longer periods can be significant. Furthermore, the heat is also important for maintaining

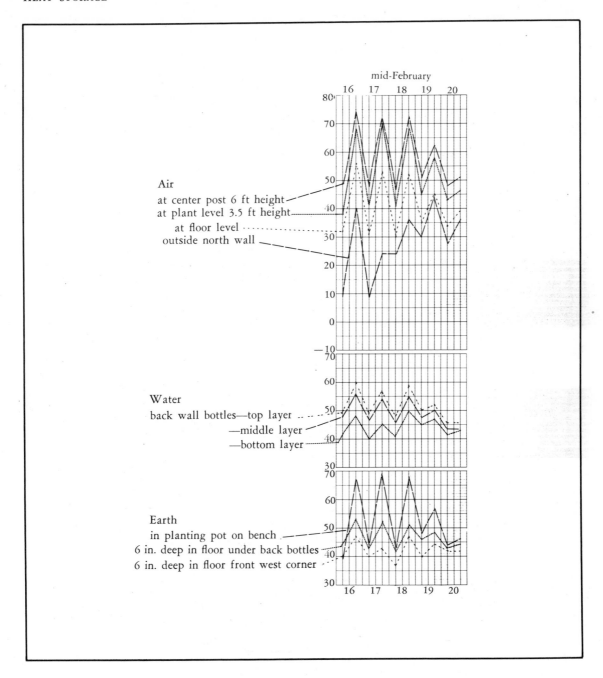

Figure 5-2b: *Air, water, earth temperatures. Maxatawny, Pennsylvania.*

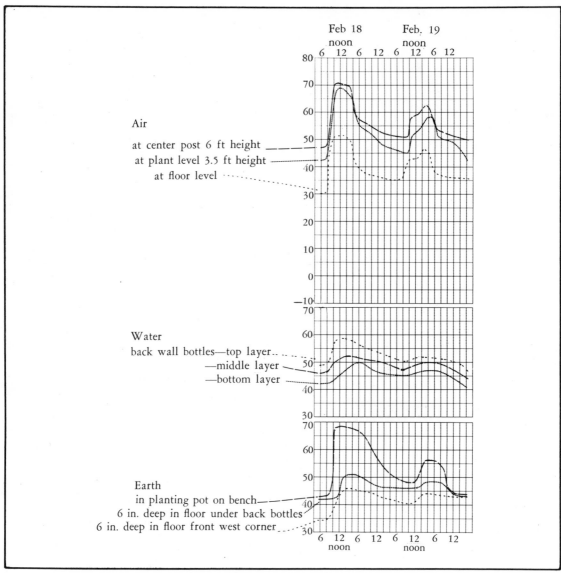

Figure 5-3: *Air, water, earth temperatures. Maxatawny, Pennsylvania (February 1977).*

high plant root temperatures.

To prevent ground-stored heat from passing to the outside, the perimeter of the greenhouse should be insulated. The thickness and depth of insulation depends on climatic severity. Perimeter insulation to an adequate depth (at least to the frost line) will eliminate the need to place additional insulation *under* the greenhouse floor as well. However, this additional step may be necessary particularly if pools of water are used for heat storage, or if the greenhouse is small.

Pools of water can store almost all the sunlight shining on them if the containing walls are dark. Some temperature stratification will occur as heated water tends to rise to the surface. Algae helps reduce temperature stratification by uniformly absorbing the solar energy throughout the volume rather than just at the walls. Evapo-ration from the pool cools the water and is a form of heat loss,* but is released again when it condenses on cooler surfaces in the greenhouse. If you don't mind "wet," there is no problem. However, venting the moisture-laden air is a significant net heat loss from the greenhouse.

Plants on the ground next to the pool are

* Evaporation of one gallon of water takes enough energy to cool 50 gallons of water 20 Fahrenheit degrees.

These graphs are data from the Maxatawny greenhouse in 1977. The five days from January are extremely cold. On the last two days from February the night temperatures moderate to near-freezing levels. Both five-day periods start with three sunny or partly sunny days and end with two completely overcast days on which there was some snow.

The air-temperature lines show the strong tendency of heat in air to stratify. The difference between air at ground level and at six feet remains a very constant 15° to 20°, regardless of sun or cloud cover, day or night. Between the six-foot level and the nine-foot peak the difference would be greater.

The data from the water storage is taken from the 372-gallon jugs stacked about six feet high along the north wall. The small containers and the good contact between them distribute heat well horizontally and vertically, while retarding severe stratification which occurs in large free masses of water. Notice that after the second day of low solar input, the temperatures at all three levels move close together. The most readily available heat has been removed.

The measurements taken in soil show how the earth can react to energy even on cloudy days. Most of the floor in this greenhouse is shaded and so the data is not directly comparable to sunlit floors. Most of the solar energy aimed at the floor is blocked by the benches, plants, and soil containers at the 3½-foot level. Expect to see considerably more energy absorbed by ground-level beds.

The point in the front west corner is only a few inches from the walls and receives direct light for half the day. It is consistently colder than the shaded point, illustrating heat losses through the insulation and to the cold air of infiltration at the glazing. But apparently the morning of January 21 was sunny enough for that point to surpass the soil temperature in the rear of the greenhouse. Though the shaded point receives no direct radiation, it is closer to the center of the mass and receives some radiation constantly from the warm water in the bottles.

The data taken in the plant pot illustrates the effect of direct radiation, a position in a warmer air layer and a large surface area exposed to warm air. The extremes could be stressful to plants if they go much beyond the ranges shown.

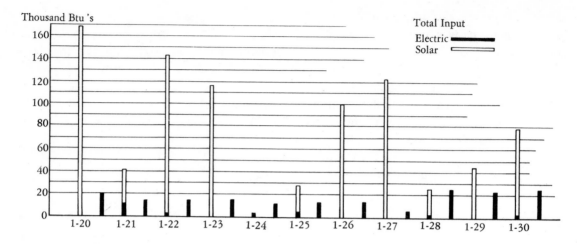

Figure 5-4a: *Comparative energy input—solar, electric.*

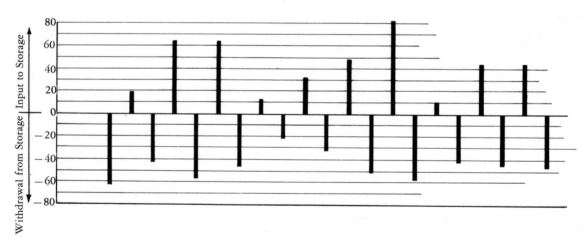

Figure 5-4b: *Changes in energy storage.*

heated fairly well. Plants farther away lose the benefit of the warmth and heat radiation from the pool. Some air circulation may be required to pass heated air to these isolated plants. Plants above the pool are in the best location, but too many could shade the pool.

Photo 5-1: *Earth storage. Cape Cod Ark (New Alchemy Institute).*

Photo 5-3: *Water storage. Fiberglass cylinders. Ark, Prince Edward Island (New Alchemy Institute).*

Photo 5-2: *Pool storage. Pragtree Farm, Ecotope Group, Seattle, Washington.*

Reflectors can increase heat gain to pools. Some greenhouse structures are specially designed to focus light striking the back wall into the pool.

Water containers, placed in the floor, which are not transparent are not much better than the bare ground. Certainly the water when heated can store more heat than the ground in the same volume. But water containers heated on the top do not circulate and store heat as fast as when heated from the bottom or side. Clear containers would be better but only if directly illuminated by the sun. You should carefully consider your heat-storage placement. It can sometimes be tricky, but no matter what you do it probably will work satisfactorily.

Photo 5-4: *Water storage. Fiberglass cylinders. Cape Cod Ark (New Alchemy Institute).*

Heat Storage in Walls

The areas bordering the inside walls of the greenhouse are excellent places to stack heat-storing materials (see Figure 5-1). These areas not only receive direct light from the sun, but also, when occupied by warm heat-storing material, deliver heat radiation to more of the plant area. Heat-storing material can be part of the greenhouse wall construction, or added after the insulated shell is erected.

55-Gallon Drums

One of the most common objects used as a heat-storing wall is the 55-gallon steel drum filled with water. The main advantage of the 55-gallon drum is that a lot of water can be stored in one container. Another advantage is that water itself can hold a lot of heat in a relatively small volume. These are the main advantages of the 55-gallon drum.

However, the round drum itself wastes space that could be used for additional storage: square drums placed side by side would be better in this

Photo 5-5: *Fifty-five-gallon drum water storage. Pittsfield, Massachusetts.*

respect. There are more serious problems.

As the sun illuminates the drum, the water within heats and rises to the top of the drum; the unheated water remains at the bottom. This separation of the hot and cold water is rather dramatic and can be noticed by sliding your hand on the outside drum surface from top to bottom. The separation creates two problems. First, the bottom half of the drum is less effective thermal-storage space because it does not heat. And second, the hot portion of the drum loses heat at least 15- to 20-percent faster than it would if the

water was well mixed throughout the drum. Furthermore, large amounts of exposed surface on the sides and top of the drum create high convection losses to the air and heat radiation losses in directions that do not strike the plant-growing area, overheating the air and poorly using the precious energy stores.

Since the 55-gallon drum is in such common use, there are some ways to improve its heat-storing efficiency. The separation of hot and cold water probably cannot be prevented, but the heat lost to the air by convection can be reduced.

Photo 5-6: *Drum and tank storage. McMinnville, Oregon.*

Photo 5-7: *Water storage. Used water heater. Milwaukee, Wisconsin.*

Small Water Containers

Most of the problems associated with the 55-gallon drums can be eliminated by making the wall of relatively small, water-filled, square containers. These containers can be metal or plastic, opaque or transparent (filled with dyed water), and can vary anywhere from one to five gallons. It should be emphasized that the containers should not be placed on separate shelves. Stack bottles so that a bottom bottle has good contact with a top, as shown in Figure 5-5a. Normally

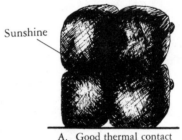

Sunshine

A. Good thermal contact creates uniformly heated wall.

Figure 5-5a: *Stacking small water containers.*

Those surfaces of the drum which are not heated directly by the sun should be insulated; these include the top of the drum and the back half. In this way, the convection losses to the air are reduced and heat-radiation losses that do not strike the plant area are eliminated. The stacking of drums upright one on top of the other would help heat the bottoms of drums from the tops of others, tending to uniformly heat and more efficiently use the storage. Because there is usually a flange on the tops and bottoms of the barrels, the contact and subsequent heat transfer between stacked drums will nevertheless be poor.

this would eliminate plastic containers, but some can take the load. Some shelving can be used with plastic containers, but the containers should be stacked at least three rows per shelf. In any event you should test containers *under load* for a month or so before you buy 500 to 1,000 of them.

Since there appears to be no situation where you have too much storage of this type, containers should be chosen and stacked to give the greatest depth or thickness for a given wall area. The five-gallon square metal can, stacked on its side, seems to be an ideal unit for a container wall, meeting all the desirable requirements.

Photo 5-8: *Water storage. Small containers. Flagstaff, Arizona.*

Some containers require additional support, so plan on it.

A wall, two or more containers thick, can be formed, but it is certain that the heat will be inadequately transferred and extracted from the back units unless you take special precautions in stacking. Figures 5-5b and 5-5c give some examples.

Contrary to our expectations, when the bottles in each layer, stacked as shown in Figure 5-5b, were separated, the bottles as a unit collected more energy than they did tightly packed. We included an adjustment for the increase in solar

Sunshine

B. Poor thermal contact prevents uniform heating of total water volume; creates heat waste similar to that of 55-gallon drums.

Figure 5-5b: *Stacking small water containers.*

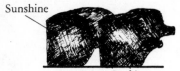

Sunshine

C. Better Stacking
than B for
multiple-thickness
wall.

Figure 5-5c: *Stacking small water containers.*

energy collected when the bottles were spaced.

These experiments, carried out for 13 days at Rodale's Maxatawny greenhouse, consistently

Photo 5-10: *Water storage. Small containers. Maxatawny, Pennsylvania.*

Photo 5-9: *Water storage. Small containers. Maxatawny, Pennsylvania.*

showed this effect. Apparently, bottles stacked according to Figure 5-5c allow much better contact and uniform heating than the stacking shown in Figure 5-5b.

Nonetheless even though we apparently made a mistake in our bottle stacking, these bottles helped the Maxatawny greenhouse plants survive one of the coldest Januarys on record (1977).

With 500 one-gallon water bottles stacked according to Figure 5-5a, my Flagstaff greenhouse maintained an average January *low* temperature of 49.8°F. while the average low outside was 12.4°F.

Photo 5-11: *Water storage under growing beds. Maxatawny, Pennsylvania.*

Container Walls under Raised Beds

In order to increase total storage volume we placed water-container storage under raised beds in the Maxatawny greenhouse (see Photo 5-11). This storage collects solar heat on the front face, transmits heat into storage among bottles, and delivers heat as hot air to the beds above. We are not certain how effective this type of storage is, but it does raise the plants up to the warmer air

levels in the greenhouse. When using this type of storage the bottles should not be placed close to the clear front face. Heat radiation from the bottles tends to be lost right through the front wall without heating any plants. At night, insulating the clear front face reduces this form of energy loss.

Masonry Materials

Rock, adobe, and masonry walls, like the soil itself, are not particularly efficient materials for absorbing and storing solar heat directly. The problem stems from two facts. First, these materials hold less than half as much heat as water in a given volume. Second, these materials do not conduct the heat away from the sun-heated surface into storage fast enough before the heat is lost as heat radiation and convection to the air. The heating of the water in a container, unlike the solid material, sets up circulation currents which extract the heat from the sun-heated surface before significant losses occur.

Nevertheless, masonry walls of all sorts directly illuminated by the sun and in the shade

Photo 5-12: *Water storage under growing beds. Maxatawny, Pennsylvania.*

are found as part of the heat storage in many solar greenhouses. These walls can be solid, or bins and pallets of loose stones. It is unfortunate that hot air is difficult to circulate through stones without fans. The circulation of air through stone helps store the heat contained in the air.

A water wall in front of a masonry wall is an excellent combination.

Comparison of Relative Efficiencies of Solar Heat Absorption for Water (Container) and Masonry Walls

An actual experiment to compare the relative efficiencies of solar-heat absorption for water and masonry walls would be extremely difficult and expensive to design and carry out successfully. The next best approach is computer simulation, using experimentally obtained material properties and accurate mathematical descriptions of heat flow. In order to test the accuracy of the simulation, I used two entirely independent mathematical descriptions to calculate the heat absorptions: the two descriptions yielded results which agreed to within one-tenth of one percent.

The simulation assumes that the water or masonry wall is in an empty room maintained at 54°F. The back of the wall is insulated so that no heat is lost there. The front of the wall absorbs 90 percent of the sunlight, equivalent to any black painted surface. The sun shines at normal greenhouse winter levels and remains on for 10 hours.

The results are expressed as the percent of the solar energy absorbed into storage as a function of time and given for two wall thickness, ½ foot and 1 foot, respectively. The percent of solar energy absorbed is also a measure of the effi-

Photo 5-13: *Rock storage. Noti, Oregon.*

ciency of heat absorption for the wall material.

Figures 5-6 and 5-7 compare the efficiences for a concrete (and adobe) wall (a), a wall composed of opaque and transparent water containers (c and e, respectively), and walls of two other materials, graphite (b) and steel (d).

The concrete (adobe) rapidly loses efficiency, because of the relatively low heat conductivity of the material. Most masonry materials have characteristics similar to adobe and concrete: bricks, rock, soil, and so on. However, adobe has a very favorable additional feature not

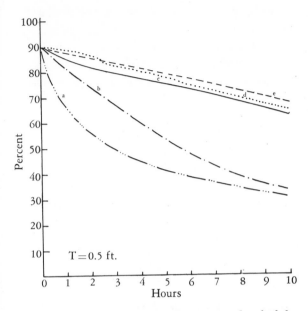

Figure 5-6: *Percent of solar energy absorbed by exactly similar walls of 0.5 ft. thickness as a function of time (hours) for a constant solar-heat flux of 200 Btu./hr./ft.². The walls are composed of: a) concrete (adobe), b) graphite, c) opaque water containers, d) steel, and e) transparent water containers. Each wall absorbs 90 percent of the solar flux. Heat loss is from the solar-heated side of the wall by means of radiation and convection to a uniform temperature and radiation environment maintained at 53.6°F. The back of the wall is perfectly insulated.*

wonder the old adobe homes and the new solar adobe dwellings are such energy-efficient structures. Thick adobe walls have both properties of heat storage and insulation wrapped into one unit. Only recently has a government study supported this concept. The study showed that the most energy-efficient masonry wall for keeping heat in a structure is a composite wall of masonry on the inside (for heat storage) and insulation on the outside (for preventing heat loss to the outside).

As Figures 5-6 and 5-7 show, only 30 to 35 percent of the solar heat can be stored directly into the "dry" masonry walls by sun heating after 10 hours. This is poor and leads to strong overheating when such walls are used in greenhouses (and homes).

I should emphasize that the walls can store a lot of heat once heated, but they cannot absorb the solar heat as fast as it's made available.

The water-container wall is not sensitive to container size provided the containers are not too small (smaller than beverage cans) or too large (near 55-gallon size). The opaque and transparent container should be painted or dyed to absorb 90 percent of the sunlight (common black paint or black Rit dye will work). Figures 5-6 and 5-7 show that the transparent container is slightly better than the opaque container. The transparent container can absorb the solar light throughout the volume, while the opaque container absorbs the solar light at the container surface before the water can absorb the heat. The uniform volume heating is more efficient than the surface heating of the container. In the latter case, some solar heat is lost by radiation and convection to the air before the water absorbs it.

A good dark liquid for the transparent container is Rit dye. I found that three standard, two-ounce boxes can dye 500 gallons of water.

shown in the Figures. Adobe stores more heat but conducts heat slower than concrete. For adobe these two opposing properties balance out, giving adobe a heat-storing efficiency similar to concrete. However, the slow transfer of heat in adobe gives it a self-insulating quality not found in concrete and other masonry materials. No

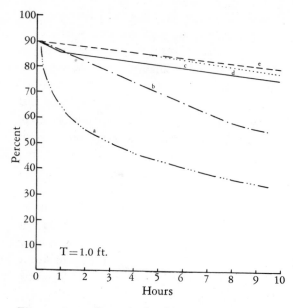

Figure 5-7: *Percent of solar energy absorbed by exactly similar walls of 1.0 ft. thickness as a function of time (hours) for a constant solar-heat flux of 200 Btu./hr./ft². The walls are composed of: a)concrete (adobe), b) graphite, c) opaque water containers, d) steel, and e) transparent water containers. Each wall absorbs 90 percent of the solar flux. Heat loss is from the solar-heated side of the wall by means of radiation and convection to a uniform temperature and radiation environment maintained at 53.6°F. The back of the wall is perfectly insulated.*

The concentration of dye should be no more and no less than that required to absorb the sunlight through the length of the container. I determined this concentration by placing the dye-filled container in front of the sun's disk (be careful of the eyes) on a clear day and noting the concentration at which the light is just no longer visible.

Small amounts of antifreeze or rust inhibitor should be added to the metal containers to maintain a long life. Of course, no dye is added. The opaque container should be painted a dark color to absorb the solar light. Containers painted dark red and blue instead of black will reflect small amounts of red and blue light back to the plants, yet will heat almost as well as black containers. The red and blue light are important for plant growth and fruiting.

As Figures 5-6 and 5-7 show, the water-container wall is perhaps the most efficient, least expensive storage medium available for solar greenhouse use.

Other Materials for Heat-Storing Walls

Many researchers are concerned about improving heat storage of solid walls which is fairly poor. Improvement can come by increasing the heat conductivity of the wall, the ability to absorb heat fast. Another improvement can come from increasing heat capacity, the amount of heat stored in a given volume.

There are a few other materials which have properties that could improve heat storage in solid walls, most notably, steel and graphite.

Steel has both a high heat conductivity and high heat capacity, the latter only 15 percent less than water. Unfortunately, steel (and other metals) is heavy, almost eight times heavier than an equal volume of water, and is expensive.

Rodale Press sponsored research at Lehigh University which showed that embedding steel rods in a concrete wall, with a spacing between rods no more than two or three times the diameter of the rod, could significantly improve the heat-storing properties of the wall. Furthermore the volume occupied by the rods is 40 percent or less, which reduces steel expense and weight.

Further research showed that mixing iron filings, generated by the waste from steel mills and fabrication plants, with limestone cement did not improve the heat conductivity of the composite material, but did improve its heat-storing capacity. For this reason metallic wastes could be recycled into building materials to improve heat-storing qualities.

Figures 5-6 and 5-7 show the efficiencies for the solid steel wall. Not surprisingly the steel holds 70 to 85 percent of the solar heat after 10 hours, depending on wall thickness.

Graphite is a naturally occurring rock that has a heat conductivity about 100 times greater than masonry, even three times greater than mild steel; unfortunately it has 25-percent lower ability to store heat in a given volume than masonry. But unlike steel it is 20 percent lighter than concrete. Graphite will absorb heat into storage almost as fast as the sun can make it available. However, after a few hours of sun heating, the graphite wall, depending on thickness, will gain more heat than it can store. As a result, the efficiency of heat storage goes down rapidly. After 10 hours, a ½-foot wall of graphite holds only as much heat as concrete (see Figure 5-6). Increasing the wall thickness and the total storage volume reduces graphite's heat saturation problem, as Figure 5-7 shows. Notice that thickness has little influence on a masonry wall's efficiency of heat storage, provided the wall is ½-foot thick or greater (compare 5-6 and 5-7). A masonry wall thinner than ½-foot would have a lower efficiency than shown in Figure 5-7. Also a masonry wall thicker than 1 foot would have a negligibly higher efficiency than shown in Figure 5-7.

Graphite could be used in rod form and inserted into walls as I discussed for steel earlier. The flaked or powdered form, as is found naturally, would be no better than iron filings, and would reduce the heat capacity of the masonry wall if added. So graphite would only be good as large pieces, such as rods and bricks. Industry does manufacture such products, but I suspect they would be too expensive.

Although at one time actively mined in 25 states, graphite is now mined only in Texas. Apparently foreign sources are more economical.

Oils (and waxes) from crankcases, electrical devices, or whatever can be used as heat storage in place of water. Oil has a heat capacity from 13 to 42 percent less than water, depending on the type. Further, oil is more viscous, a feature which reduces the efficiency of heat extraction from the sun-heated container surface. All in all then, oil is a significantly less-efficient, heat-storing material than water.

Waxes and salt hydrates (and their eutectics) are being studied for use as a chemical form of heat storage. These materials have the highest ability to store heat in a given volume of all the materials discussed to this point (up to eight times higher than water). These materials absorb and release enormous amounts of heat by changing from a solid to a liquid (heat gain) and then back again (heat release). Water has a similar behavior but at a low temperature (water to ice). The costs for the chemicals are not prohibitive. However, after a period of time, the material has a tendency to remain liquid and not give up its heat when needed. Researchers, such as Marie Telkes, have been working with these materials for many years, and it will still be sometime before they are perfected for general use.

Waxes are relatively expensive, but salt hydrates are relatively inexpensive. The former we probably cannot afford, while the latter has serious design problems not yet overcome.

Eventually, materials and methods should become available which will greatly simplify the way we must store heat now, with massive volumes of rock and water.

Collecting and Storing Hot Air

As I have shown, simple rock and water objects are the easiest and most effective way we now have of collecting and storing heat for the greenhouse.

A lot of the solar heat goes into heating the air by contact, creating an excess which is vented to the outside, except when the greenhouse is attached to the dwelling. If your climate requires you to collect every calorie, the next simplest step, after you have added passive heat-storing objects, is to consider collecting and storing hot air.

The solar heat that has been converted into hot air is more difficult to collect and store, because the heat in the air is so diffuse. Storing heat requires air to pass over objects that are both cooler and capable of holding far more heat in a given volume than air. Again, the most common materials used for this purpose are water and rock.

The air must be spread thin enough over the rock (or water) so that hot air does not pass through the heat-storing area uncooled. This is best assured by providing a large surface area in the storage for the air to pass over. With rocks this is achieved by a large bin of stones about fist size through which the hot air can pass. Passing small bubbles of hot air through a water tank may be one way water can be used for this type of storage. In this method, the water would occupy less volume than the stones for the same amount of heat stored, particularly so when half the storage volume occupied by the stones is air.

Each of these methods (air through stone, air bubbled through water) has the disadvantage of requiring pumps or fans to pass the air through the storage medium. The amount of air that must be pumped through the storage volume is often enormous, on a clear day at least 100 or so greenhouse volumes of air per day.

Another related disadvantage is the relatively low temperature at which greenhouse air is drawn into storage, typically less than 90°F. Since the efficiency of heat extraction from the air is proportional to the difference in stone and air temperature, the efficiency of heat extraction from greenhouse air will be low.

Herbert Wade, now with the Arizona Solar Energy Research Commission at this writing, has suggested an interesting greenhouse design that may store the sensible heat contained in the air in a rock bin without fans. His design places an inverted pyramid of river stones in back of the greenhouse. The wall of loose stones, retained by a rigid frame, rises like a canopy above and over the floor with the greatest mass of stone near the ceiling (where the hot air is) and the least at floor level. Hot air rising up to the ceiling from the greenhouse interior passes through the rock, cools and sinks into a channel in the back of the bin where it is vented out at floor level, and the cycle starts over again.

Hopefully, the natural air-circulation cycle created by the cooling of the stones will be strong enough to pass 100 greenhouse volumes through the bin during a clear day. The rock bin also absorbs solar light directly for additional storage. Fans may still be necessary to assist the heat-storage and extraction process, but far less fan energy may be required by this system than other rock storage systems which force the hot air against the natural flow.

In a less elaborate way, some researchers in Noti, Oregon, are trying this approach (see Chapter Eight).

A rock or water storage bin (except for the natural circulation type) can be placed just about anywhere. However, installing the storage in the greenhouse may take up too much room, under the floor may require too much excavation, or outside may involve complicated and expensive ducting and insulation problems. The best storage locality is in the greenhouse or under the floor where most of the heat losses from storage will go into the greenhouse. These trade-offs should be considered carefully.

Heat Collected and Stored Outside the Greenhouse

Methods which collect and store energy outside the greenhouse are complex and expensive and I will not spend much time discussing them. I refer you to any of many solar-home building books which treat such problems in detail.

Climatic criteria may indicate a particular greenhouse design cannot collect sufficient solar energy internally to operate year-round. Solar energy can then be collected outside to be stored outside (or inside) the greenhouse for additional heating requirements. Outside collection and storage is expensive, because of the mechanical devices typically required to collect, transfer, and store the heated medium (water or air). Any of these systems can be integrated with existing heat-storage and delivery systems.

The simplest system for outside collection and storage is operated on a natural circulation cycle. An air or water solar collector can be placed below a heat-storage area. Ductwork between the collector and storage is provided, so that the heated medium from the top of the collector goes into the storage to force cooler medium from storage to the bottom of the collector. This process continues by natural circulation. At the end of the day, the storage area is filled with heated rock or water whose energy can be recycled to heat the greenhouse. Hot water heaters, working on this principle, have been operating in Japan, Australia, and Israel for years. If outside collection is required, then every attempt should be made to design it as a natural circulation system.

For various reasons, it may not be feasible to install a natural circulation system. In particular, it may not be possible to place collectors below storage. In such cases pumps or fans must be used to circulate and store the heated medium. This, of course, is a step higher in cost and complexity above the natural circulation system.

A rather interesting method of outside collection and storage for greenhouse heating is being studied at Ohio State University. Here a large, deep pond of water is mixed with common table salt. By a special mixing process, layers of the pool are infused with salt whose concentration increases with depth. As the sunlight heats the pool of water, the heated water tends to rise, but the salt layers prevent this occurrence. The result is hot water stored deep in the pond protected from heat loss by the layer of water above. Over a summer season the pool will collect and store enough heat to provide most of the greenhouse's winter-heating needs. This form of solar heating is planned for commercial operations where it is most economical.

On a smaller scale, certain parts of the country could use swimming pools for storage. Certainly salt should be avoided, but a darkly painted pool with a daytime cover and added nighttime insulation could collect, store, and supply a greenhouse with additional heat.

The cost of these external collection and storage systems should be carefully weighed against costs for conventional heating both now and in the future. In any event, before external solar and conventional heating systems are considered every attempt should be made to collect and store solar energy within the greenhouse itself.

General Rules of Thumb for Heat-Storing Walls within a Greenhouse

1. First choose materials which have a high capacity to store heat and then materials which have a high ability to conduct heat. For common materials, choose liquids first, solids (or masonry material) second.
2. Within the limited room available in a solar greenhouse, as much heat storage as possible should be added. However, massive heat storage alone will not insure performance, heavy insulation must be provided to retain the heat stored.
3. Water containers: Either opaque or transparent water containers (metal or plastic) can be used. Containers should be thin walled, especially if nonmetallic.
4. Containers ideally should be square and stacked for good thermal contact: five-gallon square tins seem to be most ideal.
5. Heat storage should be placed around all interior walls (except in front of clear walls) and stacked as high as possible. Some support may be required for this purpose.
6. Heat storage should be painted dark colors.

7. The perimeter around the greenhouse floor should be well-insulated, especially if the greenhouse contains pools of water used for heat storage.

Integrating Backup Heat Systems with Heat Storage

The backup heating system should not be integrated into the existing storage, whether the storage is inside or outside the greenhouse. The backup should provide heat directly to the plant area as needed to maintain temperature. Why?

Suppose a storage unit is capable of holding enough heat to last four days of cloudy weather. For a period of five cloudy days, one additional day of heating is needed. If the backup system heats the storage first, then it may have to supply two to four days of equivalent heat to the storage before temperatures of the storage are high enough to deliver heat to the greenhouse. Then, on the clear day following the cloudy period, when charging of storage begins, the storage already has a partial charge and may now become overcharged . . . a waste of heat. If the one day of extra heat is supplied directly, then both the conventional energy and solar energy would be conserved.

The backup system can be integrated *with* the storage. Backup heat can be integrated at the point where the existing ductwork takes heat from storage to supply the greenhouse.

The best method of uniformly heating the greenhouse for storage is provided by heat radiation; radiant heating would also be the best form of backup. But most solar storage systems outside the heat-storing walls do not deliver radiant heat to the greenhouse, and therefore, a radiant heating system would be difficult to integrate with existing delivery systems. Integrating a radiant heating system with a masonry or container wall would heat the storage and create wasted energy. Most likely, the radiant system should be a completely independent unit.

A soil-heating backup system can be integrated into the planting area if soil temperatures drop below those optimum for plant growth (about 50°F.). Electric heat tapes are probably the most efficient and least costly.

Chapter Six

The Weather and the Solar Greenhouse

David J. MacKinnon

Weather refers to the current state of the atmosphere, such as the temperature, humidity, wind, visibility, cloudiness, and atmospheric pressure. How you use all this information depends on your purposes. Certainly you ask whether it's raining or not before you step outside to wash the car or water the lawn. Or you might call the weatherman to get an idea of weekend weather for that bicycle ride you planned.

When you decide to build a solar greenhouse, you ask similar questions: What weather conditions influence the greenhouse? Am I adding enough insulation? How much sunlight occurs during the winter? Can I provide year-round heating just with solar energy? All these questions are important, but they can all be boiled down to two fundamental elements: temperature and light. A plant can survive at low light levels but most will die when temperatures drop to winter levels. I have seen plants frozen on the clearest, sunny days during a fall cold spell. The plant temperature is the most important element, and during the winter you want to maintain good growing temperatures in a greenhouse regardless of light levels. The costs of artificial lighting and heating have forced us all to look at alternative technologies: the solar greenhouse is one.

How much heat a greenhouse, or for that matter any building, needs depends on a number of things including: how well the structure is insulated and sealed from the wind; how warm the inside is maintained above the outside temperature; and the amount of exposed surface area. The warmer a greenhouse is than the outside, or similarly, the colder the outside is than the inside, the faster heat is lost. Insulation reduces the rate of heat flow, but a flow of heat continues from hot to cold, no matter how much insulation is added. A poorly sealed, but well-insulated greenhouse, can lose tremendous amounts of heat as the wind blows cold air in and hot air out through many tiny cracks.

So you see that the temperature of the plant environment is fundamental to plant survival and growth. And light is also fundamental to plant growth. How this temperature is maintained and light supplied in an economical way is the essence of a well-designed solar greenhouse.

Once the solar greenhouse has been designed to prevent the heat from escaping too fast, you might ask: How much solar energy is available for heating and how do I use it? Since the sun is "off" during the night and on heavily overcast days, and has a short period of illumination during the winter, you cannot expect heat when you need it. You also find when the sun does shine, a well-designed greenhouse receives energy faster than it can use it, so as the old saying goes "why not save some for a rainy day." In fact, by simple methods, you can store enough solar energy in a day or two to give many days and nights of heating during cold cloudy weather without burning any fuel for additional heat.

Designing the greenhouse to maintain the ideal light and temperature conditions for the plants using solar energy alone can be difficult, depending upon the climate and time of year. There are many trade-offs between how much light should go to the plants and how much should be stored directly as heat.

The most fundamental challenge you should consider in designing your greenhouse is: Can the greenhouse collect and store enough solar energy to maintain adequate growing temperatures (and light) through the coldest, cloudiest, and windiest conditions normally expected during the winter? If it can, then you can be reasonably confident the greenhouse plants will survive your winters. And if the solar light level is adequate for plant growth, so much the better.

An answer to questions about the coldest, cloudiest, and windest conditions, as well as the amount of sunshine, lies in the records of the United States Weather Bureau.* The climatic records not only describe the long-term average of the day-to-day weather, but also include information about the variations of the day-to-day weather from the average. Obviously, the green-

house responds to the weather on a daily basis, but rarely does the daily weather assume average conditions. It is for a sequence of extreme daily variations or a period of extreme weather (coldest, cloudiest, windiest) that the solar greenhouse must be designed.

Using the climatic records assumes that the climate of the future will remain essentially similar to the climate of the past. You can certainly raise many objections to this assumption. Not only can climate change from place to place, but over many time scales as well. For example, on the small space and time scale, the rise in average urban temperature is associated with wasted heat released from increasing energy utilization in these areas within the past 75 years; on the large space and time scale, scientists suspect a gradual return of an ice age, caused by who knows what. The weather records can only indicate so much about these changes.

It must not be assumed that these climatological averages should provide the only basis for greenhouse design. Local long-term warming or cooling trends do occur; the greenhouse site may have a local climate significantly different from that at the weather-bureau station and most importantly, variations in weather severity from year to year are large and must be considered. Therefore, you are encouraged to consider the climatological information and the minimum design criteria in Chapter Seven in relation to the greenhouses discussed in Part II.

Winter Design Criteria

As described earlier, the three essential weather elements that determine the winter operation of the solar greenhouse are: *sunshine, temperature, and wind.* Sunshine (and cloudiness) determine the amount of solar light available for

---

* Your local weather bureau makes these records available for your perusal. In addition, you can purchase detailed summaries of local climatic data by writing the National Climatic Center, Federal Building, Asheville, NC 28801. A small payment of 15¢ is required for each station summary; remittances should be made payable to the Department of Commerce, NOAA.

plant growth and the heat. Outside temperature and wind determine how much heat the greenhouse needs to maintain its environment at some given temperature. Outside humidity is of less importance, but low outside humidities indicate areas where humidification of the greenhouse may be necessary. Other weather elements, such as rain and snow, have only a small part to play, unless, for example, you suspect snow will cover the transparent walls of the greenhouse. Upon searching the records, I found that most of the extreme weather conditions occur during January. And it is for this month that the extremes should be studied closely.

How do we determine the extreme conditions likely to occur in January during an average winter? One way is to record, for each year of weather records, the conditions during the period of harshest weather. Then we can take the conditions for the period between the least and most harsh (the median or average) as representative for an average January. To consider all-time record conditions may overdesign the greenhouse for situations that may never occur again within the life of the greenhouse. So designing the greenhouse to survive the median or average of the annual extremes will assure that the greenhouse has a good chance of surviving January, and therefore the winter, using solar energy alone.

Sunshine

I found the sunshine conditions most difficult to describe. There have been a few studies correlating sunshine and the percentage of cloudiness. Unfortunately, the percent of cloudiness does not distinguish between thick and thin clouds, which greatly influence the amount and distribution of the sunshine. However, by assuming that the clouds during January are thick, I feel confident I am not underestimating sunshine conditions. Be that as it may, the correlation is good enough that if records of clear, partly cloudy, and overcast days are available, some idea of sunshine conditions can be obtained. For accuracy, actual solar radiation measurements are much more useful. Unfortunately, there are very few places where such measurements are made.

The United States Weather Bureau has long-term records of clear, partly cloudy, and overcast days for each month of the year for many cities in the United States. A clear day assumes that zero to three-tenths of the sky is cloudy, partly cloudy—four-tenths to seven-tenths, and overcast—eight-tenths to ten-tenths. Figures 6-1 and 6-2 show the average number of overcast and clear days, respectively, in January based on records from 1931 to 1960. These Figures give only the clear and overcast days, the number of partly cloudy days for a given locality can be obtained by adding the clear and overcast days and subtracting the sum from 31. For example Waco, Texas, has 16 overcast days and 9 clear days, leaving 6 partly cloudy days. I assumed the partly cloudy days themselves do not influence the greenhouse one way or the other. During a partly cloudy day, the greenhouse gains just enough energy to get to the next clear or cloudy day. Of course, this really depends on how well the greenhouse is insulated and how cloudy the day is. But what concerns us here is the number of consecutive clear days available for collecting heat, followed by the number of consecutive overcast days through which the greenhouse must operate with no sun. In turn this information will enable us to determine the minimum amount of insulation and heat storage required in the solar greenhouse.

I searched for simple methods which utilized

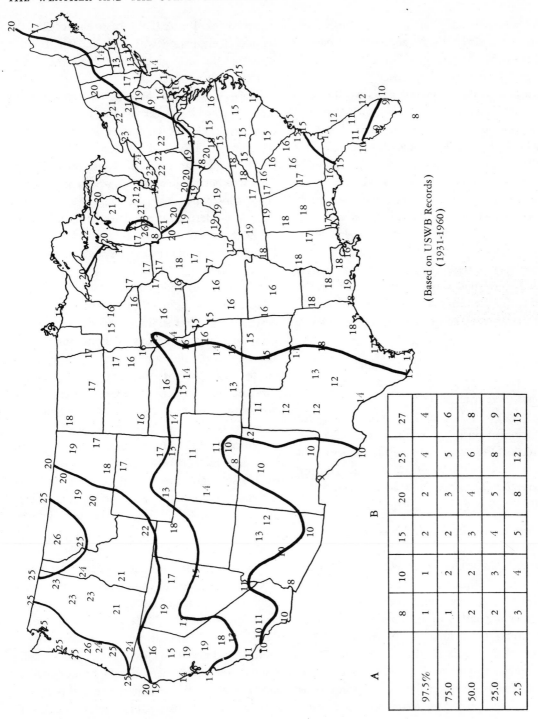

(Based on USWB Records)
(1931-1960)

A		8	10	15	20	25	27
97.5%		1	1	2	2	4	4
75.0		1	2	2	3	5	6
50.0		2	2	3	4	6	8
25.0		2	3	4	5	8	9
2.5		3	4	5	8	12	15

B

Figure 6-1: *Table 6-1: Average Number of Overcast Days in January*

the Weather Bureau's data for the average number of clear, partly cloudy, and overcast days. I found a paper by Irving I. Gringorten (1966) who presented a useful approach.

Gringorten found that one day's weather conditions depended very strongly on the weather of the previous day. He developed a mathematical model which describes these dependencies for weather parameters, such as wind, temperature, and pressure, to name a few. He also found his model able to predict the likelihood (or probability) that any weather situation, like rain, will persist for a given number of days. He tested his model against actual weather records across the nation: the results showed remarkable accuracy. The method was also tested and proven accurate for determining the probability of a given number of consecutive clear or overcast days.

I followed Gringorten's procedures and calculated the probability of having a given number of consecutive overcast (no sun) and clear (full sun) days, given the average number of days for each expected during a month. Tables 6-1 and 6-2 record this data for specific intervals of average number of overcast and clear days during January, *but they can be used for any other month.*

Again, let us take Waco, Texas, which has an average number of 16 overcast days, as shown in Figure 6-1. In Table 6-1, 16 is closest to 15 entered in row B; then in column A the probability of expecting a continuous period of overcast of a given length can be obtained. According to Table 6-1 column A, Waco has a 97.5-percent chance (excellent) of two days of continuous overcast. And Waco has only a 2.5-percent chance (poor) of five days of continuous overcast. Since the extreme conditions are being

designed for, I took the 2.5-percent level as the longest likely period with no sun. It is for this level that the solar greenhouse should be able to operate with no solar gain.

Waco, Texas, also has on the average about nine days of clear weather. In Table 6-2, nine clear days is nearest ten entered in row B. Then, according to Table 6-2 column A, Waco has a 97.5-percent chance of two consecutive days of clear weather. It also has a 2.5-percent chance of eight consecutive days of clear weather. But again, considering the extreme condition, I chose the 97.5-percent level or two days as the most likely number of clear days before the next cloudy period.

According to the scheme just developed, a solar greenhouse in Waco, Texas, should be designed to collect sufficient energy in two clear days to survive five days with no sun. What about some of the more cloudy localities as indicated in Figure 6-1, such as the Pacific Northwest and areas bordering the Great Lakes? These regions have at least 20 overcast days and only as many as five clear days in January. According to my 2.5-percent overcast criteria (Figure 6-1) and my 97.5-percent clear criteria (Figure 6-2), a solar greenhouse in these areas should be designed to collect and store enough solar energy in one day to last at least eight days with no sun.

What about those areas with nearly 25 overcast days? In this instance, solar greenhouses should be designed to collect enough solar radiation in one day to last 12 or more days of continuous overcast. Quillayute, Washington, on the Olympic Peninsula has an average of 27 overcast and only two clear days in January, and a solar greenhouse here should be designed to survive at least 15 consecutive overcast days with only one day of solar gain. Such extreme con-

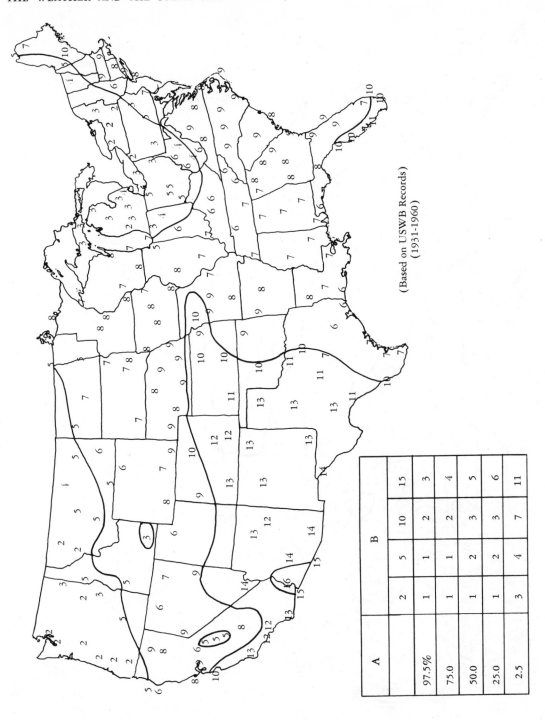

(Based on USWB Records)
(1931-1960)

A		B		
	2	5	10	15
97.5%	1	1	2	3
75.0	1	1	2	4
50.0	1	2	3	5
25.0	1	2	3	6
2.5	3	4	7	11

Figure 6-2: *Table 6-2: Average Number of Clear Days in January*

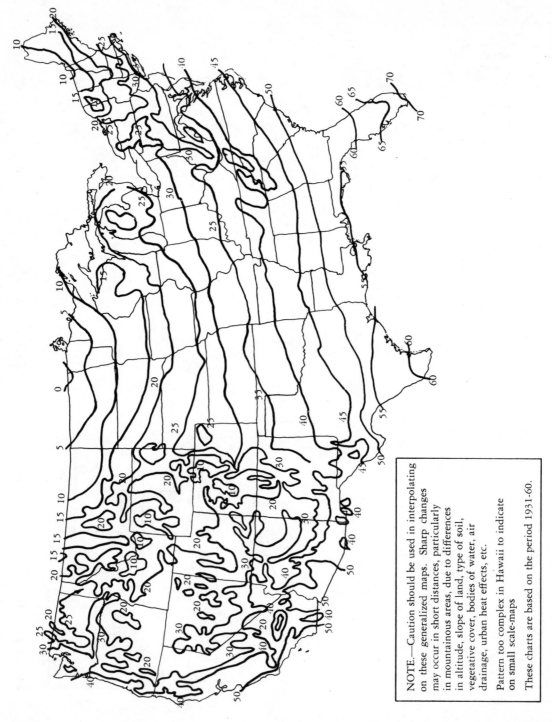

NOTE.—Caution should be used in interpolating on these generalized maps. Sharp changes may occur in short distances, particularly in mountainous areas, due to differences in altitude, slope of land, type of soil, vegetative cover, bodies of water, air drainage, urban heat effects, etc.

Pattern too complex in Hawaii to indicate on small scale-maps

These charts are based on the period 1931-60.

Figure 6-3: *Normal daily average temperature: January.*

ditions require methods for storing heat for long periods of time; these were discussed in Chapter Five.

Temperature

Assuming we can store most of the solar energy during a clear period, how fast will the energy pass out of the greenhouse? Recall that this depends on how well-insulated and wind-proof the greenhouse is, as well as the difference between the inside and outside temperature. The insulation and inside temperature are variables that we can adjust when we finally determine how much heat we need to operate the greenhouse. The outside temperature and wind are variables we cannot adjust to remain a constant factor. When low temperatures and high winds combine during a cloudy period, the greenhouse is subjected to its hardest stress, but this is what we have to design it for.

To specify the lowest temperature conditions likely to occur during the overcast periods is somewhat arbitrary. Typically, January cloudiness is associated with strong weather fronts passing from west to east. During these cloudy periods the temperature remains at or near normal levels (with little daily fluctuation) until the passage of the front. The normal January temperature is the average of the normal high and low and is more or less representative of the average temperature during an extended cloudy period. After the front passes, the temperature often drops to the lowest experienced in a normal year (January). Given that these conditions are typical, I then assumed the normal January temperature is representative of the average outside temperature during a continuous cloudy period, and the last day during the overcast period I assigned the lowest temperature experienced in a normal year. For the clear days before and after the overcast period, I also assigned the normal January temperature. Figures 6-3 and 6-4 show the normal January temperature expected in a normal year, respectively, for the continental United States. These temperatures can be used to determine the amount of insulation required on the greenhouse to retain the stored solar heat for the expected overcast period provided we know the inside temperature as well (see Chapter Seven).

Waco, Texas, has a normal January temperature of 45°F. (interpolated from the 40°F. and 50°F. lines in Figure 6-3), while the lowest temperature experienced in a normal year is about 10°F. (from Figure 6-4). Thus, Waco will have two clear days at 45°F., followed by five overcast days, the first four at 45°F. and the last at 10°F. Kalispell, Montana, on the other hand, will have one clear day at 20°F., followed by 11 overcast days, the first 10 at 20°F. and the last at −30°F. before the next clear period.

The wind criteria is the final climatic condition needed to design the solar greenhouse for winter operation.

Wind

The wind at any particular locality is very difficult to determine, because it is influenced by topography, trees, buildings, and other obstructions. Figure 6-5 shows the average direction of surface winds in January. Generally the arrows point from the west to the east indicating the influence of strong westerly winds associated with passing frontal systems. Figure 6-6 shows the average wind speed for January in miles per hour based on records from 1931 to 1960. I assumed

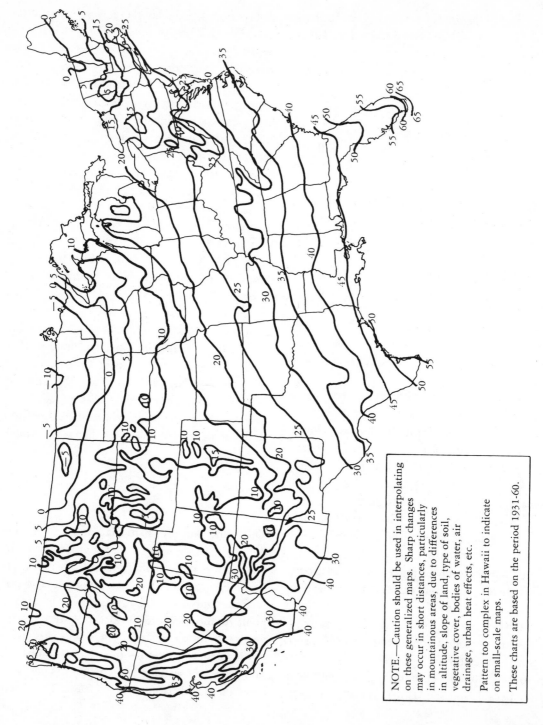

NOTE.—Caution should be used in interpolating on these generalized maps. Sharp changes may occur in short distances, particularly in mountainous areas, due to differences in altitude, slope of land, type of soil, vegetative cover, bodies of water, air drainage, urban heat effects, etc.

Pattern too complex in Hawaii to indicate on small-scale maps.

These charts are based on the period 1931-60.

Figure 6-4: *Normal daily minimum temperature: January.*

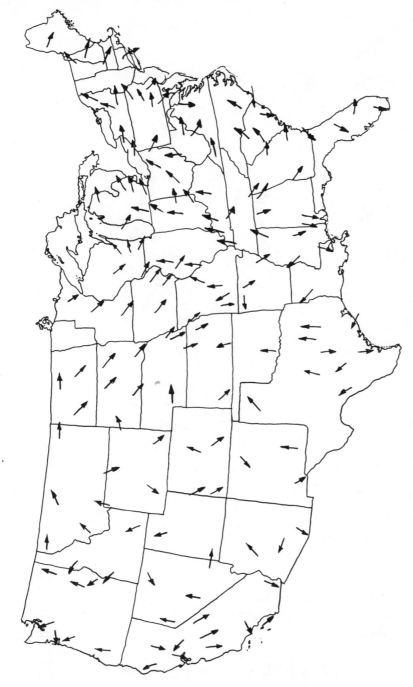

Figure 6-5: *Normal surface wind directions in January.*

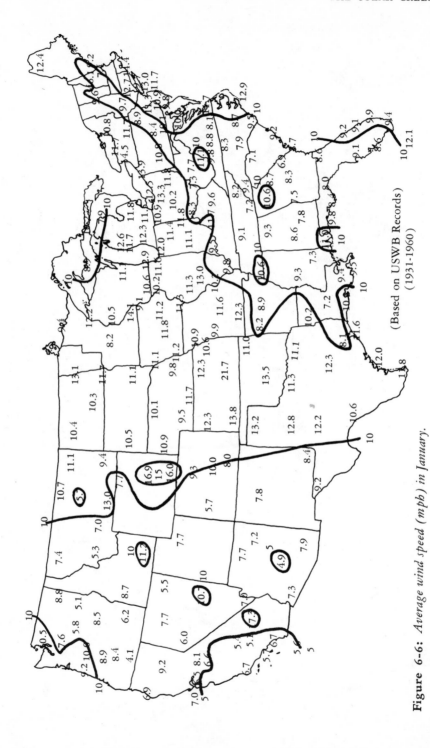

Figure 6-6: *Average wind speed (mph) in January.*

(Based on USWB Records)
(1931-1960)

this average wind speed occurs during the cloudy period, but then doubles in intensity during the last (and coldest) day of the overcast period. Certainly, the coldest nighttime temperatures occur during *calm* conditions after a cold front has passed, but designing the greenhouse to survive through the coldest expected conditions with a strong wind factor gives an extra margin of protection. Protection against the wind blowing cold air into and warm air out of the greenhouse is probably the single most neglected factor in greenhouse design. I cannot overemphasize the importance of this protection.

In summary, the winter design criteria for a solar greenhouse in Waco, Texas, includes the following: in two clear days collect and store enough solar energy (temperature 45°F., average wind, 12 miles per hour) to survive five overcast days, the first four of which are at 45°F. and an average wind of 12 miles per hour, followed by one day at 10°F. and a wind of 24 miles per hour. Climatic criteria for any part of the country can be developed in this way by using the previous Figures and Tables.

Humidity

In the areas of the Southwest where winter greenhouse overheating can be a problem, humidification is often necessary. When cool or cold outside air enters the greenhouse to prevent overheating, the air's humidity lowers drastically as its temperature rises to greenhouse levels. When the outside humidity is 50 percent or less, the humidity of the entering air can drop to 10 percent or less. Humidity should be maintained at 40 percent or more to combat plant wilt. Additional spraying of walkways and plants is required to keep humidity up. In Flagstaff, I water the walkways and plants on almost every clear day during the winter. If you live in regions where winter humidification is a problem, refer to Figure 6-7.

Some general observations can be made about the winter climate design criteria at this time. More care will be necessary in designing completely solar-heated greenhouses for the Pacific Northwest, Montana, and the Great Lakes states (and New England?) than Florida and the Southwest. The eastern states and the upper central Plains states will be difficult localities for the solar greenhouse; the southern states should be relatively easy. Particular attention to wind-proof construction should be paid in the central states, the Great Lakes region, the Atlantic seaboard, and the Rocky Mountain states.

While the previous Figures and Tables give an indication of the broad-scale climatic criteria, the local variations should be considered in many cases. Extra-cloudy conditions could exist in the mountains and the lee sides of large water bodies. Higher winds could exist on ridges, next to highways and other open areas. Lower temperatures could occur in valleys and other low-lying areas. My Flagstaff greenhouse is in an open field and receives some of the strongest winds and coldest temperatures in the vicinity. My local climate is not as severe as the climate some of my friends must endure a few miles up the road on the San Francisco peaks. They were lucky last year: they had a 47-day growing season.

One final note: In those regions where difficult climatic conditions exist, you may feel defeated in not being able to meet the January design criteria for solar heating alone. Still, if the greenhouse is designed as well as possible to meet these conditions, then perhaps you only need to delete December, January, and February from the greenhouse growing season. However,

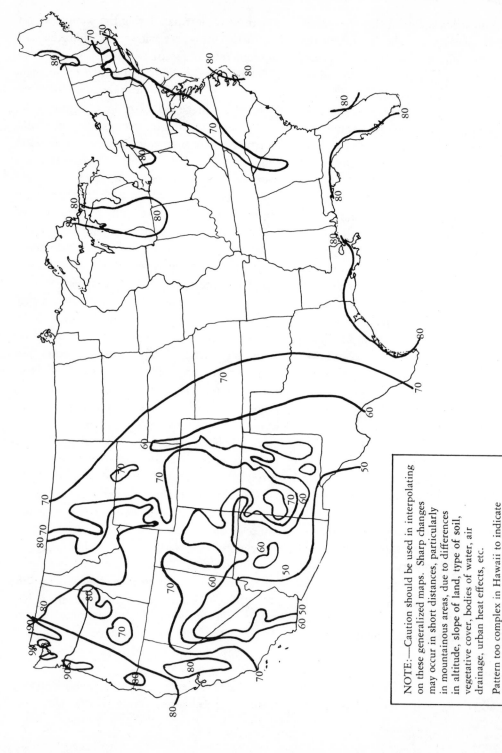

NOTE:—Caution should be used in interpolating on these generalized maps. Sharp changes may occur in short distances, particularly in mountainous areas, due to differences in altitude, slope of land, type of soil, vegetative cover, bodies of water, air drainage, urban heat effects, etc.

Pattern too complex in Hawaii to indicate on small-scale maps.

These charts are based on the period 1931-60.

Figure 6-7: *Average relative humidity in January.*

for the well-designed greenhouse only a small supplement of conventional energy will be needed to get it through the coldest month.

Spring and Fall Design Criteria

These periods are difficult for greenhouse operation, because of the rapid variations in weather from one extreme to the next. Even clear weather is difficult, typically characterized by warm days and cool or cold nights. It is for these periods primarily that daytime opening and nighttime closure of vents is required to prevent alternate overheating and freezing. Humidification may be frequently required. I spend much more of my time adjusting the greenhouse during these periods, especially in Flagstaff, where outside temperatures can go from 5° to 55°F. in six hours on a daily basis.

Summer Design Criteria

Except for a few localities in the United States (mountainous areas primarily), summer greenhouse operation will be difficult. If a good summer garden can be grown in the local area (tomatoes are a good indicator) on a regular year-to-year basis, summer operation of the greenhouse may not be worthwhile. In such areas an early-spring planting should be made with the intent to transplant outside as soon as the normal growing season begins. Such a program will yield early vegetables started from the greenhouse and late vegetables grown from seed outside.

For those who do insist on summer greenhouse operations there are some common-sense factors to consider. Normally if daily temperatures remain below 85°F. and there is a light wind, then partial shading of the greenhouse and all vents full open is sufficient for cooling. I found old bed sheets made good shade. However, as the outside temperature approaches the tolerance level of the plants (around 90° to 95°F.) some alternate cooling must be considered. When outside temperatures are at the tolerance level, natural ventilation is not adequate, no matter how much shading or how strong the wind. Figure 6-8 shows the normal July daily maximum temperatures. The West Coast, the Rocky Mountains, and the northern tier of states seem the most reasonable areas for summer greenhouse operation (temperatures 85°F. and below). Some additional cooling can be provided in areas with low outside humidity by regular water soaking of plants and walkways in the greenhouse. The cooling is provided by the evaporating water, working on the same principal as the evaporative coolers used in the southwestern states.

Again, humidification will be needed in those areas whose outside humidities are below 40 percent. Since the outside air does not heat up as much as in the winter, spring, and fall, the humidity of the outside air does not drop too severely when it reaches greenhouse temperatures. Figure 6-9 shows the July average minimum relative humidity which occurs during the hottest part of the day. Those areas with the July minimum below 40 percent will certainly need humidification.

Of course, it is not necessary or desirable to grow the same plants in the summer as in the winter. For the home greenhouse, choose plants which fit the greenhouse environment; don't force the environment to fit the plants (see Chapters Twelve and Thirteen).

I have tried to give you a simplified view of climate from the standpoint of what the greenhouse is subjected to while it tries to keep your

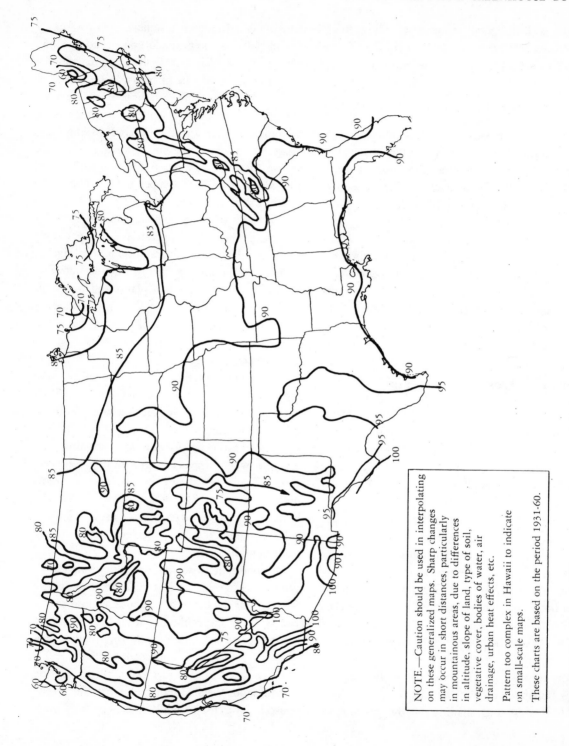

NOTE.—Caution should be used in interpolating on these generalized maps. Sharp changes may occur in short distances, particularly in mountainous areas, due to differences in altitude, slope of land, type of soil, vegetative cover, bodies of water, air drainage, urban heat effects, etc.

Pattern too complex in Hawaii to indicate on small-scale maps.

These charts are based on the period 1931-60.

Figure 6-8: *Average daily maximum temperature in July.*

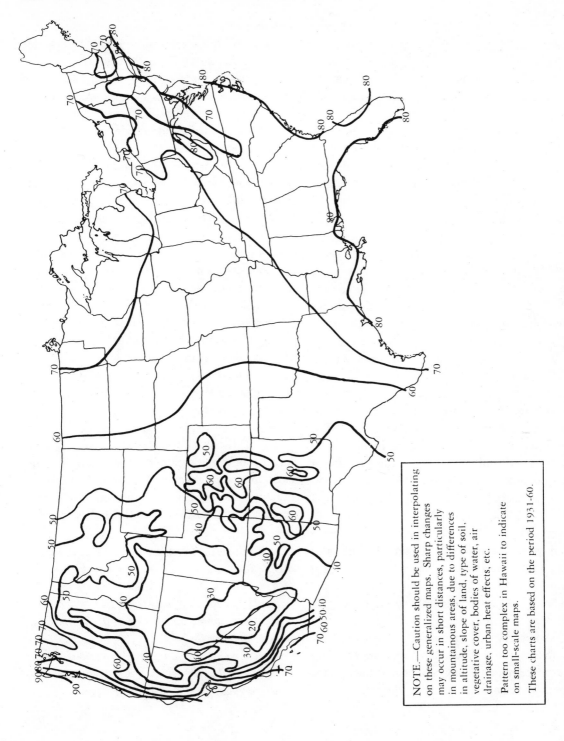

NOTE.—Caution should be used in interpolating on these generalized maps. Sharp changes may occur in short distances, particularly in mountainous areas, due to differences in altitude, slope of land, type of soil, vegetative cover, bodies of water, air drainage, urban heat effects, etc.

Pattern too complex in Hawaii to indicate on small-scale maps.

These charts are based on the period 1931-60.

Figure 6-9: *Average minimum relative humidity for July.*

plants alive and growing. Let me give a relevant example.

Suppose you live in Kalispell, Montana, a severe January climate indeed. You know the greenhouse should ideally collect and store enough energy in one clear day to provide heat for 12 continuously overcast days. But you would like to continue those healthy tomatoes you started in fall by keeping the temperature at least to 40°F. or higher. First, you need to calculate how much solar energy comes into the greenhouse during one clear day. Second, you should determine the total energy required (regardless of the source) to keep the greenhouse at 40°F. or higher for *both* the one clear day the greenhouse is collecting solar energy and the 12 cloudy days it loses heat. For this simple calculation, all you need to know is the greenhouse size, the insulation of the solid and clear walls, and finally the difference between the average inside and outside temperature for each day.

Let's see how a well-designed greenhouse would perform in this harsh winter climate. The first thing I would try to assure in my greenhouse is well-insulated solid walls. I'd try at least six-inch-thick fiberglass batts, a common enough material. Then, I would make sure I had at least two thicknesses of glass (or clear fiberglass) on the south face. All storm windows are constructed this way. I would also put up a night blanket every evening and leave it up until the sun shined again 12 days later. I would measure the area of my clear face, say 200 square feet and then measure the area of my solid walls, say 400 square feet. These are typical areas for a 10-foot by 20-foot freestanding solar greenhouse. I now assume that the average greenhouse temperature on the clear day is 60°,

but drops to 40° by the last cloudy day, an average of 50°F. for the whole period. The outside temperatures we know, again from the previous charts. The amount of heat needed to maintain the inside temperatures is a simple product of the insulation value, the wall areas, and the difference between inside and outside temperature.

Interestingly enough, the above greenhouse could ideally receive 92 percent of its energy needs from the sun. Obviously, the greenhouse cannot collect every calorie of energy, and it cannot be entirely sealed against the wind. But certainly what this should tell you is an entirely solar-heated greenhouse can almost grow tomatoes year-round in one of the coldest and cloudiest areas in our country.

In reality, you would be doing well to store 50 percent of the available solar energy, and the light levels would be too low for tomato growth. But you more sensibly can grow lettuce, radish, and other cool-weather plants that do well in low light and let the temperature drop near freezing. Thereby you would have an excellent chance of growing year-round, even in Kalispell.

The Kalispell example should give you some idea of how the weather information is translated in design criteria. In the next chapter, I use the same weather information to calculate specific values for insulation and heat storage.

It is important to realize that all design recommendations are based directly on the weather charts. The actual translation of chart information into specific design criteria involves complex calculations which in the interest of simplicity have been done for you.

Therefore, the minimum design criteria found in the next chapter can be considered a valuable guide to solar greenhouse construction.

Chapter Seven

Minimum Design Criteria for Solar Greenhouses

David J. MacKinnon

As you have seen in Chapter Five, the simplest way to store solar heat in the greenhouse is in massive objects, such as water-filled containers and earth, directly illuminated by the sun. The water-filled containers are the most effective storage and are considered the primary storage. The ground in the greenhouse can also hold a lot of heat, but it heats up slower because it is usually shaded from direct illumination; this type of storage is referred to as secondary storage. Secondary storage is important and should be included in greenhouse design.

As the greenhouse passes into a continuous overcast period, the primary and secondary storage provides all the heat. First, the primary storage provides the heat until the greenhouse temperature drops to the level of the secondary storage at which point both the secondary and primary storage provide heat.

You can develop relationships among the required amount of heat storage, the insulation value of the walls, and the allowed amount of wind infiltration for the greenhouse, if you know the typical temperatures of the primary and secondary storage that can be achieved, the inside greenhouse temperature desired on the last cloudy day of the overcast period, and the accompanying winter design criteria developed in Chapter Seven.

From these relationships, I wanted to find the minimum values of insulation and heat-storage mass in order for a greenhouse to maintain a minimum temperature of 40°F. for all climatic locations in the continental United States. All of these relationships can be expressed by one term which I call *the heating design factor*.

First, I calculated the heating design factor with no wind infiltration, equal heat capacity for primary and secondary storage, and temperatures of the primary storage ranging from 60° to 80°F., and values for the secondary storage ranging from 50° to 70°F. I arbitrarily assigned specific storage temperatures within the above ranges depending on climatic location and the likelihood of achieving the storage temperatures. For example, I chose low storage temperatures for cloudy and/or northerly locations, and high storage temperatures for sunny and/or southerly locations.

The results were developed into a map of the United States divided into 47 zones with different heating design factors. This data was further simplified and generalized into results which should give you a good idea of minimum con-

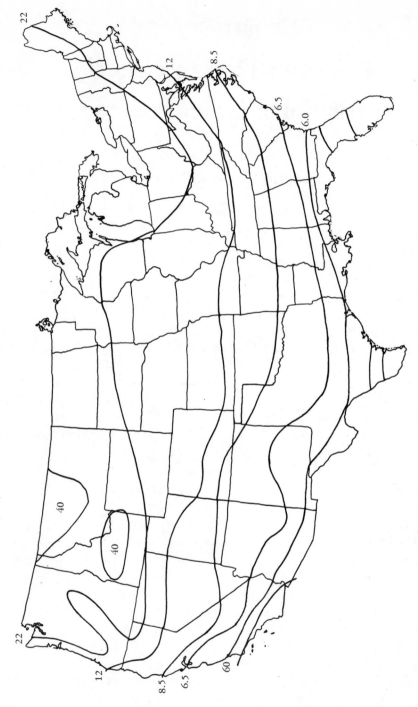

Figure 7-1: *Minimum average R-value for aboveground walls (no wind effects).*

struction features for your greenhouse. These data are presented in Figures 7-1 through 7-3; Figures 7-4 and 7-5 are supplementary data which I am recommending as guidelines which seem reasonable. For these later two figures, I have not developed a rigorous analysis as I have for the previous four.

Figure 7-1 shows the minimum average R-value for the aboveground walls, including a nighttime blanket, with which you should build your greenhouse. A nighttime blanket is a cover placed over the clear walls at night and during cloudy periods. The R-value is a common measure of the insulation value of the wall. Refer to Chapter Three to become reacquainted with its definition. The average R-value is related to the component surface areas and R-values for each of the greenhouse walls. The minimum average R-value is the least average R-value which your greenhouse should have.

The average R-value for your greenhouse can be calculated in the following way. Measure the areas of each of your aboveground walls and divide into each of these areas its R-value. Add each of the resultant values together and divide this figure into the total wall area. This is the average R-value.

The Flagstaff greenhouse, which is discussed in Chapter Eight, has a double-glazed clear wall with an uninsulated night blanket (R-3). The roof has six inches of fiberglass batt (R-19); the side walls have 3½ inches of fiberglass batt (R-11). Placing these values into the relationship yields an average R-value of 6.25. This value is slightly lower than the 6.5 to 8.5 range suggested by Figure 7-1. As you shall see in the next example, I can improve the average R-value of the Flagstaff greenhouse by adding an insulated night blanket.

The Maxatawny greenhouse, which is also discussed in Chapter Eight, has a double-glazed clear wall with an uninsulated night blanket (R-3). All the other walls have the same insulation value, consisting of seven inches of recycled newspaper (R-22). The resulting average R-value is 8.2 which is significantly less than the range of 12 to 22 shown in Figure 7-1 for Maxatawny's location. If you look at the relationship for the average R-value closely, you will see that the low component R-value for the clear walls causes the average R-value to be low. For this reason, an insulated nighttime blanket is recommended for the clear face having an R-value of at least 10 or greater. Such a blanket will increase the average R-value for the greenhouse to 17 or greater. Recommended R-values for nighttime blankets are presented in Figure 7-3.

Figure 7-2 shows the minimum recommendation for the volume of primary heat storage in terms of the floor area of the greenhouse. The insulation values shown in Figure 7-1 were adjusted according to the minimum heat-storage volumes recommended in Figure 7-2. You can reduce your required average R-value by increasing your storage, provided the increased storage intercepts more sunlight as well. It is important that you place primary storage to receive as much direct sunlight as possible. Storage should be placed to intercept at least 30 to 40 percent of the sunlight passing into the greenhouse. The water containers (primary storage) in the Flagstaff greenhouse are stacked along the interior walls and receive at least 37 percent of the sunlight passing into the greenhouse during the winter.

The Flagstaff greenhouse has a floor area of 240 square feet. From Figure 7-2 the recom-

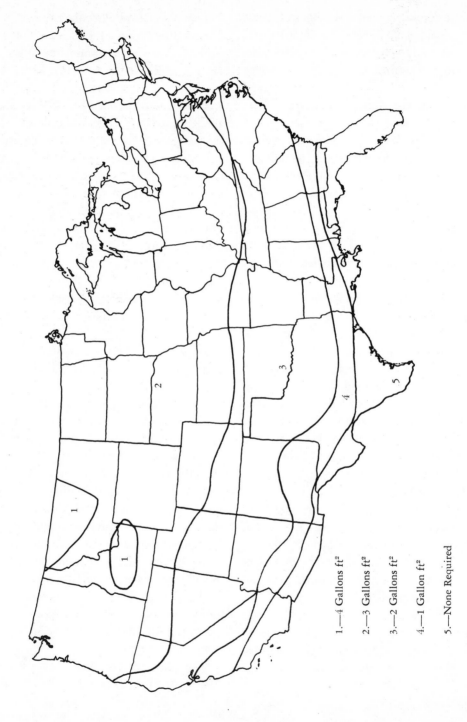

1.—4 Gallons ft²

2.—3 Gallons ft²

3.—2 Gallons ft²

4.—1 Gallon ft²

5.—None Required

Figure 7-2: *Minimum recommendation for the volume of primary heat storage.*

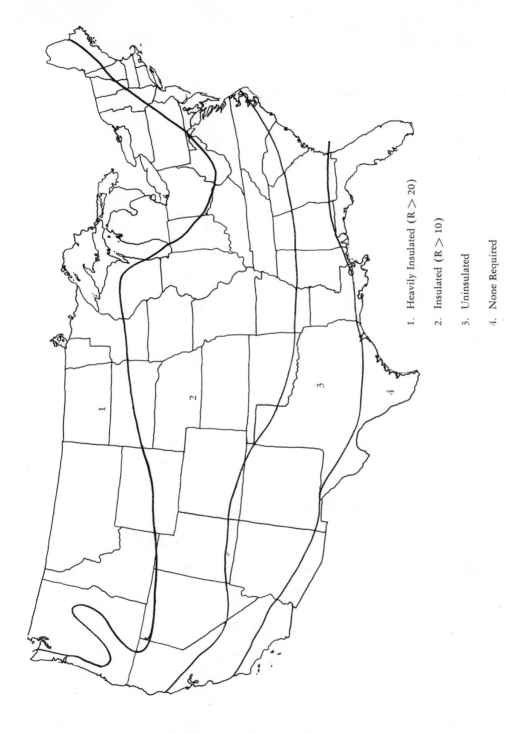

1. Heavily Insulated (R > 20)

2. Insulated (R > 10)

3. Uninsulated

4. None Required

Figure 7-3: *Recommended R-values for nighttime blankets.*

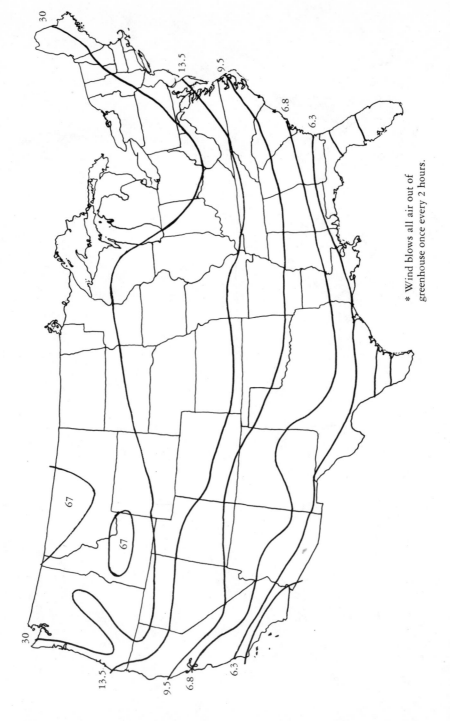

* Wind blows all air out of greenhouse once every 2 hours.

Figure 7-4: *Minimum average R-value for aboveground walls, including night blanket (wind effects included).*

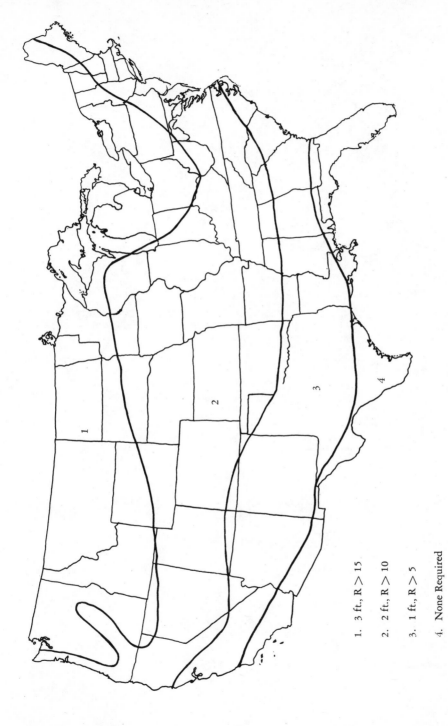

1. 3 ft., R > 15.

2. 2 ft., R > 10

3. 1 ft., R > 5

4. None Required

Figure 7-5: *Minimum ground perimeter insulation: depth and R-value.*

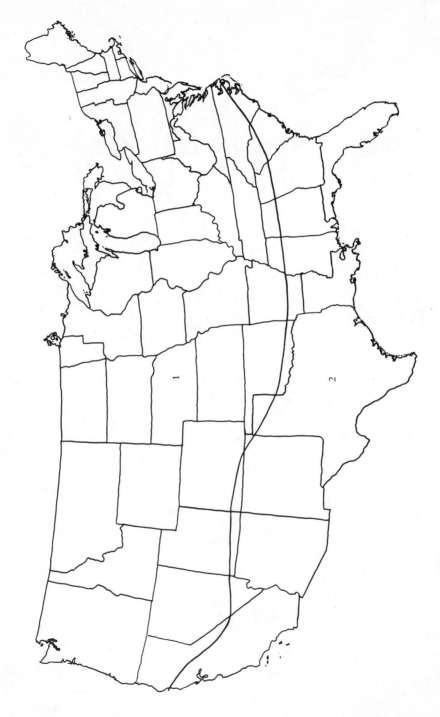

Figure 7-6: *Minimum number of glazings on clear walls.*

mended minimum storage is 480 gallons (2 gal./sq. ft. × 240 sq. ft. = 480 gal.). Currently there are 500 gallons (1976–77 season), but storage will be increased to 1,000 gallons. For Maxatawny, the floor area is 256 square feet. From Figure 7-2, the recommended storage is 780 gallons, currently there is 800 gallons and no room for any more.

The volume of the secondary storage whose effects are included in all the data is assumed to be the entire floor area of the greenhouse down to the two-foot level.

Figure 7-4 shows the effects of wind on the minimum average R-value required to maintain the greenhouse at 40°F. or greater. The insulation value of the walls must be increased to balance the heat blown out of the greenhouse by the wind. This was just one of many ways to demonstrate wind effects. The colder the outside temperature, the greater the heat lost for a given infiltration rate. And the higher the outside wind, the greater the infiltration rate.

Figure 7-4 was developed for a wind sufficient to infiltrate and change the greenhouse air once every two hours. I calculated the infiltration rates for the Flagstaff and Maxatawny greenhouses during the average wind conditions indicated by Figure 7-6. Both rates were close to one greenhouse volume every two hours. This rate was used for all locations in developing Figure 7-4.

On the last cloudy day of the design overcast period the wind doubles, but the infiltration rate for both the Maxatawny and Flagstaff greenhouses triples. This adds on extra stress in the greenhouse not shown in Figure 7-4. I was surprised that the wind created such strong effects on what I thought were fairly airtight greenhouses. It appears that the only simple way to prevent such large infiltration rates is to install outside battens over vents and doors during the winter.

Those of you in particularly windy areas (refer to Figure 7-6) be advised that you can put 10 feet of insulation in your greenhouse walls and your plants will still freeze if your greenhouse is not as airtight as possible.

Figure 7-5 is a recommendation for ground insulation: depth and R-value. The insulation should be placed around the perimeter of the greenhouse. The best insulation for this purpose is rigid closed-cell foam, such as polystyrene or polyurethane, that does not crush under weight.

Figure 7-6 is a minimum recommendation for the number of glazings (number of layers of glass or plastic on the transparent walls). During one test, the Flagstaff greenhouse survived a unusual sequence of 12 stormy days in which only one of the 12 days was clear (the middle of the period) and the rest virtually solid overcast. During this period in January, the average temperature was 24.4°F. with a crackling −7°F. during the night following the last day. All this was achieved with one glazing (fiberglass) and an uninsulated night blanket. During the −7°F. night, the greenhouse temperature did drop to 34°F. . . . but it survived. For the rest of the winter the minimum greenhouse temperatures remained above 40°F.

One final note: Chapter Six contains "large-scale" climatic information. If you have local climatic information for your area, compare it with the charts. If your weather is greatly different from that depicted in the charts, go to a zone with similar conditions. Then return to this chapter to find your adjusted minimum design criteria.

Of course, you should weigh the recommended minimum criteria against actual working designs for a given area. In the final analysis, a working

greenhouse is your best standard. A number of
working greenhouses from various regions of the
country and Canada are discussed throughout the
remainder of the book.

Part II

Constructing the Solar Greenhouse

Chapter Eight

The Freestanding Greenhouse

Jack Ruttle

At this time there are perhaps no more than a few truly solar greenhouses in operation in this country—and most of these are attached greenhouses. The reason for this development is obvious. Attached houses are relatively inexpensive to construct and convenient to maintain. Furthermore, attached houses can provide a significant amount of heat and food.

On the other hand, although a freestanding house won't offer all the above advantages, many are being constructed and many more contemplated. There are a number of reasons for this phenomenon. Some people might want a larger growing area than an attached house potentially provides. In some cases, the existing home might not have an orientation suitable for an attached house, which is true of the Mackie and McDougall houses discussed in this chapter. Or in some cases, there might be adjacent obstructions, such as trees and outbuildings, that make construction of an attached house inadvisable.

Or perhaps a school, such as the Canyon Park Junior High School in Seattle, Washington, wants a greenhouse to serve as an interdisciplinary tool; in this case a freestanding greenhouse is desirable.

Or perhaps a community group wants a large solar greenhouse for vegetable production. In this case also, a freestanding house might be in order.

Or perhaps people are simply excited by the "solar" and aesthetic challenge inherent in the freestanding greenhouse idea.

Reflecting all the above reasons, most of the solar greenhouses featured in this chapter have been built by individuals with an interest in applying passive solar technology to the greenhouse. Several of these people have affiliations with organizations: the New Alchemy Institute and their various benefactors, David MacKinnon with the support of the Museum of Northern Arizona and Rodale Press, Inc., and Bear Creek Thunder with the Ecotope Group and Pragtree Farm. Consequently, they can all draw on people, talent, and money beyond themselves, applying formal research and development techniques to solutions for low-technology living.

What has pressed these designers into such research projects is that they envision the solar greenhouse as an essential tool for the future. Though they have worked independently, they all anticipate an increasing need for locally grown fresh produce in winter, as the fuel for growing and shipping vegetables from the semi-arid regions far to the south becomes prohibitive.

The Brace Design

The first real testing began four years ago at the Brace Institute in Montreal. The climate there

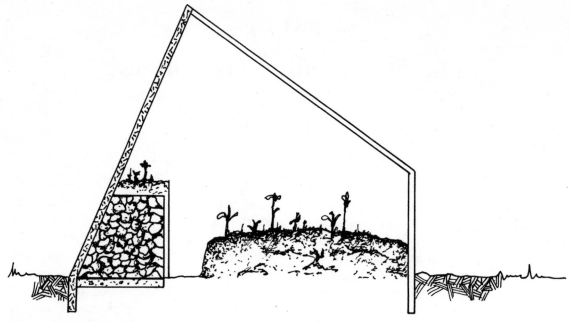

Figure 8-1: *The Brace design.*

is so severe that local greenhouse growers even then were finding it hard to operate. Researchers at Brace wanted to help them continue in business and help Montreal become a little less dependent on the south for food.

Brace focused on just one aspect, reducing the need for fuel by insulating the north wall. Actually, there was no doubt that insulating large expanses of glass wall would drastically cut heat losses. But how much? And would the resultant reduction in light cut into plant production? They probed those questions with a simple test which was conceived as a demonstration for local growers. Everyone likes a race; the Brace people built the new greenhouse next to a conventional design and ran one.

Both houses were heated to a level necessary for a crop of commercial tomatoes in Montreal's winter. The new design required one-third less

fuel. Beyond the impressive reduction in fuel costs, the crop in the solarized house grew faster. Though a little less light entered that greenhouse, none could pass on through a clear north wall. The Brace design provided more total light for growth by bouncing light back to the plants with a reflective coating on the insulated wall. Few people anticipated superior growing conditions in a greenhouse that had less clear surface. Therefore, the Brace findings represented an important advance in greenhouse knowledge.

Unfortunately, the commercial growers that Brace wanted to influence have been slow to recognize the significance of the design change and adopt it. But for several of the freestanding solar greenhouse designers, the work at Brace was the maverick break with tradition; it breathed life into a dream of low-energy vege-

Photo 8-1: *The grape house. Lyman Estate, Waltham, Massachusetts.*

table production during cold seasons.

Historical Designs

In each of the greenhouses in this chapter you can see some of the lines of the Brace design. Moreover, these greenhouses hark back to some simple designs of centuries ago.

The old "grape house" (1804) at the Lyman Estate in Waltham, Massachusetts, is typical. The shape would constitute a classic prototype for a commercial-sized modern solar greenhouse. There are other similarities. Unlike modern commercial practices, the old greenhouse runs east to west to capture the sun effectively. People then knew that plants would grow illuminated by just the southern half of the sky. It was heated by a wood furnace separated from the growing area by a thick brick wall. A gently sloping flue runs the length of the house to a chimney at the far end. Warm air in the flue heated the wall. The furnace in the back room also radiated heat into the wall, top to bottom. The plants were warmed not by occasional blasts of hot air, but by steady radiant heat from the bricks, a fine structural material for absorbing

Photo 8-2: *Freestanding greenhouse. Lyman Estate, Waltham, Massachusetts.*

energy. Today, if using fire to supplement heat in a solar greenhouse, we would recommend burning intensely to charge up the mass in the greenhouse rather than burning it slowly all night.

The large house was a monster to run. A smaller and older (1800 or earlier) freestanding greenhouse at the estate is more characteristic of forcing structures commonly used in eighteenth-century America and Europe, where the design comes from. It is a tool for starting early vegetable and flower plants for the nearby kitchen garden, and is really midway between a green-

house and a cold frame. A tall person has to stoop to walk in it. A much smaller wood furnace works the same as in the large greenhouse. Even better, it and the flue are built into the rock wall which retains the waist-high growing bed. The rock radiates heat directly into the soil of the growing bed as well as the air. On the shallow-glazed face, there are channels for two layers of sash. Ventilation was as easy as opening a window. The house might have been double-glazed though it isn't now.

More than anything else, such similarities between the oldest and newest greenhouses hint at the simplicity of the techniques which make free-standing houses work. But the array of versatile insulating materials we have to work with and the skillful integration by modern designers of measures for admitting, containing, and storing heat, set us far ahead of vegetable growers 200 years ago.

Contemporary Designs

Looking to the future, it is tempting to say that we will not see better technology for solar greenhouses developed than what these designers have worked into their freestanding passive structures. The study of solar heating is not new, and the people represented in this chapter are well schooled in the methods. Materials for glazing may improve—plastics have some wonderful properties. But for admitting light energy and trapping heat radiation, there is hardly a finer material than glass. Nor is there a readily obtainable substance that comes close to water for its heat-absorbing capacity. Considering the abundance of water, it is hard to imagine a replacement. Brick, stone, and concrete absorb radiation reasonably well while doubling as part of the structure.

So the materials and know-how for fine solar greenhouses are at hand. The solar features are not costly or subject to failure because the structures do not need collectors, pumps, pipes, or power. Technology per se is purposely designed out of passive systems.

The similarities among solar greenhouses are in the large features: two glazing layers, generous amounts of insulation above and below ground, and large masses of water and earth for heat storage, much of it in direct radiation. By no means does each greenhouse use all of them. However, common use suggests a consensus that these few techniques are essential in any climate

which requires a large structure, attached or free-standing, in order to significantly extend the season.

The principle achievement of solar greenhouse designers has been in putting all the elements together to create passive systems that work through the winter. It is only natural that these people should all be attracted to the challenge of freestanding greenhouses. That many situations are only suited for freestanding greenhouses is reason enough. Moreover, by solving the problems of the most demanding design, they have evolved techniques and insights which are appropriate for all applications right down to attached greenhouses and solar cold frames.

The optimum combination of parts into a passive greenhouse for any climate is not clear cut, nor can an ideal design be abstracted from the buildings treated here. There are intriguing differences among all of them. Each system is a compromise between the builders' ideas and the demands of quite different climates, between economy of space, money, and convenience of operation.

Because almost every greenhouse was specifically designed to be entirely passive and to operate through the winter, you have a very neat basis for comparison. Examining all of them allows you, in some measure, to learn things which go beyond the one or two examples built for a particular region. This will help as you anticipate features you will need to incorporate as you design your own. And it is why this chapter presents detailed information concerning weather, interior climate, and design features. To the extent possible, that information is presented uniformly for each greenhouse.

Collectively, the principles of successful integration of the essential features as detailed in Part I will become clear. The key is to look for the balance in each system. Systems that work well do so because the parts all complement each other not solely because of great quantities of insulating or storage materials. Many of the designers will confess to relying a little too heavily on some feature or other at the outset of their work. Changes are contemplated for all of them. The trend is not to alter the larger aspects of the design, but to amplify parts or add features that were omitted. Though there may be room for improvement, each of these greenhouses has worked and has worked well.

One essential feature they all share, though not very visible, is careful craftsmanship. It's free and within the reach of every builder. There is absolutely no point in giving meticulous attention to shape and materials, then losing energy through careless cuts and joints. The better the greenhouse is insulated, the more its total heat loss will be due to infiltration of cold air. These designers report that they anticipated seams, especially around openings and glazing joints, in the planning stages and reduced them as much as possible. Once the greenhouses were complete, cracks have been hunted down like vermin and sealed.

At first glance, several of these greenhouses will appear so expensive as to make the vegetables grown within a luxury for the rich only. Remember that they were built from all new materials and sometimes with outside labor for the sake of saving time and probing ideas quickly. As research projects go, they are cheap. Several others here have put up solar greenhouses with some salvaged materials that are cheaper than traditional all-glass hobby or commercial greenhouses. Using permanent materials, you should be able to construct a solar greenhouse like these that will outlive you.

Because the winter of 1976-77 was the first winter of operation for half the greenhouses, it is used as a reference point for all cases. That season was also unusually cloudy in the Southwest and bitterly cold in the Northeast. Average weather extremes are provided as well. Consequently there is common ground for comparing the performance of these greenhouses among themselves as well as to your own projected design. Notice, too, the reliability of the rules of thumb in Chapter Six in providing accurate extreme design conditions.

As a guide to actual construction, details of techniques for each step along the way are provided for David MacKinnon's Flagstaff greenhouse. Not only does this one embody every essential feature of a solar greenhouse, but his very simple techniques guarantee a well-sealed, permanent, and reliable structure. This description is not a recommendation or endorsement of MacKinnon's particular blend of elements, such as the amount of insulation, storage, and type of curtain. Specific components will be different in every climate. Likewise, there are different construction techniques appropriate to solar greenhouse building. For example, MacKinnon's foundation is best suited to a dry climate. Accordingly, useful alternate techniques are highlighted in each of the greenhouse cases cited. In turn, the construction as well as the design information presented here is intended to have direct bearing on subsequent chapters featuring attached greenhouses, pit greenhouses, and solar cold frames.

David MacKinnon

Flagstaff, Arizona

35° North Latitude

David MacKinnon has studied solar greenhouse and cold frame design for several years. Working with Rodale Press he has built two free-standing greenhouses in Arizona and Pennsyl-

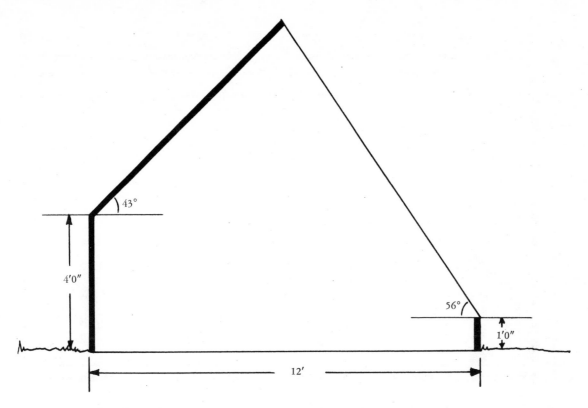

Figure 8-2: *Greenhouse dimensions.*

vania. In operation for one winter, his second design at the Museum of Northern Arizona at Flagstaff, maintained an excellent interior climate throughout the season. Bountiful crops grew and were harvested steadily. The average nighttime lows inside hovered around 50°F., with no need for heat from outside sources.

Orientation: Due south

January Climate Outside: Overcast days average 13 this month. Two consecutive overcast days are likely. Five consecutive cloudy days is the longest stretch in an average year. Flagstaff also gets an average 13 clear days in January. Three clear days in succession is usual. The average temperature is 30°F. The lowest temperature for the month averages −10°F. Average wind speed is 7.7 mph.

These guideposts for designing a solar greenhouse constitute a fairly accurate prediction of the real conditions in Flagstaff for the winter of 1976-77. It was slightly more cloudy than expected, but it was a little warmer too. The temperature reached −7°F. on two nights. The average outside low was 12.5°F. Fifteen days were cloudy, 14 days were clear. Twice, however, they experienced five-day cloudy periods. The first of these at the outset of the month was actually part of an extremely rare 11-day period.

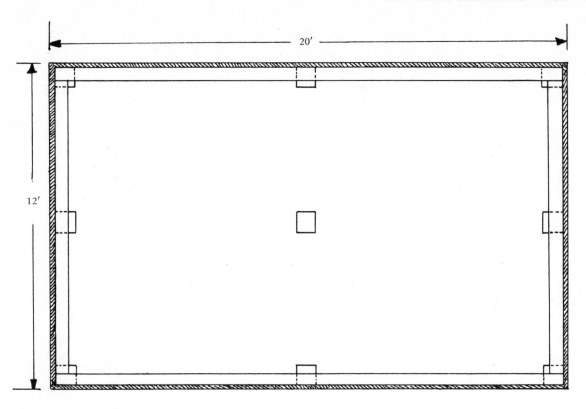

Figure 8-3: *Floor plan and perimeter insulation.*

Climate Inside: The greenhouse did not require extra heat. The average nighttime low was 49°F., very good for cool-season leafy greens. Once the temperature dipped to 34°F., on the last night of an 11-day period with little energy from the sun.

Configuration: The greenhouse is 12 feet wide

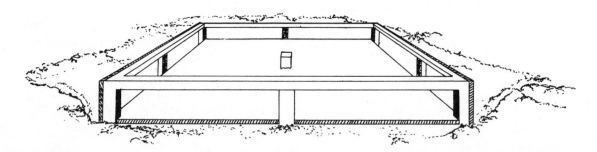

Figure 8-4: *Foundation with insulation installed.*

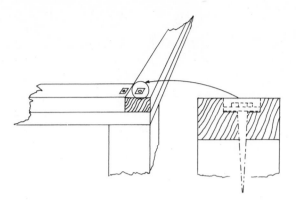

Figure 8-5: *Piling detail.*

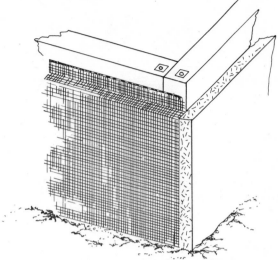

Figure 8-6: *Detail: Wire mesh installation.*

and 20 feet long. The peak is over the midpoint of the north-south axis and rises 9½ feet above the ground. The clear south face is 10 feet high, from the 1-foot vent wall in front to the peak, and is sloped at 56°. The rear roof is sloped 43° down to the 4-foot kneewall in back.

There are 240 square feet available for growing space and walkways, illuminated by 200 square feet of clear surface.

Construction: The foundation is sturdy, cheap, and constructed with minimum materials. Sections of railroad ties serve as pilings. The foundation was excavated to a depth of 3 feet (frost

Figure 8-7: *Framing detail. Front and rear walls.*

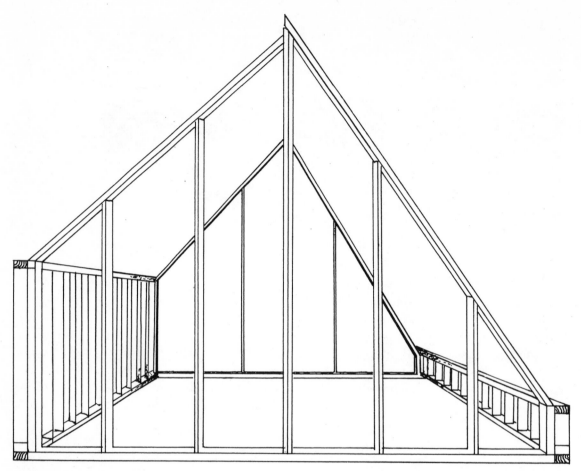

Figure 8-8: *Framing detail. End walls.*

line) so that the insulation could be installed. The pilings were set at each of the corners and at the midpoints of the two 20-foot walls, with the tops of each piling at ground level. One piling was set in the middle of the house to support the center post.

To support the insulation below ground, ½-inch wire mesh was attached to the perimeter of the piling foundation (outside the insulation). The wire also serves to prevent rodents from destroying the insulation and getting into the greenhouse. More insulation was laid over the excavated floor and the earth was replaced. Flagstones cover the excavated floor.

Six-by-six-inch fir beams were bolted to the tops of the pilings around the perimeter. This framework supports the building. This particular foundation is best suited to greenhouses in dry climates. However, any similar cost-saving shortcuts are desirable; the conventional poured-

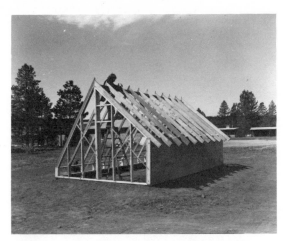

Photo 8-3: *Framing detail. Roof.*

Photo 8-4: *Rear roof detail.*

Photo 8-5: *Completed greenhouse.*

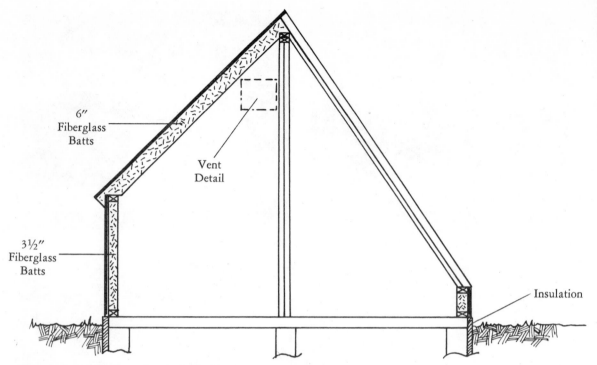

6″
Fiberglass
Batts

Vent
Detail

3½″
Fiberglass
Batts

Insulation

Figure 8-9: *Section—Insulation in place.*

concrete-and-block foundation is much stronger than is necessary to support most solar greenhouses.

Standard 2 x 4 framing practices were followed, with studs on 2-foot centers. The roof was constructed with 2 x 6s to allow for thicker insulation. The interior and exterior are sheathed with plywood. All wood in the building is treated with a preservative nontoxic to plants. The exterior is painted white, and the interior walls are covered with aluminum foil to direct light back to the plants. The roof is covered with tar paper and rolled roofing material.

Insulation: The foundation is insulated from the

Photo 8-6: *Insulation installed. Interior.*

Photo 8-7: *Curtain stored.*

ground outside by planks of polyurethane foam 1½ inches thick. Insulation extends 3 feet into the ground and covers the bottom of the foundation. MacKinnon reports that he would not cover the bottom with insulation again since the earth temperature inches below the frost line is in the low 50s which is what his insulated earth achieves at the deepest levels. Instead, he recommends using thicker foam planks (2 inches) and extending them deeper into the ground, about 6 inches below the frost line.

The walls contain 3½-inch fiberglass batts.

Photo 8-8: *Raising curtain.*

The ceiling is insulated with 6-inch fiberglass batts.

A homemade curtain insulates the clear face at night and on cloudy days. The fabric is parachute material from an army/navy store. Over one side of it, ordinary aluminum foil has been glued with contact cement. It is lightweight and has proven very durable. During the day it lies in a bunch along the bottom of the glazed wall. In the evenings it is raised up by a pulley at the peak. It is supported by guy wires strung parallel to and a little below the rafters.

MacKinnon reports that the curtain prevents heat losses which amount to 10° higher nighttime minimum temperatures. That is testimony to the significance of radiation losses through glazings. The curtain is thin and has a relatively low R-value. It does restrict air flow over the surface. But it could do a better job of that too since about a foot and a half of glazing on each end is left uncovered, simply because the wires to move the vents would be obstructed. MacKinnon says that the curtain undoubtedly would block even more heat if it covered the entire glazed surface, were sealed somehow to prevent drafts, and included some truly insulating material. As is, though, the greenhouse has maintained good growing temperatures.

Glazing: The exterior glazing is 5-ounce regular Filon sheets fastened vertically (from peak to ground) to the top of the 2 x 4 rafters on 2-foot centers.

Inside the second layer is 5-mil acetate. The acetate is glued to 3½-foot-by-2-foot wooden frames with silicone sealant to make a taut panel. The frames are nailed to the bottom of the rafters creating a 3½-inch dead-air space between glazings. MacKinnon used acetate because it

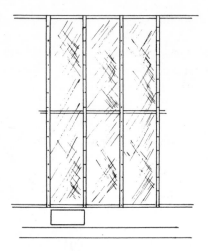

Figure 8-10a: *Exterior glazing installation.*

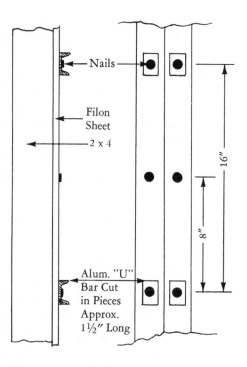

Figure 8-10b: *Detail: glazing installation.*

Photo 8-9: *Water storage: 500 gallons.*

acts more like glass than polyethylene does: it admits more light and lets less radiation back out.

Heat Storage: 500 gallons of water in 1-gallon translucent plastic jugs are stacked on their sides along opaque walls. The water has been dyed black with Rit dye to absorb heat better. The stack on the rear wall is 4 feet high and receives direct radiation most of the day. The stacks on the side walls are 6 inches high and receive direct radiation part of the day. For each one Fahrenheit degree rise or drop in water temperature, the storage takes in or gives back 4,165 Btu's.

The bottles are stacked on their sides for two reasons. First, it presents to the sun a dense pack of water. If they were stacked on their bottoms, the area around the neck would be open and energy would not be captured in those spaces. Second, there is close contact on all sides of the containers, so when more heat is stored in one area it can migrate to an area with less heat. The bottles are kept in place on their sides by wiring

Photo 8-10: *View of heat motor at top vent and wire-spring configuration for opening bottom vent.*

the necks to chicken wire stretched between furring strips on the wall. The only disadvantage to the system is that the bottle tops don't seal well. Stacked on their sides, some tend to leak under pressure.

The floor also can store energy because it is insulated from the outside. Daily, only the top 6 inches (about 120 cubic feet) exchange heat with the greenhouse air. How much heat that space holds varies with the amount of water in the soil. Assuming that one-degree temperature change in the soil involves 20 Btu's per cubic foot, the entire floor has a daily capacity of 2,400 Btu's for each one-Fahrenheit degree change. The soil in the planting containers also captures and releases some heat.

Over longer periods, heat stored throughout

the 3-foot depth of soil is important for maintaining greenhouse temperatures.

Vents: Since the greenhouse holds heat so well, it is prone to overheat in the warmer and longer days of spring and autumn. Vents are essential for long-season operation, but the cracks around the insides become prime heat-loss spots in cold, windy weather. MacKinnon located vents near the peak at both ends of the greenhouse and a series of smaller ones in the wall along the ground at the south face.

The vents are lightweight, made of a single piece of plywood with styrene foam glued to it. The styrene fits the vent opening tightly, but the plywood is larger than the opening so it overlaps to batten the joint. Crushable foam weather strip surrounds the perimeter of the styrene door. The vents are operated by a heat motor that exerts 50 pounds so they are held tight and the foam weather strip fills the cracks.

Heat motors mounted at each of the end-wall vents operate all the low vents as well (via pulley and cable) automatically without outside power. Temperature-sensitive metals do the work. MacKinnon recommends the particular ones he is using. Their starting temperature is adjustable, and they work with great force. By adjusting the location of the heat motors, the distance they will move a vent can be controlled as well. They are made by John Hoffman, Inc., Sierra Madre, CA 91024.

Gardening: MacKinnon tried a variety of crops in the greenhouse. Compared to their production in a summer garden outdoors, some thrived and some grew very poorly. Bush squash grew into nice plants, but the fruits were tiny and not worth the time and space. Neither did onions or bulbs, broccoli, spinach, or beets do well.

Tomato, lettuce, and radishes all produced abundantly. Tomataoes, in fact, will yield better in a solar greenhouse during early and late winter than they do as an outside crop in Flagstaff's dry and very short summer. MacKinnon started his tomato plants for the greenhouse in the summer and by Christmas, harvest began. Ripe tomatoes were picked regularly for two weeks. For a three-week period in mid-January, none ripened, then harvest began and continued steadily.

Radishes and lettuce were seeded in the greenhouse on October 25. More were seeded three weeks later. Beginning at Christmas, both were picked bi-weekly all winter.

This system shows that relatively small amounts of storage can work. The reason is twofold. The greenhouse is well constructed and insulated, and Flagstaff can depend upon plentiful and intense sunlight. Despite a cloudier January than normal, the solar greenhouse created good growing conditions. After the longest cloudy stretch, the temperature dropped to 34°F., but no supplemental heat was needed to keep the plants producing.

Still, MacKinnon plans to double the amount of water storage in the greenhouse. Though more isn't absolutely necessary, there is room to double the amount without infringing upon the plant-growing area. MacKinnon will replace the plastic jugs with rectangular, metal five-gallon containers painted black to get 1,000 gallons stacked against the walls.

In addition, the greenhouse floor will be converted to rectangular beds and pathways. Plants will be planted directly into the ground. MacKinnon foresees better use of the greenhouse area for higher plant density than pots allow. Pots also shade the floor from direct radiation, so beds may allow more efficient heat collection by the soil (especially when plants are small).

MacKinnon has strong feelings about the reflective coatings used inside to redirect radiation. His greenhouse uses aluminum foil glued to the walls. Foil focuses radiation in a much narrower pathway. Most of it is aimed right back to the floor and plants. He reports that when he looks into his greenhouse from the outside it looks black, a sign that little radiation is pointed back out. White paint scatters the radiation, and some of it will pass out through the glazing so that the greenhouse appears white viewed from the outside.

On the other hand, white paint won't cause radiative "hot spots" in the plant beds as foil can. Furthermore, aluminum foil conducts 10 percent more heat through the walls than white paint will. In effect, it decreases the insulation MacKinnon feels both substances have their advantages and recommends a choice based on economics, ease of care, and aesthetic preferences.

Bill and Marsha Mackie

McMinnville, Oregon

45° North Latitude

Bill and Marsha Mackie have operated their solar greenhouse since the winter of 1975-76. Initially their goal was to get some vegetables for the table through the winter and to raise some fish in the tank which contained water for thermal mass. They would have liked to attach the greenhouse to their home. But their primary concern has been that the greenhouse be entirely solar heated, and there is no room on the side of their

Photo 8-11: *Freestanding greenhouse. McMinnville, Oregon.*

house that faced the sun. So they devised a passive solar greenhouse which has done a good job of trapping and retaining heat and growing plants.

They salvaged materials for the greenhouse zealously to keep costs down. A high-quality double-glazing is essential in their opinion, so they bought new materials. They also had to buy roofing and foundation materials. Of the $437 total cost, these three items took the largest share.

The heat-storage system has undergone several transformations. Early in their venture they mounted a solar collector to help put extra heat into the water tank. They found the gains weren't worth the costs, and they removed it. Over the first winter they learned that the water temperatures in the tank were too cold for bass or tilapia, the fish they wanted to work with. The Mackies decided not to fight relatively low water temperatures (which they would always have since little direct radiation strikes the water), and removed the fish. In the middle of the second winter, a time of extreme drought in the

Photo 8-12: *Interior.*

Northwest, they saw the tank as a way of saving some of their greywater, a system with multiple advantages for the greenhouse and garden.

Orientation: Due south. They would change this. There is less light available in the greenhouse during spring than during fall because spring mornings are consistently very cloudy and afternoons tend to be clear. They start plants for the garden then, so they feel the greenhouse would work better if the greenhouse faced slightly west of south.

January Climate Outside: The reference winter (1976-77) was a little colder and much drier than usual in McMinnville. The average daily high was 48° and the average low was 27°. The coldest it got was 13°F. Normally the winter is very wet with only about three clear days to collect solar energy all month. Twenty-three days are normally overcast. In January (1976-

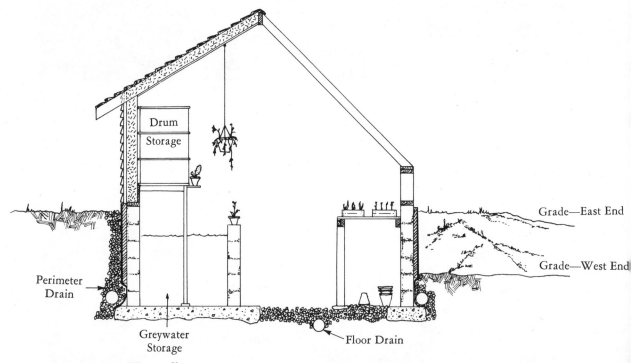

Figure 8-11: *West wall.*

77) only 17 days were completely overcast and nine were very sunny. Compared to other areas of the country, that is still not very much available solar energy. However, the relatively moderate temperatures do permit successful greenhouse growing.

Climate Inside: For the first year the greenhouse was single-glazed. The second layer was not added until February. Still, the temperature at night rarely dropped below 50°F. Normally in the day, the temperature would climb into the 60s or 70s and occasionally even the 80s.

During prolonged cloudy weather, which is fairly common, the temperature remained in the 50s day and night. The lack of sun seemed to have noticeable ill effects on the plants. To alleviate this they later painted the interior white and gained reflected light.

With two layers of glazing, the greenhouse never goes below 50° at night. Usually it stays around 55°F. The temperature is ideal for raising plants. Insufficient light is the biggest problem for winter gardening.

Configuration: The greenhouse is 11 feet wide and 15 feet long with glazing on only the south side. It is built into a shallow slope so that on the north side and east end, the greenhouse is sunk about 3 feet. The glazed face is sloped 45°.

Construction: The foundation is a block wall on concrete footings. Because of the wet climate, special attention was given to drainage. A vapor barrier was placed against the block wall and drainage tile was laid below the north and south foundation walls. As they back-filled, they put 6 inches of gravel beside the wall all the way up. In the center of the greenhouse floor they dug a shallow trench for a pipe which drains out the

west end. They then covered the floor with polyethylene, laid the pipe in the ditch and covered all with a layer of gravel.

The Mackies bolted a 2 x 6 around the top of the block foundation. The crack between the block and this wooden plate is a fairly large heat-loss area. They recommend applying some fiberglass or caulk between the two during construction.

Standard framing (2 x 4s on 2-foot centers) was used for the greenhouse, except for the clear south face. Since the fiberglass sheets were 5 feet wide, the rafters on the front face are on 2½-foot centers. There is one 2-foot-by-2-foot vent high on each end wall, and there are two more vents under the eave of the north wall. All vents are screened for summer and all have hinged shutters on the outside of the greenhouse. Each vent has 3 inches of fiberglass insulation squeezed between the screen and exterior shutter. The vents are permanently closed during winters.

One change they may make is to replace the fiberglass insulation with a sheet of 1-inch Styrofoam cut to size and glued to the inside of the shutter. This would allow wintertime venting which is occasionally necessary, especially with the humidity caused by warm greywater.

Insulation: The opaque walls and the north roof of the greenhouse are all insulated with 3½-inch fiberglass batt. Originally, the foundation was not insulated. For the second winter, however, they dug down 2 feet along all walls and placed 1 inch of Styrofoam against the concrete block. They don't use any insulating material against the glazed face of the greenhouse.

Glazing: The greenhouse is double-glazed with 30-mil Kalwall. The layers are 3½ inches apart, one on the outside of the rafters and the other

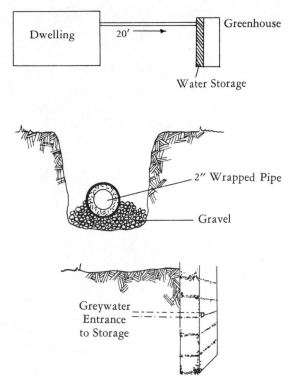

Figure 8-12: *Detail: gravity drain.*

on the inside. The Kalwall was drilled before nailing. A bead of caulk was laid on the outside edge of each rafter before the Kalwall was installed.

Heat Storage: The greenhouse contains 1,640 gallons of water. On a shelf several feet above the water tank, 440 gallons in eight black drums receive direct radiation all day long from mid-September through mid-March. The drums absorb much more of the energy that strikes them than does the much greater volume of water in the tank.

The concrete blocks intercept the direct radi-

ation but do not transfer much to the 1,200 gallons of water inside. Consequently, the water in the tank does not get as warm as it could. The water temperature stays around 50° in the winter and rises to 60° in the summer. Fish can "winter over" at that temperature, but they won't grow. Nonetheless, 1,200 gallons of water at 50°F. contains considerable heat which is important for keeping the greenhouse warm at night.

Aquaculture in the solar greenhouse is a popular concept, but none seem able to keep water warm enough for fish to gain weight. The experimentation continues in other greenhouses, but the Mackies decided to turn their fish tank into a greywater holding tank in the middle of their second season. With such a suitable tank just 20 feet from the home, conversion was simple. Water from all sinks, the shower, and the washing machine go into the tank. Since most of this is hot, the system neatly captures otherwise wasted energy and warms the greenhouse considerably more than the tank's solar-collection ability. A shower in the house can raise the temperature in the tank five Fahrenheit degrees.

The tank is fed by a gravity drain. The 2-inch pipe, insulated with fiberglass batt, tar paper, and polyethylene, lies in a 1-foot sloped trench from the basement to the greenhouse.

The tank is drained by siphoning. Since the original drain in the greenhouse floor empties out the west end above the garden, the tank could be emptied onto the greenhouse floor and the garden watered from the drain exit. Because greywater contains some fats, however, the Mackies now use a longer hose to siphon the water directly from the tank to the garden. They have made shallow trenches near vegetable and berry rows to direct the water where it is best used. To water plants uphill nearer the home,

Photo 8-13: *"Six Pack." New Alchemy Institute, Cape Cod, Massachusetts.*

they simply run the pump which is ordinarily turned on only a few seconds to start the siphoning. Mackie reports that so far plants watered this way look fine. He anticipates problems that sodium (from lye) might accumulate, and so he is having the water checked as "agricultural irrigation water" for a reasonable fee at the state extension service.

Gardening: The first winter they raised lettuce, radishes, and a variety of herbs successfully. They also had fuchsias and geraniums blooming all winter. Tropical house plants prospered.

The second winter they brought large broccoli in from the garden in containers. It continued to grow in the solar greenhouse, providing one harvest a week. The greenhouse is also a means for extending the summer tomato production season. Parsley has grown beautifully.

Lettuce, which they expected to yield food steadily, actually grows very slowly in the middle of winter. Spinach has not grown well at all. They plant new crops in the greenhouse in fall. These will begin to produce two months later. Besides some greens for the table in winter, Marsha Mackie is successfully raising flowers for cutting. These she sells to a restaurant in town. Starting great numbers of plants for the outside

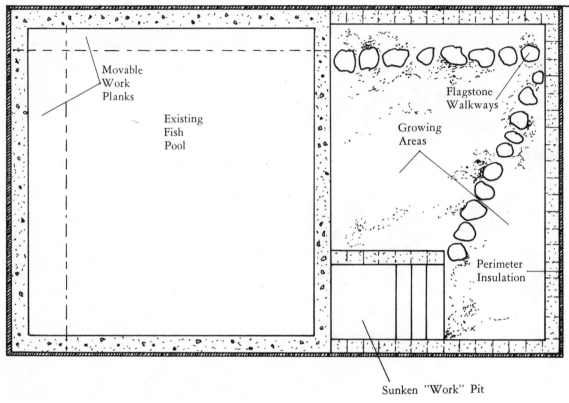

Figure 8-13: *Floor plan for "Six Pack."*

garden very early is one of the greenhouse's primary uses. The Mackies report that it serves this function best of all.

New Alchemy Institute

Falmouth (Cape Cod), Massachusetts
41.5° North Latitude

The New Alchemist's family-sized solar greenhouse has grown vegetables through two winters as a completely passive system. It is one of the most intensively planted and productive free-standing solar greenhouses. The most notable feature is the very large volume of water for heat storage. The pool covers half the floor space and receives direct radiation on the surface most of the day. There is no night curtain to hold in heat.

Orientation: Due south

January Climate Outside: At Falmouth, the average high temperature is 38° and the average low is 24° with the lowest expected extreme -7°F. But January (1976-77) was about 8°

colder than normal. There are usually one eight very clear days and 15 completely cloudy days.

Climate Inside: The January daily high temperature averaged in the 60s. But prior experience has shown that on a warm sunny day in midwinter the greenhouse can reach 90°F. The greenhouse was in the high 30s most nights and never got colder than the low 30s. During the day the soil temperature at four inches deep was 53° on sunny days. The water temperature in the pools stayed around 40°.

Configuration: The greenhouse is 25½ feet long and 15½ feet wide. The clear front wall slopes to within 1 foot of ground level. The peak is 12 feet high and the opaque roof slopes steeply down to a 4-foot kneewall in back. The east and west walls are double-glazed back to the peak. The growing area is 150 square feet.

Construction: The greenhouse was designed around an existing fish pool 15-feet-by-15-feet and 4 feet deep. The walls and floor of the pool are 4-inch poured concrete. The foundation extension that encloses the growing beds is concrete block about 2 feet deep. The double-glazed portion of the east and west walls consists of 2 x 4 mullions. The rest of the sides as well as the roof and kneewall, use 2 x 4 studs and rafters. The ridge beam is a 2 x 10 supported in the center. The rafters on the glazed face are 2 x 6s. The rafters are wide to allow for three secondary layers of glazing with about an inch and a half between each layer.

Insulation: All opaque surfaces are insulated with 3½-inch fiberglass batts. The concrete-block and fish tank foundations are insulated to their bases with 2 inches of foam on the outside.

Glazing: The end walls are glazed with Kalwall inside and out, spaced about 3½ inches apart. The front face is glazed with .04 Kalwall on 2-foot, 8-inch centers. The Kalwall is arched (45° grooves are cut in the rafters to receive the ends of the fiberglass), like a convex "barrel vault," to make the surface stronger, reduce flexing, and shed snow and rain.

The New Alchemists report that the system sheds the water onto the wood in between, increasing the rate of deterioration. On their larger greenhouse they reversed the arc, making it convex, so moisture would drain on the plastic. Either technique requires more glazing to cover the surface and thus slightly increases the heat-losing surface area. It is also more complicated construction, though in some situations, the extra strength may be an important advantage. On the Prince Edward Island Ark, the New Alchemists have applied the fiberglass on the glazed south face flat.

Behind the Kalwall are three layers of a Tedlar-like film. It is thin and very clear so it transmits much more radiation than three layers of polyethylene would. The three dead-air spaces that are created are very important for holding heat in at night since no night-curtain system is used.

Heat Storage: The tank holds 6,750 gallons of water. Two-hundred-and-twenty-five square feet of surface receive direct radiation all day long. The water is dark, nearly black with algae. The water temperature stays very close to 40°F. in the dead of winter with little change between day and night. That is a low temperature, but a one-degree change in this pool involves 13 times more heat energy than a one-degree change in storage in the Flagstaff greenhouse and 10 times more than the CET greenhouse in Pittsfield. On

Photo 8-14: *Glazing. "Six Pack."*

Photo 8-15: *Growing area. "Six Pack."*

the other hand, the large mass has a small surface area so it is relatively difficult to get heat in and out of it. Water at the surface contributes more than water at the bottom.

The soil receives direct radiation where leaves don't shade the ground, and this also has considerable heat-storage capacity.

Gardening: This is a very cool running greenhouse, though temperatures are quite stable. It is full of plants. Flats of seedlings for transplanting line the rear wall. A flagstone path cuts diagonally from the doorway to an observation

Photo 8-16: *Ark. Cape Cod.*

Photo 8-17: *Interior. Cape Code Ark.*

pit (2 feet deep) near the pool. All the rest is space for food production which can be gardened from the pit or the pathway.

The New Alchemists grow cabbage, beets for greens, onions and garlic for tops in salads, chard, kale, turnips for greens, Chinese cabbage, parsley, endive, and lots of lettuce. So far Ruby and Bibb lettuces seem to perform best in the low light of midwinter. In January the greenhouse provides salad greens several times a week.

The experience gained with this greenhouse helped the New Alchemists plan and build two

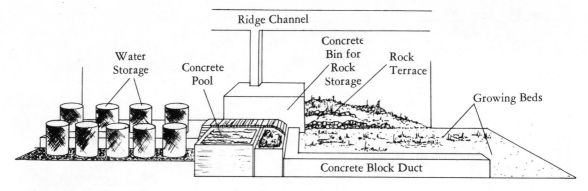

Figure 8-14: *Floor plan.*

much larger structures they call "Arks." One is a freestanding house 100 yards away. The other is integrated with a multifamily dwelling on Prince Edward Island. About a third of the floor space of the Cape Cod Ark is reserved for water storage rather than growing plants, compared to a little more than half in the family-sized unit. The larger greenhouse also uses a fan to help store heat in a large rock bin. Plants grow on top of the bin.

The greenhouse is approximately 90 feet long and 30 feet wide. The north side is heavily bermed right up to the eaves of the opaque roof. The walls below ground level are 8-inch concrete insulated with 2 inches of foam. Aboveground the opaque surfaces have 6 inches of fiberglass insulation. The expansive south face has two layers of Kalwall spaced 1 inch apart.

The soil temperature in this greenhouse was almost exactly the same as in the smaller one. In early January it had been flooded with frigid water, which took a lot of the stored heat out of the ground; and thus, perhaps the 53°F. recorded at the end of January is lower than normal as a result.

The air temperatures are always a little warmer. Nighttime temperatures average in the low 40s. Occasionally, it can dip into the high 30s. The daily high temperature is usually in the middle 70s even when it is in the 20s outside.

The structure itself stores heat in the concrete walls that are exposed to sunlight and in exposed soil. There is also a small concrete pool which holds about 3,000 gallons of water which stays

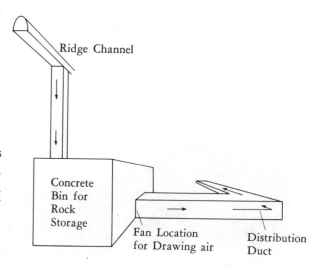

Figure 8-15: *Schematic. Forced-air heating.*

around 50°F. in winter. More water is held in large transparent fiberglass drums in the west end of the structure. Each is 5 feet high and 5 feet in diameter; five are on the ground and four are above them on a ledge. Altogether they hold about 6,600 gallons. The water is dark with algae and receives direct radiation all day on the tops and sides. Water temperature in these averages between 45° and 50° in the winter months with between two to five Fahrenheit degree changes between night and day. In summer the water can reach the mid-70s.

Partly because it is so large, the greenhouse is very high. Accordingly, there can be great temperature differences between the peak and the growing beds. To help create better growing conditions near the ground, the New Alchemists move the air with a fan. It is convenient to extract heat from the air at the same time. The air which collects in a channel built into the ridge is drawn down and through a concrete bin which has a volume near 1,600 cubic feet. It is filled with fist-sized stones. The fan runs from 9:00 A.M. to 3:00 P.M. collecting heat. Typically the air temperature drops 10° going through the system. The heat is given back to the greenhouse between 3:00 A.M. and 6:00 A.M. Not only does the system help make fuller use of the heat which the greenhouse gathers, but it also improves photosynthesis by increasing carbon dioxide transfer between air and leaf. It may inhibit fungus attack.

The large mass and the forced air moderate temperature extremes in this greenhouse, and the air is relatively warm at all times. Since the growing conditions are superior to those in many solar greenhouses, production is higher and a greater range of plants is possible. Chard, parsley, kale, lettuce, and New Zealand spinach do especially well in this greenhouse. Nasturtiums, marigolds, geraniums, and impatiens were blooming profusely in the middle of winter.

The Ark is a fine model for a community- or commercial-sized solar greenhouse. This one was expensive to build, around $25,000, but the production potential is high. The advantage is that the great volume of air helps prevent overheating; the ground in the center of such a large building will remain more evenly warm than in a smaller building, and proportionately less land is taken up by walkways and work spaces. One suspects that the costs could be cut slightly. Expenses could be reduced by using a cheaper inner glazing in conjunction with curtains to retain heat at night. This would permit less insulation. Combining the greenhouse with a large building, as the New Alchemists have done on Prince Edward Island would also help. A farmer, for example, might consider growing winter crops along the south side of his dairy barn.

New Organic Gardening Experimental Farm

Maxatawny, Pennsylvania

40° North Latitude

The Maxatawny greenhouse, which is David MacKinnon's first solar greenhouse design, has operated over two winters; the second was the most severe ever recorded on the East Coast. The experience has shown that this greenhouse can maintain minimum temperatures near 40°F. throughout the winter as a passive system. Growth of greens crops continued through January, though slowly, and harvest began in early February.

Despite outward differences, most critical

Photo 8-18: *Maxatawny, Pennsylvania, greenhouse.*

design features of this first greenhouse are identical to its sister greenhouse in Flagstaff. The only major change that would be made is to slope the north-facing roof more steeply for more light reflected to the plants, less volume to heat, and slightly lower costs for materials.

Orientation: Slightly east of due south

January Climate Outside: The average daily high temperature was 26° and the low temperature averaged 11°. The coldest it got was −5°F. Eleven days were very clear and 13 were cloudy.

Climate Inside: On sunny days the temperature

inside the greenhouse would usually reach the mid-50s. Cloudy day temperatures were very regular, with the high around 47°. In January the greenhouse had a little less than half of the total primary mass (containers of water) in place. To keep the environment stable an electric heater was installed to maintain minimum air temperatures of 40°. Still solar energy provided 80 percent of the total heat required for the month to maintain 39°F. inside. In early February the rest of the storage went in and supplementary heat was unnecessary.

Configuration: The greenhouse is 16 feet by 16 feet. The peak is about 9½ feet high and it

Photo 8-19: *Venting detail.*

slopes down only about 1 foot to the 8½-foot opaque north wall. The glazed kneewall in front is 4 feet high; the panels are hinged at the top so they can be opened for venting in the summer. The rest of the south face rises from the top of the kneewall to the peak at a 45° angle. There are 180 square feet of glazing to 210 square feet of floor. The plants are raised on benches some 3 feet off the ground; actual growing space is 91 square feet.

The front face of this greenhouse is quite unlike MacKinnon's second greenhouse. The Maxatawny design, he feels, is a sound one because the vertical kneewall combined with the 45° angle represent a good compromise of angles for light collection over a long season. The shape allows plenty of room to work in the front. Without the kneewall, the bench-growing system would not be very economical of space.

Construction: The greenhouse rests on a concrete-block foundation. The foundation, the insulation, and the glazing are the major costs in this greenhouse. The walls and opaque roof are made of 8-inch lumber and sheathed inside and out with plywood. The lumber is treated with Cuprinol, sealed and painted white. There is a post in the center to support the ridge piece.

The south kneewall is made of 4 x 4s, one at each end, at the center and across the top. This wall supports all the rafters from the ridge to the kneewall as well as the two hinged, glazed kneewall panels.

The rafters for the sloped south wall (on 4-foot centers) and the frame of the movable sections and 2 x 4s. Only the exterior glazing is permanent. To support the replaceable interior glazing and to brace the rafters, length of 1 x 4 are used to divide the space between rafters into 2-foot-by-4-foot sections; wooden frames holding the polyethylene interior glazing pop in or out of the sections.

There are vents near the peak on both the east and west walls.

The total cost for materials was about $1,500.

Insulation: The foundation is insulated from the ground with 2-inch polyurethane foam slabs. These cover the sides 2 feet deep and the entire floor. Earth was then filled back in to the top of the foundation. We learned that the insulation would have been better used if it had been made thicker around the foundation walls and extended deeper into the ground, rather than put under the floor.

The reason is that more heat is lost through the sides than down to the deeper levels of ground. Temperature probes showed that the insulated earth 12 inches deep was 10 Fahrenheit degrees cooler than constant earth temperatures a distance below frost line. So the bottom of the greenhouse probably didn't benefit much from insulation.

The walls and roof are filled with 7½ inches of loose cellulose fiber insulation, creating an R-22.

Glazing: Kalwall is attached to the rafters

Photo 8-20: *First curtain.*

horizontally. The strip nearest the ground was put on first so that higher strips overlap lower ones like shingles on a roof. This technique would not be used again because it is difficult to batten seams between rafters. Installing the glazing strips vertically makes for better caulking and battened seams.

The original plan for the interior glazing was that two polyethylene panels could fit behind the Kalwall between rafters. This would allow the amount of multiple glazing to be suited to the weather. Wooden frames were wrapped with polyethylene, so each one contained one dead-air

Photo 8-21: *Curtain in place.*

Photo 8-22: *Fiberglass batt.*

space by itself. Putting one set in made two dead-air spaces, and the second set made four dead-air spaces.

The reduction in light transmission by all the polyethylene was not worth the relatively small improvement in insulating value. For the second season, the panels were changed so just one layer of plastic was in place all the time. This gave 81-percent light transmission, and the one dead-air space held heat in well for the daytime when there was no shortage of energy. At night, a movable curtain did the work of the dead-air spaces. The curtain is easy to operate and can be made to have a much higher R-value than multiple air layers.

The first curtain was a sheet of thin fabric covered with an aluminized paint. It was hung along the ridge of the greenhouse and was rolled down at night on 2 x 2s put in parallel to the rafters just to hold the curtain. Another one was wrapped on a stick and unfurled across the kneewall. Both of these were fastened to the glazed walls with clothing-type snaps. That curtain had about an R-5.2 compared to R-3.6 for the double-glazed wall alone. In addition the curtain kept the warmer air inside from passing over the cool glazing, and it stopped infrared radiation. The aluminized paint, however, began to flake off towards the end of the winter.

Considering that such a large part of the lost heat, about a half of the total losses, was going out the glazed surface meant that it was also a prime area for improvement. Late in the winter, Diane Matthews and Bob Flower began work on a better curtain for the Maxatawny greenhouse. The new one was made from Duct Wrap, a fiberglass batt 1½ inches thick and covered with aluminum foil on one side. The foil is reinforced with fiber mesh, so it can take repeated bending. The batt is wrapped in polyethylene,

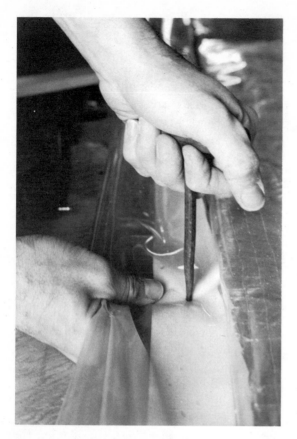

Photo 8-23: *Batt covered with polyethylene.*

Photo 8-24: *Applying canvas strips.*

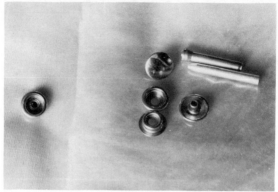

Photo 8-25: *Pop rivets.*

which protects it, keeps loose fibers in, and adds two thin dead-air spaces. The polyethylene is fastened to the batt by pop rivets and the snaps. These pierce the batts, the plastic, and 2-inch-wide canvas strips at the sides. The canvas prevents the fasteners from stretching the plastic and pulling out. This curtain snaps to the walls and several points along the wooden rafters like the first curtain, but it isn't on a roller. During the day, sections swing back and fasten to the opaque roof. The new curtain has an R-value around 10.5.

Heat Storage: Against the north wall 372 gallons of water, dyed black and in plastic jugs, are stacked on their sides. They are attached just as in MacKinnon's Flagstaff greenhouse, except that halfway up there is a wooden shelf to take weight off the bottom bottles. The bottles near the east and west walls receive direct radiation for most of the day. Bottom-level bottles receive about as much direct radiation as top bottles. The mass is in fairly small, separate containers, but these are in tight contact with each other. As a result, energy is distributed evenly. Mea-

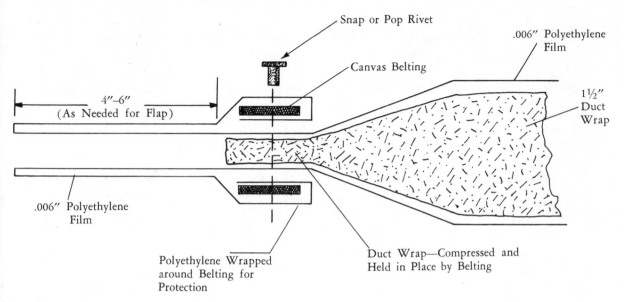

Figure 8-16: *Detail: canvas belt installation, thermal curtain.*

surements show very little of the temperature layering in this mass which there is in large tanks or barrels. This mass exchanges 3,100 Btu's for one Fahrenheit degree temperature change.

There is a lot of space under benches in any greenhouse which can be filled with water, though much of it won't receive direct radiation. In early February 1977, the bench parallel to the south wall was rebuilt to hold 504 gallons of water. Between the wooden bench frames, ¼-inch wire mesh was used to make two shelves which would support three tiers of the bottles. Here they are stacked on their ends instead of sides for easier construction. The top of the bench is also made of wire mesh so that light which passed the leaves and pots would strike the mass. The front rank of bottles receives direct radiation all day. The bench, then, has a heat capacity of 4,200 Btu's for each one-degree tem-

perature change. With the increased mass the greenhouse has maintained 44° at plant level in the face of −3°F. outside, on solar energy alone.

Flower and Matthews later found that the space left between levels of bottles for convenience somehow helped to increase the amount of heat stored. Originally the plan was to get as much water as possible into the available space. Heat would be distributed, as was happening successfully along the back wall, by direct contact between bottles. Since there was no contact between levels, however, the flow would be horizontal instead of vertical. The mass under the bench was also much thicker, seven bottles wide.

Lea Poisson suggested that heat transfer could be improved if the bottles were separated a little. Flower and Matthews removed a few bottles from half the bench and left the west half alone.

Temperature measurements over several weeks showed that the spaced bottles were able to absorb more energy than the others even though the total volume of water was slightly reduced. This was a surprise, and we are still not sure how much of the increase is due to the flow of warm air and how much to reradiation of energy among the bottles and the rest of the greenhouse interior.

Diane Matthews also compared a bottle of clear water to one with black water for a week and a half. The results are inconclusive, but the temperatures of water in the two bottles were surprisingly close. The black bottle was often but not always a degree or so warmer by the end of the day. If radiation can penetrate beyond the first rank of bottles through clear water, heat energy may be transferred better. The idea will be tested further next winter. Paints and dyes are messy to work with. They may not be necessary for thick water masses in translucent containers like under the bench at Maxatawny.

The insulated earth in the floor has considerable heat-storage capacity. Temperature probes have shown that at least the top 12 inches of ground, even though it is shaded by benches, can

Photo 8-26: *Placement of containers.*

exchange some energy daily. On a sunny January day, the change was usually 6°, from 37.5° to 43.5° and back to 37.5°F. by dawn. That means the greenhouse has 210 cubic feet of soil with a capacity near 4,000 Btu's for each one Fahrenheit degree change. Naturally, the top few inches of that foot of soil gain and release more heat than the botton few inches. But over several days, the entire 480 insulated cubic feet of earth can give energy back to the greenhouse. The planting pots hold another 25 cubic feet of earth which warms and cools almost as quickly as the air.

The benches shade almost all of the floor in this greenhouse, so the potentially effective thermal mass in soil is much less important here than it might be. The advantages of the bench system for using energy in the greenhouse is that it allows greater volume of water for storage per square foot of floor and it elevates the plants to a warmer air layer in the greenhouse.

In a solar greenhouse with no fans and no venting, there is little mixing of air. At the hottest part of the day when air currents are strongest, there is still generally a 20° difference between the floor and the 6-foot level. Between 6 feet and the peak, the separation is greater. On very cold nights, dishes of water resting on the ground, which was 37° 12 inches deep, would freeze while the air up among the leaves was 40°F.

Gardening: For its second season the greenhouse was planted with a variety of crops to see what would do well and what wouldn't. Penn State horticulturist John White helped determine the range of plants to try and picked out the particular cultivars of each that he felt would do well in the space and season in the Maxatawny greenhouse. Almost all were vegetables that thrive in cool weather. Though we felt that tomatoes and peppers should be planted in summer for fall and early-winter greenhouse harvests, a few were planted as seedlings in early December. They withered and died one by one under the low light and cool temperatures.

The greenhouse provided a very cool environment. In the middle of winter, air temperature ranges at the level of the leaves usually would reach between 55° and 60° any clear day. At night it was around 40°. The soil in the pots followed the air temperature very closely because the soil was quite moist and the volume was small and surrounded by air. In the day the soil would usually come within 4° of the high air temperature. At night it would be about 8° or 9° cooler partly because it was in an air level about a foot lower. This meant, though, that on occasion the root zone would actually drop below 32°F.

Still most of the leafy crops grew steadily. The cole crops did best. They increased fairly rapidly in size through December and January and looked healthy. Broccoli, cauliflower, and kohlrabi began to be harvested in mid-February. Kale was seeded in a flat in early January, germinated well, and thinnings were ready by the end of February. Leafy cole vegetables like kale and collards are probably the best choice for the greenhouse since ones like broccoli produce an abundance of inedible green matter before they bud.

Lettuce and endive started in early December also grew very nicely. Outer leaves were ready for harvest by end of January, though we waited until the middle of February. The entire heads were cut a month later. An early January lettuce seeding also germinated and grew very well.

Photo 8-27: *Growing containers.*

Spinach sown in early January grew slowly. This was another surprise. Since spinach is a very frost-tolerant plant, we expected it to be one of the best in the greenhouse. In late February, it began to grow strong, and though the plants never got stocky, the thinnings and small leaves were plentiful for salads.

Beets and Swiss chard germinated poorly in a midwinter planting. The plants grew slowly and spindly; by May, they were big enough to permit harvest of a few leaves. The bottoms were the size of big marbles.

Most of these vegetables would have been more productive, we are sure, if planted in late summer and early fall to fill the greenhouse with green food before the days became very short and cold. On the other hand, the first season of closely observed winter gardening at Maxatawny has shown us some of the crops that are able to continue growing at the most difficult time of year. In the next season, we will try what now looks to us like a sound planting schedule for maximum food production in fall, winter, and spring.

Pragtree Farm

Seattle, Washington

48° North Latitude

Howard Reichmuth and Jeffrey Barnes of Bear Creek Thunder designed a greenhouse with a parabolic north wall for the Ecotope Group's Pragtree Farm. The purpose of the greenhouse is to greatly extend the season for raising food and warm-water fish. Since the light levels are too low for vigorous vegetable growth and the fish need very warm water, the objective in the middle of the winter is just to keep things alive until warmer weather. The greenhouse was complete enough to plant in the fall of 1976.

Orientation: Due south

January Climate Outside: The average high temperature each day was 45° and the low was 35°F. for January 1977, and that is about normal for Seattle. Twenty-two days were fully overcast and only four were completely clear.

Photo 8-28: *Parabolic greenhouse. Pragtree Farm, Seattle, Washington.*

Climate Inside: In January, the greenhouse maintains temperatures in the high 30s most nights. On the occasional sunny day the air can reach the 80s. During cloudy days the expected high is 60°F.

Configuration: The floor area is 32 feet long and 12 feet deep. The rear 6 feet are devoted to the fish tank. A raised wooden catwalk runs the length of the greenhouse over the fish tank, so all of the remaining 6 feet is available for gardening. The peak is 12 feet high. The opaque rear wall is a section of a parabola which was calculated to deliver the most solar energy

directly into the water during the winter months.

All the light that hits the reflector ends up in the pool. This allows the pool, which is located in a relatively out-of-the-way spot in the greenhouse, to get a large share of the only occasional direct radiation in winter. For most of the year, the sun is high enough in the sky so that no light hits the reflector, but instead shines directly onto the water. The reason for such precision is to keep the water warm enough for the tropical fish to survive the winter.

Jeffrey Barnes reports that the curve is so carefully tailored for a given latitude that the wall is not an easy thing to design. Building it is

Photo 8-29: *Detail: parabolic curve.*

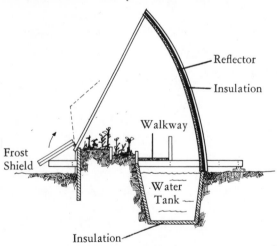

Figure 8-17: *Section—east wall.*

comparatively simple. But, he says that the effect of the curve can be successfully approximated by a series of three or four straight lines.

Construction: Techniques for erecting a parabolic north wall are beyond the scope of this book, especially considering that the primary function of the parabola here is to create an environment for aquaculture. Instead here is a breakdown of their expenses.

Glass	salvaged
Reflector	salvaged
Lumber and brackets	$924.65
Insulation	909.79
Wood preservatives and caulking	217.96
Hardware	65.22
Equipment rental	60.51
Concrete materials	37.03
Building permit	14.00
Total	$2,229.16

or $5.80 per square foot

Insulation: The opaque walls, on all of the north and parts of the east and west, have 3 inches of polystyrene on the outside. The concrete foundation also has 3 inches of foam. But the fish tank has 4 inches on all four sides and underneath it.

Glazing: The greenhouse is single-glazed with salvaged greenhouse glass. They plan to build a folding shutter which will cover the lower half of the glazed surface at night, acting as a frost shield for the plants. To shutter the entire face, they feel, it not worth the trouble and expense, with their climate and goal of 9 or 10 months of active food production.

Double-glazing is reportedly the last addition they would make to the greenhouse. In a low-light region, they feel that maximum transmission is important. The glass by itself seems to be surprisingly airtight. They installed the glass tightly and minute cracks are filled by the water which condenses on the glass.

Heat Storage: The 5,760-gallon water tank in this greenhouse, though it is an extremely large mass and collects heat very well for a ground-level pool, is not designed to give the heat back to the greenhouse very rapidly. It is so heavily insulated on all sides that only the surface can exchange heat over a night. The primary aim is to keep the water itself very warm in the middle of winter, rather than to heat the soil and air for plant growth. As it stands, the greenhouse has prevented frost through one winter even without the shutters. Cool-season crops will winter-over nicely.

The system has not trapped and held enough heat to keep the fish, which they plan to raise, healthy. They expect to supplement solar heat during 3½ months of winter with an attached sauna that will be built.

Gardening: The greenhouse will allow two distinct crops. Cold-hardy vegetables, primarily greens, will be established in fall for harvest beginning at the end of winter. The first season they planted two-dozen heads of Bibb lettuce in each of six beds at five-day intervals. Picking began in late March and lasted a month. Spinach was planted in the beds just as soon as the lettuce came out; it was all picked by the end of June. In other beds, fall-planted bok choy

did extremely well and was harvestable by the end of February.

Heat-loving vegetables, melons, cucumbers, tomatoes, and the like, are barely productive around Seattle. Melons usually won't mature without great pains to shelter them from early and late frost. Eggplants, tomatoes, and peppers are usually killed just as they hit full stride. The first-season, tomatoes were put into the greenhouse in August, a late start, but the plants continued ripening fruit until December with the grace of an extremely sunny autumn. Normally, cucumbers will be set into the greenhouse at the end of April, melons will be started some time towards the end of May, and tomatoes, eggplants, and peppers will be planted in June just as soon as the large crops of spring greens are harvested.

The greens crop came in quite quickly, and there was more than the people at Pragtree Farm needed. Southern California, the usual source of produce for Washington in winter was in the middle of a severe drought. Salad vegetables were scarce and high priced so there was a ready demand for all the greenhouse produced in local groceries.

Ed McDougall

Bellport (Long Island), New York
41° North Latitude

Ed McDougall decided to build a solar greenhouse two years ago around the same time that he greatly expanded his garden. The greenhouse was to provide plenty of large transplants for a jump on the summer as well as some greens in

Photo 8-30: *Freestanding greenhouse. Long Island, New York.*

the fall and winter. He could not attach it to his home because the driveway and garage were in the way. So using what he knew about heat conservation, he devised his own freestanding greenhouse. Though it is not as heavily insulated as most completely passive systems, and so relies on auxiliary heat in winter, it does work well. It cost only $160 to build. To keep the air temperature inside in the high 30s with a small electric heater costs about $25 a season. McDougall also maintains low 40s soil temperature with a heating cable imbedded 9 inches below the planting beds; it cost about $3 per

month to operate last winter.

Orientation: Slightly east of due south

January Climate Outside: The reference winter was very cold, 9½ degrees colder than usual. The average daily high was 28° and the average daily low was 16°. The lowest was −1°F. There were 10 cloudy days. Eleven days were clear, several more than in a normal year.

Climate Inside: The electric heater and the soil cable kept the air in the high 30s and the earth

Photo 8-31: *Interior.*

in the low- to mid-40s at night. The high temperature averaged in the upper 80s, as measured during the last two weeks in January 1977.

Configuration: The greenhouse rests on concrete blocks sunk almost to ground level, rather than on a conventional foundation. The insulation extends a foot into the ground on the inside of the block.

Because McDougall was insulating with 2-inch foam panels, he could use 2 x 3 studs. The glazed south wall is made of 2 x 2 studs. The exterior is covered with Homosote composition board.

Insulation: All the opaque walls are insulated with 2 inches of polystyrene foam board, about R-10. With the Homosote, the R-value is around 12. One inch of polystyrene extends 1 foot into the ground around the perimeter.

Glazing: The exterior glazing is Kalwall attached parallel to the rafters with a piece of battening board over seams. On the inside, McDougall fastened polyethylene to the bottom of the rafters, creating a dead-air space of about 2 inches. He found this wasn't quite enough during the first winter. So he attached 1-inch lumber to the bottom of the rafters and put up another layer of polyethylene. He has no insulating material for nighttime.

Heat Storage: Directly behind the glazed knee-wall he has five 55-gallon drums. In the rear northeastern corner he has a 40-gallon reservoir for preheating domestic hot water that also doubles as heat storage. The total is 310 gallons. He plants directly in the floor so spaces between plants get direct radiation.

The holding tank receives direct radiation most of the day. The drums at the kneewall are sunken into the ground one-third of their height; two-thirds receive direct radiation all day. The drums are painted black in front and white behind. The drums are sunken to accommodate the black plastic pipe of the hot-water preheating system. The earth holds it in place. The pipe comes from the well, wraps around each barrel as many times as possible, then leads into the holding tank and back to the hot-water heater in the home. The system does not operate in

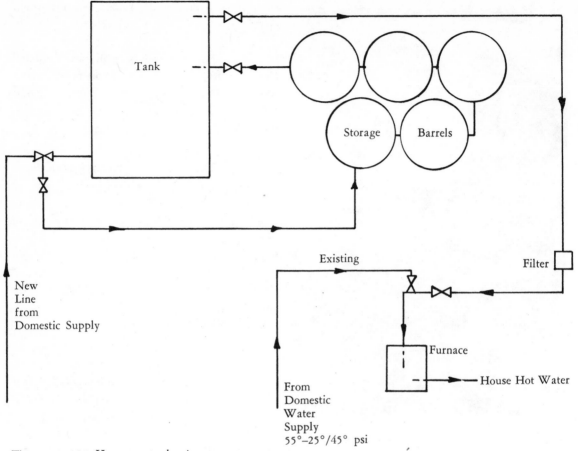

Figure 8-18: *Hot water preheating system.*

winter, so the water in it is part of the heat storage.

Gardening: In the fall and winter, McDougall grows lettuce, Swiss chard, turnips for greens, some green onions, and spinach. He plants directly in the soil and puts a few flats on top of the barrels in front. He also starts plants for the garden quite early. Cauliflower and head lettuce were seeded in late January. By the time they were set into the garden in late April, the cauliflower plants were eight inches tall and stocky. The lettuce plants were around six inches in diameter. McDougall also gets an early start for 50 tomato plants and great numbers of marigolds.

The greenhouse would probably work even better than it does for wintertime food production if it were insulated more heavily. As it is, the nighttime temperatures are fairly cool for a system with a soil-heating cable. Daytime temperatures are a little too high. Together it makes

Photo 8-32: *Center for Ecological Technology. Pittsfield, Massachusetts.*

for a wide daily temperature change.

The soil would be warmer if the insulation extended at least another foot into the ground. Two inches would give better performance than one. Warmer soil temperatures would improve growth significantly. Most freestanding solar greenhouses in similar climates have walls with higher R-values and cost less to heat. Of course, such a wall costs more to build. A curtain over the glazing, though, might improve two things at little extra cost. First, much less heat would be needed at night to keep the greenhouse in the high 30s. Second, the third layer of glazing could then be removed. The result would be more light to the plants and greater daytime heat losses through the glazing. Greater daytime losses would not be critical since 80° is a little too warm for cool-weather crops.

McDougall, however, counts on the overheating to preheat domestic hot water from April through September. By the end of May, all the plants are out and he closes up the greenhouse to superheat. At the beginning and end of the preheating season, the system puts 60° water into the hot-water heater instead of 55°. At the peak, it preheats the well water to 105°F. Over six months, McDougall estimates that he can save as much as $150.

Center for Ecological Technology

Pittsfield, Massachusetts

42.5° North Latitude

The Center for Ecological Technology is the
work of Ned Nisson and Mark Charde. They
decided to build a solar greenhouse after reading
about Dave MacKinnon's work and a visit to
Maxatawny for a close look. Between them,
they had the designing and engineering ability to
put up a fine structure in a very short time. They
improved on the shape of the Maxatawny greenhouse by sloping the rear roof down to a kneewall making a good reflector and requiring less
materials. Their approaches to reducing heat
losses are especially noteworthy. A lot of their
resources were spent on insulation. In design
and construction, crack areas were minimized
and sealed well. The result is a greenhouse that
maintains a good cool-crop environment with
two layers of glazing but no nighttime curtain or
shutter system.

Photo 8-33: *Interior (CET).*

Orientation: Due south

January Climate Outside: Past weather records
suggest that Pittsfield should expect only eight
clear days this month with a good chance that
two will come in a row but little chance that three
will. Usually 15 days are completely overcast
and seven are partly cloudy. Two cloudy days in
a row are common, and there is a 25-percent
chance of four cloudy days together. The average temperature for the month is 30°, but most
years it still dips to near −20°F. at least once.
Average wind speed is 12 mph.

Even though in 1976-77 the area experienced
the severest winter on record, the greenhouse
designers had prepared well for the extremes.

There were seven clear days for solar collection
and 15 were completely overcast. There were
two five-day cloudy periods, more than expected.
The temperature never got colder than the average extreme. However, the average highs and
lows for the month were much lower than
normal, 13° at night and 32° during the day.

Climate Inside: CET began monitoring the
greenhouse February 1. For the first two weeks
of February the extreme weather patterns experienced in January continued. But the average
daytime high was 71° inside. The greenhouse
collected almost enough energy during the day

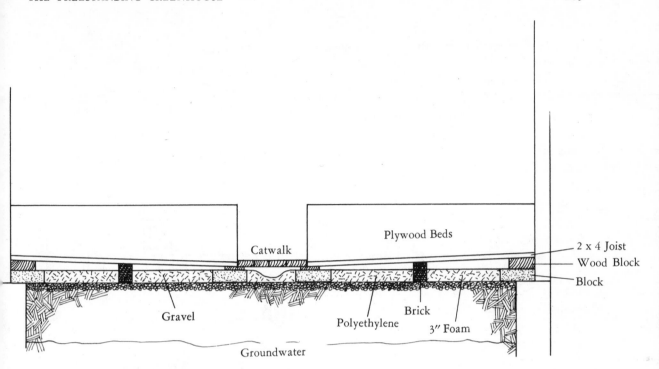

Figure 8-19: *Section—South wall.*

to maintain the desired temperature at night, 43° at leaf-canopy level. An electric-resistance heater was put in to maintain that temperature, and it only ran about 20 minutes each night for the first two weeks. After that the weather warmed. The heater stopped contributing energy early in March. The total expense for electric heat was $4. The average nighttime temperature through February was in the high 40s. The daytime high on a sunny day was mid-70s.

Three inches below the soil surface, CET never recorded any temperature below 52°F. On a sunny day it can rise 8° to 10° above that.

Configuration: The CET greenhouse is 16 feet long by 16 feet wide. The peak is 12 feet high.

In front there is a glazed kneewall 2 feet, 8 inches high. The glazed slope is set at 45° and rises 12 feet to the peak. The opaque north roof extends down 9 feet at 30° to the 8-foot kneewall in back. There are about 235 square feet of glazed collector area to 256 square feet of floor space. Some of the collector area, as in most greenhouses, is blocked by the wood rafters and some of the floor area is used for walkways and stacking heat-storage materials. Space in this one is used economically. Walkways are minimized and the beds are worked from planks that are moved around the beds.

Construction: Standard practices were followed. In this case, however, 2 x 8s were used throughout to accommodate all the insulation they wanted. The lumber was salvaged from an old building.

The foundation is of interest. They had planned to insulate down into the ground well below the frost line. However, they hit groundwater at 18 inches. So the structure rests on pilings, like MacKinnon's Flagstaff greenhouse, made of sections of telephone pole. The depth of the pilings depends on the frost line. In Pittsfield they had to sink them 3½ feet.

CET had to insulate the foundation on top of the ground. On top of the pilings, the plate which supports the structure is actually a hollow box made of four pieces of the 8-inch lumber. Later they drilled holes and injected foam insulation. Inside, they put several inches of gravel over the ground and covered it with a polyethylene film. The greenhouse has no true floor; everything rests on concrete block set around the floor area to support joists. The joists slope from the east and west walls down to within a foot and a half of the center so that the raised growing beds drain to the center.

Along the back wall the joists are parallel to the ground so they will support a catwalk and the 55-gallon drums.

With the floor blocks and joists in place, they covered the entire area with 3 inches of foam insulation.

Directly behind the glazed portions of the east and west walls, are vents. One is made of insulated panels that slide up and down like a window for adjustable wintertime ventilation. The one on the other wall is the same size, 18-inches-wide-by-3-feet-high, and is completely removable. It is plywood backed with polystyrene foam. One-foot-square vents are planned for the peak on each end wall.

The sloped rear wall is foil covered. The rest

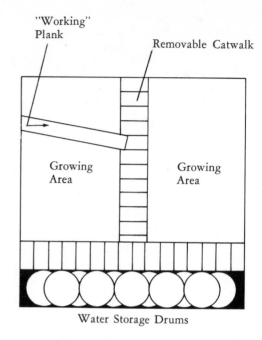

Figure 8-20: *Floor plan and drum storage.*

is natural wood panel.

Insulation: Ureaformaldehyde foam is used in the floor walls and roof. Strips of fiberglass were laid between pieces of lumber when making a seam that would open to the outside, then the pieces were joined tightly. Fiberglass was also stuffed into all chinks.

There are 8 inches of urea foam in the ceiling and walls. Urea foam does not stick, so an interior skin of polyethylene was stapled up and the foam was filled in behind it. The resistance to heat loss in the walls and roof is R-40.

Besides the 3 inches of urea foam covering the floor, there is an air space between the top of the foam and the beds, which varies from 3½ inches to 2 inches because of the beds' slope.

Glazing: The greenhouse is double-glazed with Kalwall. Manufacturers' recommendations were followed closely, and CET reports the glazing is airtight. To allow for temperature expansion, slightly oversized holes are drilled for the nails.

Eight-inch rafters were used because they were available, but 2 x 4s would suffice. The inner layer was put down first. The edges of the plastic lap, and a length of 2 x 2 is put over the seam to batten it and serve as the spacer between the next glazing layer. The second layer has the laps reversed and is battened with 2-inch furring strips.

Small panels at the front of the east and west walls are double-glazed. There was no night curtain the first winter, but some kind of quilted, insulated thermal curtain is one of the first improvements CET plans to devise.

Heat Storage: Along the back wall are eleven 55-gallon drums painted black and filled with water. For each Fahrenheit degree the temperature rises, the system gains about 5,000 Btu's. The most it has gained in a day is a 15° rise. The longest sunless stretch monitored was three days, and the heater wasn't used at all then. At the end of three days, the water had cooled down to 40°. Two fairly sunny days which followed recharged the system fully.

The soil in the planting beds stores a fair amount of heat, too. At six inches deep, CET reports a 12° temperature change on a sunny day.

Gardening: All the growing space is in two large beds in the front three-quarters of the greenhouse. Though it is a low planting level, the soil is heated by direct radiation all day and more reflected from the foil on the sloped ceiling. The lowest recorded soil temperature was

51° at six inches. Combined with a minimum air temperature of 48°F., that represents a warm environment relative to other solar greenhouses in the Northeast.

The beds are contained by plywood boxes. The shallowest soil, near the sides of the greenhouse, is a foot deep. The beds drain into a polyethylene sleeve under the catwalk. It is a good safety feature, but CET reports that so far no moisture has penetrated the collection area.

The plywood is protected by a layer of polyethylene inside. There are 2 inches of gravel on the bottom, then the 12 inches of soil, largely consisting of compost. They look to the compost to provide supplementary CO_2 as it breaks down further.

CET feels that greenhouse composting could be done in the area under the removable catwalks. The pit could even be made deeper for the purpose. The spot is both accessible for working, and economical of space.

The greenhouse was first seeded in early February. CET planted beets, Swiss chard, carrots, spinach, and turnips. All germinated well, and the first thinnings were ready to add to salads in a month.

At the same time, they brought in plants that had been started a month earlier in another greenhouse. Most were salad greens: Bibb lettuce, greenhouse lettuce, bunching onions, parsley, and corn-salad. They also set out Chinese cabbage, broccoli, cabbage, and basil.

Chinese cabbage and parsley both did extremely well in the coolest microclimate, up front under the glazing. The lettuce harvest began in mid-March along with corn-salad and spinach. The green crops were fed with manure-tea and fish-emulsion solutions. Other crops grew on just the composted soil.

The cauliflower and broccoli were ready for

Photo 8-34: *Freestanding greenhouse. Noti, Oregon.*

harvest by mid-April. Some of the cauliflower heads were 8 and 10 inches across. Turnip greens were picked lightly all along, and the plants were harvested May 1 with nice-sized globes.

Ernie O'Byrne

Noti, Oregon

44° North Latitude

O'Byrne's freestanding greenhouse was designed and built in the spring of 1976 by three architecture students from the nearby University of Oregon in Eugene, Jim Bourquin, John Hermansson, and Andy Laidlaw, under the direction of Professor Edward Mazria and Steven Baker. The aim was to build an attractive structure of recycled materials that used solar energy alone and provided a good environment for plants in winter.

The unique feature of the building as a solar greenhouse is that it relies entirely on stone and earth for heat storage. It is not a completely passive structure because a fan is used to deliver hot air from the peak into the interior of the rock mass. A sauna has been designed into one end of the greenhouse. When it is complete, heated air can be forced through the rock bed providing supplementary heat.

From an aesthetic point of view, this freestanding greenhouse is pleasing. The attached sauna expands the greenhouse as a center of daily activity. In the landscape, it is nearly invisible to the home on the north side of it because the high berm and the roof are covered with sod, presenting a green vista. A garden easily could be made part of it.

Orientation: Due south

January Climate Outside: January around Noti and Eugene usually averages near 50° during the day and 30° at night. The expected extreme temperatures, most often occurring during clear weather, are 15° lows and 55° highs. During cloudy weather which is the usual condition, nights are regularly 35° and days 50°F. Temperatures in the reference year were normal.

In January 1977 there were 19 cloudy days and 9 sunny days, more sun than usual. The Noti greenhouse was monitored between mid-January and mid-February, an extraordinarily sunny time. The longest overcast stretch was three days.

Climate Inside: The greenhouse is designed to maintain normal low temperatures of 50° and highs of 70°. The coldest temperatures they expected inside were 45° at night and 60° in the day.

During the first winter the greenhouse performed very close to these expectations. Because there was more sun than usual, it was often on the warm side; temperatures ranged from 47° to 73°F. These extremes did occur during clear weather as predicted. Radiation losses through the glazing are greater at night then, but the likelihood of recharging the next day is high too. Because cloudy nights are almost always warmer, the losses are lower, which balances the weak solar input during a cloudy day. During cloudy stretches that winter, the daytime high inside was 55°, but the low at night was only 50°F.

Configuration: The floor area is 17-feet-long-by-12-feet deep. The peak is 12 feet high. On the south side the vertical wall is 8 feet high and on the north it is about 9 feet. The greenhouse is built into the side of a south-facing slope, and the north side is sunken deep into the hill. What remains abovegrade has been heavily bermed up to the eave. Sod covers the entire north roof.

Construction: Fir post-and-beam construction provides the framework and eliminates the need for a conventional foundation. The logs were salvaged locally from recently logged land. The roof and all the walls except the north use standard 2 x 4 framing. The exterior is finished with 2 x 8 tongue-and-groove and the interior with ¼-inch cedar. The roof is covered with Homosote, building paper, and polyethylene on top to protect the materials from the moist sod roof. The door is a salvaged walk-in freezer door: cheap and heavily insulated.

The north wall is a thick mass of rock, about 3 feet wide at the bottom and 4 feet at eave level. The excavation slopes back into the hill so the flattish stones could be stacked into this dense wall, thicker at the top than the bottom. The interior of the wall is vertical and wire mesh helps keep the rock firmly in place. Thin, flat rocks stack well and provide plenty of air spaces for the essential heat exchange.

The total material cost was $900.

Photo 8-35: *North wall, berm detail.*

Insulation: The walls are insulated with 3½-inch fiberglass batts. There is no insulation extending into the ground around the perimeter, nor between the rock wall and the earth. The builders now feel that insulation should have been installed between the heat-storing rock wall and earth outside. Heat is lost steadily to the earth which has low insulating qualities and is aggravated by continual dampness in the Northwest. The same is true for the sod roof. Though nearly a foot thick, it does not insulate well. The warmest air is near the roof and insulation would hold energy in much better.

Glazing: The south-facing roof is 120 square feet of double-glazed Filon with a ½ inch between layers. Glazing in the 8-foot south wall is 36 square feet of ordinary windows which were salvaged. They can be opened for summer ventilation. In winter, polyethylene is put up inside to make a dead-air space. The designers intend to install shutters or a curtain for the next season.

Heat Storage: All the heat storage in this greenhouse is rock. On the floor are 4 tons of gravel, some of which receives direct radiation all day.

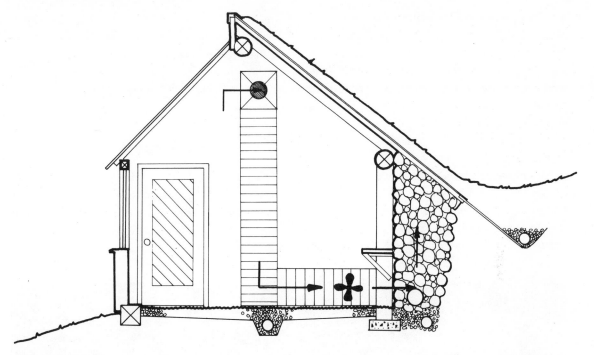

Figure 8-21: *Forced-air storage.*

The floor would retain more heat if, again, insulation extended into the ground below frost line around the perimeter.

The primary system is the 28,000-pound rock wall coupled with a fan which runs whenever the greenhouse is collecting solar energy or temperatures drop below 45°F. Typically, the fan might be used when the air is overheating, from 9:00 A.M. to 3:00 P.M. on a sunny day, and again when it is needed most, from midnight to dawn. The fan draws air through a duct from the peak where the hottest air is concentrated and delivers it to the bottom interior of the rock wall. Energy then rises naturally up through the rock. The fan is essential to the system.

The reason is that heat passes through rock slowly. The surface of the rock wall receives direct radiation all day. It cannot transmit energy to the interior as fast as it receives it when the sun is bright. The excess energy is reradiated and heats up the air. In addition, the thin surface layer, which becomes relatively warm, cannot absorb energy as efficiently as when it is cooler. The fan is needed to take advantage of the heat which returns to the air and to keep the greenhouse from overheating. Without forced air movement there would be very little warm air migrating to the middle and back of the rock wall which is coolest and has more capacity to receive additional heat than the surface.

Gardening: The greenhouse has not had a full season of gardening yet, but some house plants, wandering jew, spider plant and others, were put in for the month of January. The greenhouse kept the plants healthy, but they didn't seem to grow. At the end of the month, seeds were sown for early spring greens and for garden transplants: lettuce, radishes, cole crops and tomatoes. All types germinated quite well and grew enough to be ready for transplanting by the middle of February.

Judging by experiences of eastern solar greenhouse gardeners, the Noti greenhouse maintains fine growing temperatures. The air and the soil remain quite warm, and appear not to be subject to drastic changes or extreme cold. Accord-

ing to observations at Noti, extremely low light levels are probably the reason that growth in January is so slow.

Future Refinements

Only those freestanding solar greenhouses which have successfully grown crops in winter have been treated here. Undoubtedly, there are other fine systems which remain unknown to us. In fact, the construction of freestanding solar green-

Photo 8-36: *Farallones Institute. Occidental, California.*

Photo 8-37: *Sauna/greenhouse. Circle, Montana.*

houses is something of a phenomenon, with structures springing up in all parts of the country. Farallones Institute has recently completed one well-suited to the mild northern California coastal climate. The Domestic Technology Institute has built one in Denver and another near their headquarters in Evergreen, Colorado.

The designers of the freestanding greenhouse treated here all report that they have learned from their experiences and plan to introduce new features. For example, the Mackies, the people at Pragtree Farm, and CET, are all designing

types of curtains and shutters to insulate the glazed wall at night.

In a freestanding greenhouse, a backup heating system can be an important consideration, depending on what crops you intend to grow. Several of the greenhouses described here use electric heaters, primarily because the researchers wanted a precise monitoring of heat energy added. While that is important to researchers, it may or may not suit your system. The New Alchemists have a wood stove for maintaining the Cape Cod Ark through extremely cold periods. Perhaps most efficient are the systems that use waste heat, such as the Mackies' grey-water trap or the saunas underway at Noti and Pragtree Farm.

Remember that with electric power it is cheaper to add fluorescent light than heat. Faced with a choice of constructing a wider, higher glass front to let in precious light (and resigning yourself to supplementary heating) or leaving the glazed face small in order to insulate more, you may save the most energy by adding fluorescent light. This dilemma arises most often in very cloudy and cold climates. Fluorescent lights may be a very tempting option in the Pacific Northwest where temperatures are relatively warm and stable inside the greenhouse during winter but where plants won't grow because so little sun gets through the clouds.

Fans, too, have value in solar greenhouses beyond their usefulness in augmenting heat storage. Since they take power, they don't fit the passive mode. Certainly a system that relies on fans for success has sacrificed its essential simplicity. But as horticulture in these new greenhouses becomes as finely tuned as solar engineering, fans will likely become common, if only to get more carbon dioxide to the plants.

Earle Barnhart, of the New Alchemy Institute, suggests that plants will not do as well as they might in the perfectly still environment of a solar greenhouse. Besides insufficent light in winter, carbon dioxide can limit growth in an airtight greenhouse. Abundant CO_2 can even offset some of the effects of reduced light. When the air is stagnant, the air in the leaf zone can easily be depleted, causing photosynthesis to stop. However, a fan can remedy this situation. It will also mix warm air at the top with cool air near the ground, which is particularly significant when ground-level beds are used.

In addition, a fan can be installed in such a way as to increase the amount of heat put into storage—at no extra expense. Simply, direct the air flow so that the warmest air in the house is channeled across the thermal mass. In many instances, wind power could be harnessed to turn small fans in the greenhouse.

Finally, as our understanding of horticulture in the solar greenhouse increases, the pioneering work with compost will receive more attention. There may be no simpler way to substantially increase CO_2 in the air than by decomposition. Inside the greenhouse, solar energy "triggers" the composting process. In turn, the pile can heat up to 150°F., which also might be a significant heat contribution.

Chapter Nine

The Attached Greenhouse

James B. DeKorne

The reasons for building an attached greenhouse read like a litany of good advice for any section of the country. Greg Mackie of Snowmass, Colorado, who has constructed numerous solar greenhouses in his region and who often is paid for his services with greenhouse vegetables, offers the following reasons for building an attached greenhouse:

1. The plants complete the biosphere. They add oxygen and refresh the air.

2. The greenhouse adds humidity to the air. This is badly needed year-round in the western one-third of the country and all over in winter. Even in very humid sections of the East, when you take cold humid air in from outside and heat it, it then has a relative humidity of around 5 to 10 percent. Just how much humidity does a greenhouse add? It will increase the humidity in an adjoining room of comparable size by 5 to 10 percent.* If you have open ponds, a 10- to 20-percent increase,* and fountains will increase it even more.

3. It can heat adjacent rooms all during a sunny day and, depending on the amount of thermal storage, part of the night. As a rule of thumb for the maximum daytime heating, the greenhouse can totally heat up to twice its area in the house, given enough mass and insulation.

4. It is an aesthetical addition to the house. I can think of nothing better than having breakfast in a warm jungle in the middle of winter, or opening my greenhouse door instead of my refrigerator to get dinner.

5. Low-cost greenhouses I have built, that have been run to capacity, have produced vegetables to pay for the cost of materials in nine months.*

6. Where I live and in much of the West and North, it gets below 50°, or even freezes, every month of the year. A greenhouse is actually needed all year-round to grow things like tomatoes that will not fruit when continually subjected to nighttime temperatures of below 50°F.

7. Plants raised to large size in greenhouses with constant temperatures usually die if they are transplanted outdoors to a cold and fluctuating climate. Plants grown in solar greenhouses with moderated temperature fluctuations adjust to their new

* (Firsthand measurements.)

* (Personal case studies of three greenhouses.)

175

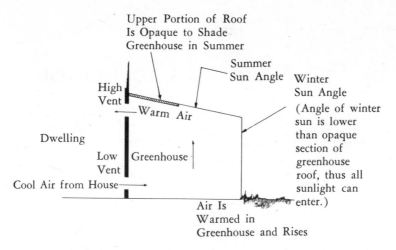

Figure 9-1: *Air circulation in typical attached greenhouse.*

environment better.

8. An attached greenhouse is an inexpensive structure, which can be constructed for approximately $2.50 per square foot.

An attached greenhouse is really nothing more than its name implies—a thermally efficient forcing structure attached to the south side of a dwelling with provision for venting the collected heat into the house. Most greenhouses which are retrofitted onto a home make use of existing doors or windows for venting the heat inside. Depending upon the type of home and the construction ability of the builder, a much more efficient ventilation system is often installed. This consists of floor-level vents which admit cool air from the house into the greenhouse. (Remember: Cool air sinks, warm air rises.) As this cool air is heated, it rises inside the greenhouse and is expelled through ceiling-level vents back into the house. In this way, cool air is always circulating from the house (bringing with it lots of essential carbon dioxide for the plants),

being warmed in the greenhouse, and then vented back to the dwelling many degrees warmer than when it entered. After sunset, the process can be reversed—the now-cooler air from the greenhouse enters the home where it is warmed, rises, and reenters the greenhouse. Some people prefer to close the vents at night, using the greenhouse primarily as a daytime heat collector during the winter rather than a place to raise plants.

When including a greenhouse as part of a new home, the floor and ceiling vents are incorporated into the design and don't pose the problems encountered in retrofitting a greenhouse to an already existing dwelling. One idea which should further improve the efficiency of the greenhouse as a solar heater, would be to install the floor-level vents from the dwelling against the far north wall of the room and use the space between the floor joists as a ventilator passage into the greenhouse.

In this way, the coldest air would be drawn from the room to be heated. The space between

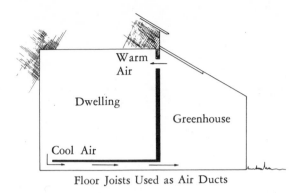

Floor Joists Used as Air Ducts

Figure 9-2: *Venting system below floor.*

the joists, of course, would have to be enclosed in such a way that only the air from the *room* would enter the greenhouse. Otherwise, the cold air under the house floor would constantly enter the greenhouse, to no advantage at all.

During the summer, of course, the last thing you want to do is heat your dwelling, so the ventilators to the house are kept closed. To keep the summer plants from cooking, an auxiliary-venting system must be employed which circulates the heated greenhouse air outside. This is accomplished by building a ground-level vent to admit cool outside air on the upwind side of the greenhouse, and a high vent to expel the hot greenhouse air on the downwind side. This orientation will insure efficient and continuous circulation of air. Some sort of windbreak in front of the low vent may be necessary in high wind areas, but since wind velocities are lowest in the Northern Hemisphere during the summer months when these vents are used most, high winds shouldn't be a problem. Bill Yanda, who has more attached-greenhouse construction experience than anyone I know, states in his book:

The total square footage of exterior vents

should be about one-sixth of the floor area of the greenhouse. The high vent is one-third larger than the lower one.

Here in New Mexico, using a hydroponic growing system, I just have never had humidity problems in my greenhouse. Obviously, in other parts of the country where the air-moisture content is higher than our semiarid environment, humidity could pose very real problems—particularly with an attached greenhouse where excessive moisture might easily cause mildew on household furnishings. Adequate ventilation in summertime, then, is a must, and in some locales might even necessitate the use of an electric blower of some sort.

Experts have determined that the most efficient use of space is to make the attached greenhouse about twice as long as it is wide. Thus, a forcing structure built against a house wall 20 feet long should have a width of 10 feet. There is a point of diminishing returns here, however. I personally would never build an attached greenhouse less than 8 feet or more than 10 feet wide, no matter what the length was. Ten feet is a good width to aim for—it gives plenty of growing space while still remaining efficient as a solar collector.

Constructing an Attached Greenhouse

The construction of a typical attached greenhouse is very simple, making use of standard stud-wall carpentry techniques. One begins by digging a trench below the frost line to the exact outer dimensions of the greenhouse. A cement footing is then poured. Two tiers of cement blocks are laid on the footing, using either mortar or the "concrete-down-the-holes" method. Space for a door is provided—keeping in mind

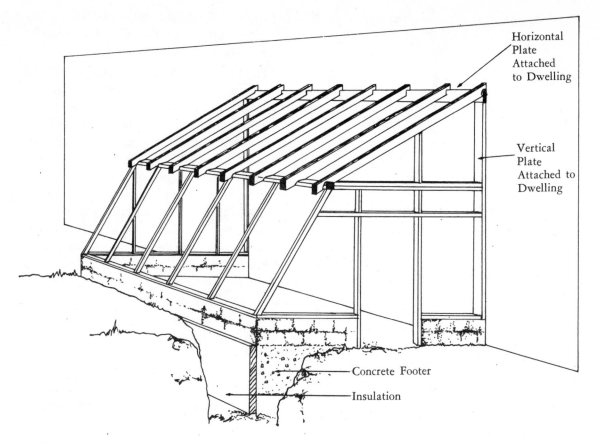

Figure 9-3: *Framing and foundation insulation—attached greenhouse.*

that the doorway should be on the side away from the prevailing winds.

After the blocks are laid, bolts are cemented in place to provide a means of attaching the 2-inch-by-8-inch wooden plates. The plates provide a nailing surface for the stud walls. The 2 x 4 studs for the clear-wall portion of the greenhouse are nailed on 47-inch centers—this is to provide correct spacing for the fiberglass, which comes in 48-inch widths.* (Techniques would vary with other glazing materials.)

Now is the time to decide whether you want your south wall at a vertical (90°) angle, or at the angle of your latitude plus 35° (see Chapter Four). Whichever configuration you use, you'll have to decide how the greenhouse rafters will attach to your home. If you aren't able to attach them to the house rafters themselves, a horizontal plate can be fastened to the wall of your dwelling by means of lag screws or expansion

---

* Note: References to use of fiberglass as a primary glazing merely reflect the extensive use of this material, particularly in the Southwest. For full details, including rating and installation hints for the various glazing materials, see Chapter Four.

bolts, and the greenhouse rafters nailed to it. Vertical plates are attached on the east and west walls of the house in the same manner, and serve as a nailing surface to which the greenhouse walls are fixed.

The east wall of the greenhouse should be clear to catch that important early morning sunlight, but the west wall is usually opaque and well insulated. The west wall studs are placed on 24-inch centers. The outside surface may consist of any convenient building material—plywood and Celotex are often used. The most important thing to remember about this opaque wall is that it must be insulated as much as possible. You can glue Styrofoam panels to the outside surface with heavyduty construction adhesive, cover this with tar paper, then nail on chicken netting to which you apply cement stucco.

Because the humidity level in a greenhouse can become very high, a wood preservative must be applied to all wood surfaces to prevent rot. The recommended wood preservative for greenhouses is copper napthenate. Not knowing any better in 1973 when I built my pit greenhouse, I generously treated all wooden members with pentachlorophenol, commonly known as "penta." This is truly a deadly substance, as anyone who has ever used it can attest—I actually felt quite ill after using the stuff, experiencing dizziness, nausea, and general malaise for several hours. According to all greenhouse authorities, the penta *should* have killed all the plants in my greenhouse. The fact is that it didn't even make them as sick as it did me. The only explanation that I have for this is that the greenhouse sat exposed to the hot New Mexico sun for a week or two before the Filon was installed, thus allowing the penta to completely penetrate the wood and dry out. Since the greenhouse was finished

in late October, the structure sat vacant until the following February when the first vegetables were planted. This gave the structure additional time to absorb and dry the poison. I have never had any problem with plants dying in my greenhouse that could in any logical way be traced to penta poisoning, but I have heard of other people who have lost everything in their greenhouse because of it.

After the wood preservative is applied, the fiberglass is cut into the proper lengths and attached to the studs with special nails. Available from the same source where you bought the fiberglass, these nails are made of aluminum (so they won't rust and stain the fiberglass) and have rubber gaskets beneath their heads which help prevent water from entering through the nail holes.

A very important design feature of an attached solar greenhouse is the fact that approximately one half to two-thirds of the upper portion of the roof—the part that butts up against the house—is opaque. This feature provides built-in shading from the high angle of the summer sun, yet allows all of the low-angle winter sun to enter the greenhouse. The lower portion of the roof consists of translucent corrugated fiberglass panels. (Although the wall sections can be covered with flat fiberglass, the corrugated type on the roof provides extra strength.) If you don't intend to do any summer growing at all, the entire roof of the greenhouse could be opaque. (It is difficult to anticipate climatic conditions in other parts of the country. Obviously, one wouldn't build the same sort of greenhouse in Needles, California, as one would in Anchorage, Alaska.)

After the interior plastic is stapled in place, and a suitable floor material installed—this can range from flagstones or tile to crushed gravel—

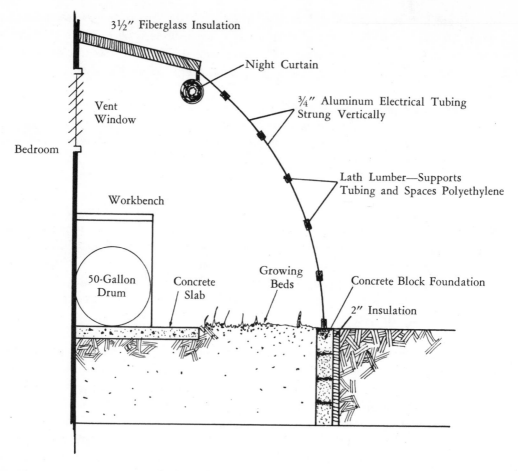

Figure 9-4: *West view, attached greenhouse. Long Island, New York.*

your attached greenhouse is essentially completed and ready for the plants. Most people build earth-filled planter boxes along the walls and suspend hanging pots from the rafters. Suffice it to say that you want to optimize the amount of growing space available.

Similarly, you also want to optimize the amount of storage space available. According to Greg Mackie, "My rule of thumb is this: if it gets above 90° in December, January, or Feb-

ruary, then you need more thermal mass. Anyone who says he has to vent in the winter is saying, in effect, that he needs more thermal mass.

"As far as water storage is concerned, I have found the following rule of thumb to be useful: in and around Snowmass, Colorado, I would use a minimum of two gallons per square foot of greenhouse space. In the warmer climates, I would use a little more. In the Midwest, for

Photo 9-1: *Solar adobe greenhouse. Chino Valley, Arizona.*

example, I might add four gallons of water per square foot (see Chapter Seven for more details).

"Actually, I go a little farther than water storage. I insulate the perimeter of my greenhouse with 5 to 6 inches to beadboard, 2 to 3 feet deep. This makes all the earth in the greenhouse a storage area. With the help of this perimeter insulation I can run a greenhouse all year-round, even at 11,000 feet, with no movable insulation. The warm soil keeps the adjacent air warm even if the greenhouse drops below freezing.

"Of course, it depends on what you are trying to grow. I grow root crops and greens. On the other hand, I know people living at 9,500 feet

Photo 9-2: *Glazing. Framing detail.*

who like to have tomatoes in January. For them, some kind of nighttime insulation is essential."

David MacKinnon, who has considerable solar-greenhouse experience states that, "Thermal storage is just as important in an attached greenhouse as in a freestanding one. In an attached greenhouse with inadequate storage there is a tendency for the temperature to swing wildly during the day, from around 100°F. to around freezing at night. And this is not good for crop production. On the other hand, adequate thermal mass has a "moderating" effect on the greenhouse environment; it encourages natural air circulation which helps complete the convection loop in the greenhouse." (See Chapter Five for complete storage information.)

Attached Greenhouses: Regional Examples

While the attached greenhouse I have briefly described here represents the standard design which was pioneered and defined by Bill Yanda and Greg Mackie for the Southwest, variations on the theme are popping up all across the country. A nice example of how a greenhouse can be integrated into the overall concept of a dwelling has been conceived and built by two Arizona architects—Michael Frerking and Bill Otwell. They estimate that 80 percent of the home's winter heat load is handled by the greenhouse.

Chris Ahrens of Long Island, New York, has a small attached greenhouse which makes use of ¾-inch aluminum electrical conduct as its supporting structure. These vertical tubes are held by means of T-joints to a horizontal tube which is attached to the foundation. Horizontal wooden laths wired to the vertical struts help

Photo 9-3: *Attached greenhouse. Long Island, New York.*

support a double layer of ordinary 6-mil plastic sheeting. Using these readily available and inexpensive materials resulted in an expenditure of about $80 for the entire greenhouse.

On Cape Cod, Massachusetts, Bill von Arx's attached greenhouse is a commercial glass (single-glazed) and aluminum unit. The original design is not "solar" in the sense defined in the book, but von Arx has added refinements which increase its solar efficiency. He installed sheets of "bubble pak" against the vertical panels of glass. (This is the same material used in the original Lama Growhole described in Chapter Ten.) Next, von Arx built two solar collectors which heat and circulate water through the greenhouse. Power for water circulation comes from a small wind electric system. One of the solar collectors, placed against the north wall of the greenhouse, is made out of panels used for circulating fluid in a refrigerator truck. The other solar collector is located outside the greenhouse. It used ethylene glycol (antifreeze) as a fluid and transfers the collected heat into water via a heat exchanger inside the greenhouse. The inside bottom of the growing bench has two

Photo 9-4: *Attached greenhouse with solar collector. Cape Cod, Massachusetts.*

loops of copper refrigeration tubing through which the solar-heated water is pumped at night. These loops are covered with about an inch of sand to hold and distribute the heat more evenly to the plant roots.

There are probably as many variations on the basic attached greenhouse as there are people to think them up, indicating the great versatility of this solar structure. For example, the Institute for Local Self-Reliance in Washington, D.C., has a greenhouse that is built on a city rooftop. The unit, which cost approximately $2,000 to build, "takes" heat from the two floors of living space below. Strictly speaking, there is no heat-storage

capacity in the greenhouse other than the brick wall at the rear (see Figure 9-5). Because the use of soil would pose problems of weight far in excess of that for which the roof was designed, the greenhouse uses an organic hydroponic system. The vermiculite and perlite used as a roof support medium for the plants are much lighter than dirt and will not exert undue stress on the structure below.

Although the construction of attached solar greenhouses has largely been evident in rural areas, there is every reason to believe that it is becoming an urban phenomenon as well. In fact, Mark Plotkin of Milwaukee, Wisconsin, built a walk-in, solar-heated greenhouse (perhaps more properly described as a solar collector) on the porch on the second floor of his home.

Each side, bottom, and top edge of the porch is insulated with fiberglass, covered with plywood, and sealed with a silicone sealant. The framing is conventional. First the back studs are secured to the house with lag bolts. Then the front face (pre-made) is set into place and secured with angle braces to the deck ledge. The windows are single sheets of pane glass.

An interesting feature of the greenhouse is

that shutters (or wings), which are constructed of 1/8-inch plywood and fiberglass and painted with hi-gloss white enamel serve as both nighttime shutters and reflectors. These can be adjusted by a pulley system to control the amount of light which gets into the greenhouse (Figure 9-8). This greenhouse, which has been in operation for three years, has never gone below 47° even when the temperature was −20°F.

Since people living in urban areas have limited opportunities for vegetable production, the urban solar greenhouse offers real hope for those who

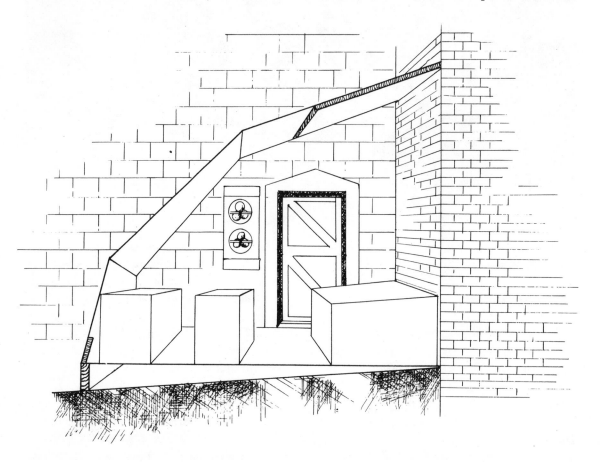

Figure 9-5: *Rooftop greenhouse, Washington, D.C. (Institute for Local Self-Reliance).*

Photo 9-5: *Rooftop greenhouse growing beds.*

Photo 9-6: *Rooftop greenhouse intake and exhaust fan.*

want to strive for self-sufficiency. And such a greenhouse has been built in center-city Milwaukee through the efforts of the University of Wisconsin, Department of Architecture, as part of an energy resource conservation course (ACCESS projects).

The greenhouse, which is attached to the southeast corner of a garage, is situated approximately 40 feet from an apartment house. In part, students were able to make use of recycled materials in the construction (storage tanks, glazing, fiber pipes, plywood).

This passive solar greenhouse has been fitted with active components, though they are not yet in use. Two 25-square-foot, flat-plate solar collectors are mounted on the south end of the garage roof. A fan forces the hot air from the collectors through a 4-inch flexible hose which runs down the inside wall of the garage into 4-inch fiber pipe imbedded in the soil. However, the greenhouse has functioned well without additional heat from the solar collectors.

The greenhouse, sunken into the ground approximately 4 feet, is double-glazed with recycled storm windows and shuttered with 5-foot-by-5-foot Styrofoam (2-inch) panels framed with wood. The wood is covered with canvas. Storage consists of two 50-gallon, hot-water tanks that have been recessed into the wall of the garage. The storage "box" is insulated with 4 inches of fiberglass. The walls of the storage "box" are lined with reflective foil.

In February, students seeded 400 vegetable plants including three types of tomatoes, beans, radishes, chives, and onions, which later were transplanted in a number of area gardens.

The greenhouse temperature never went below 44° even when the outside temperature dipped to 10°F. According to Greg Ander who helped construct the greenhouse, the interior temperature remained relatively high—even with minimum storage, because of the insulated shutters. He estimates that shutters cut night-time heat loss by 60 percent.

There is no lack of ingenuity on the part of people who want to construct a solar greenhouse. For example, Douglas Needham of New York State, would have preferred to attach a green-

Photo 9-7: *Porch greenhouse. Milwaukee, Wisconsin.*

Photo 9-8: *View from interior of house.*

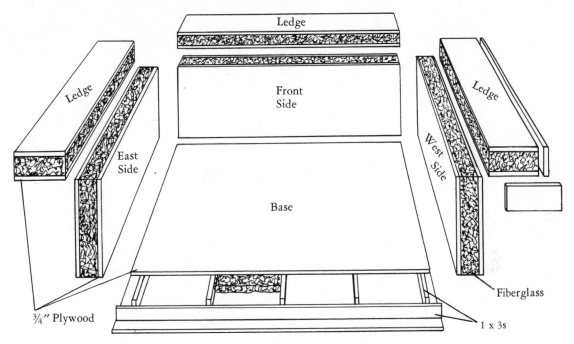

Figure 9-6: *Exploded view: shutters.*

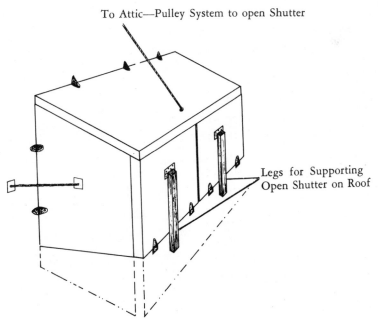

Figure 9-7: *Shutters assembled and in place.*

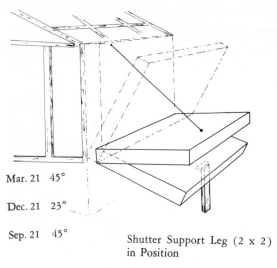

Mar. 21   45°

Dec. 21   23°

Sep. 21   45°

Shutter Support Leg (2 x 2)
in Position

Figure 9-8: *Shutter/reflector angles.*

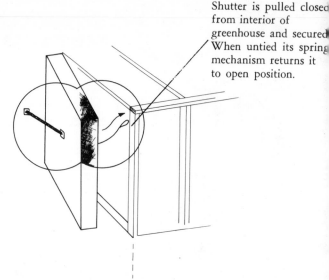

Shutter is pulled closed
from interior of
greenhouse and secured
When untied its spring
mechanism returns it
to open position.

Figure 9-9: *"Wing" mechanism.*

house to the south-facing wall of his home for the obvious heat advantage. Unfortunately, the orientation of the house was not satisfactory so he attached a solar greenhouse to the wall of his 25-foot-by-40-foot tool-implement shed which has aluminum siding. Needham poured an 8-foot-by-8-foot foundation, 30 feet long and 10 feet wide to support the east, south, and west walls. He used economy-grade 2 x 4s for wall and roof framing. The height of the south wall of the greenhouse is 6 feet; the 2 x 4s supporting the roof rose to a height of 10 feet where they were attached to a 2 x 4 stringer that was attached to the wall of the shed.

The roof and south wall of the greenhouse were covered by an outer layer of corrugated greenhouse-grade rigid fiberglass. (Use glass or flat fiberglass; the corrugated variety tends to split when nailed.) An inner layer of 4-mil plastic film was fastened to the 2 x 4 framing by 1-inch batting nailed over the film. Three roof

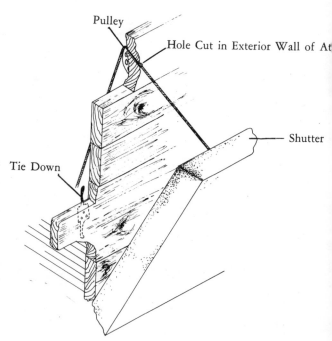

Pulley

Hole Cut in Exterior Wall of At

Shutter

Tie Down

Figure 9-10: *Mechanism for raising roof shutter.*

Photo 9-9: *Solar greenhouse attached to garage. Note solar collector on roof. Milwaukee, Wisconsin.*

vents, three window vents in the east wall, and a wall fan located next to the door on the west wall provide ventilation. To prevent heat loss he installed 9½ inches of fiberglass insulation inside the shed against the wall of the greenhouse.

Instead of using bagged sawdust or polyethylene-board insulation to prevent heat loss through the ground, around the outer perimeter, Needham buried old hay bales with tops just above the base of the concrete and extending to a depth of 2 feet. After the greenhouse was constructed, he dug up the earth inside and placed a 2-foot layer of hay about 2 feet beneath the surface, replacing the earth in layers of 6 inches,

alternating with 6-inch layers of well-rotted horse manure.

Needham planted lettuce, onions, beets, cabbages, cauliflower, sprouts, and broccoli right in the ground. He reports that "even after weeks and months of uninterrupted, subfreezing daytime temperatures and many nights around zero degrees, the plants continued to grow. The aluminum siding reflected light and heat back into the greenhouse and much of the heat was apparently absorbed and trapped in the earth bounded by the layers of hay."

All the plants grew and were harvested with exception of the sprouts. In April, Needham

planted climbing strawberries, climbing tomatoes, melons, and even two lemon trees in the
greenhouse, together with seeds in flats for transplanting in the garden.

Attached-Pit Greenhouse

If by now you think I am totally sold on the

idea of an attached greenhouse, you are only half
right. Actually, a superior design consists of a
combination of the attached and pit greenhouse
concepts. Combining the thermal advantages of
earth insulation with the advantages of home
heating results in a very efficient structure—the
attached-pit greenhouse.

One consideration before you build an
attached pit is the risk of digging a large hole so

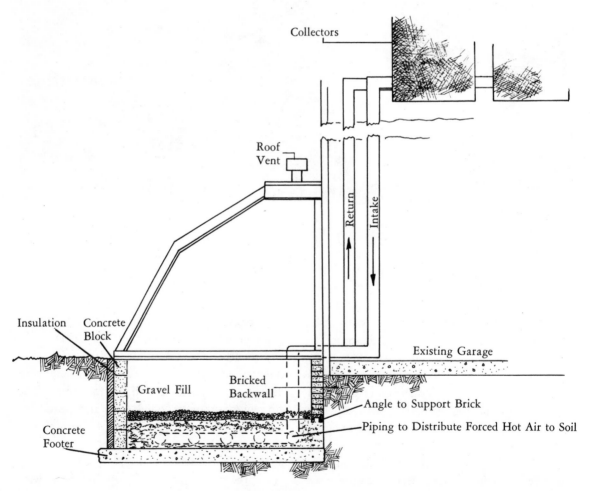

Figure 9-11: *Rendering of photo 9-9, including forced-air distribution.*

Photo 9-10: *Greenhouse attached to toolshed. Holley, New York.*

close to the foundation. In most circumstances, it would not be a job undertaken by anyone but an experienced builder.

Photo 9-11: *Interior.*

Nonetheless, there are plenty of examples of homeowners who have actually cut through the basement wall in order to attach the pit to the house. Joe and Gail White of Epping, New Hampshire, have constructed a 28-foot-by-10-foot attached pit which rises 3½ feet above the ground, exposing a little of the total surface to air and wind.

Another good example of an attached-pit greenhouse has recently been completed at Ghost Ranch, an adult-study center administered by the Presbyterian Church near Abiquiu, New Mexico. The photographs shown here were taken before the building was completely finished, but the design features are readily apparent.

Bob and Cissie Johnson of Landenburg, Pennsylvania, have a 3-foot-deep pit greenhouse attached to the southwestern wall of their home. The greenhouse dimensions are 24 feet by 9 feet and the ceiling at the rear rises to about 8 feet. The only provision for heat storage is the mass of the concrete back wall. Heated air is free to pass up and into the living area and when it gets very warm, a fan pulls air into the crawlspace under the house itself.

Homeowners who live as far north as 45° are finding that an attached-pit greenhouse works very well as a heat source and a season extender for crops. George de Alth of Clementsvale, Nova Scotia, who constructed their 640-square-foot house on an old dry-wall, stone foundation, used part of the foundation for a 14-foot-by-8-foot attached pit.

For the de Alths, the rationale for building an attached pit was simple. "We live," they report, "in western Nova Scotia which has frost-free summers of about 90 days. In order to start tomatoes, peppers, melons, and eggplants early enough for good transplantation at the end of May, people in this part of North America need

Photo 9-12: *Attached-pit greenhouse. Epping, New Hampshire.*

Photo 9-13: *Attached-pit greenhouse. Abiquiu, New Mexico.*

to plant their seeds at the beginning of March. Our vegetable garden is a quarter of an acre, and to start enough plants for it, we needed a greenhouse."

In constructing the greenhouse, its foundation, beds, and walkways, de Alth stayed within the bounds of standard carpentry. He started by pouring some concrete footings in which he placed spikes, point up, so that he could sink posts into them. In these 4 x 4 posts he notched for 2 x 8s which supported the walkways and the general lower deck of the greenhouse; these are 3 feet below ground level.

As he constructed the greenhouse, he painted every piece of wood with a wood preservative to prevent rot. Whenever earth came in contact

Photo 9-14: *Attached-pit, interior.*

Photo 9-15: *Attached-pit vent system.*

with any of this wood, he separated the pieces with two layers of 4-mil plastic to protect the earth from the chemicals in the preservatives and to counteract moisture.

De Alth doubled-glazed with glass panes salvaged from an old commercial greenhouse. He insulated with 2 inches of Styrofoam. Similarly, he constructed interior shutters of Styrofoam, strengthened with like pieces of Aspenite. He reports that this method of shuttering was unsatisfactory (small pieces of Styrofoam fell onto the plant beds) and intends to replace it with two layers of plastic on the inside of the glazing.

Clearly, there are few, if any, locations in North America where an attached greenhouse could not be built. In fact, in diverse regions of the country significant work has been done in an attempt to make the attached greenhouse part of the ecosystem of the house. A few of these examples, including ones from California and

Prince Edward Island, are featured in the accompanying photographs and illustrations.

The solar greenhouse in Occidental, California, built by Peter Hennesy and Gregory Bowen, is an ambitious and aesthetically pleasing attempt to integrate the structure with the house proper. With some help from the stove in the sauna, the owner hopes to be able to grow tropical fruit in the greenhouse.

Hennesy describes the microclimate which influenced his design as "windy, rainy, cold, foggy, occasionally all at once. It tends to be foggier in the summer than in the winter, so summer days can be cool and overcast with a lot of bright, sunny winter days.

The 10 x 16-foot greenhouse, which was built on an existing foundation, is double-glazed with 4 ounces of Filon with a 5½-inch air space between. All openings (two doors and two vents) are weather-stripped with neoprene. The doors and lower vents are insulated with 1½

Photo 9-16: *Attached-pit greenhouse. Landenburg, Pennsylvania.*

Photo 9-17: *Interior.*

inches of urethane foam and the growing bed is insulated with 3-inch foam. The greenhouse interior is sheathed in ¼-inch interior plywood, painted white. Under the exterior sheathing, the greenhouse is wrapped in 6-mil polyethylene vapor barrier to prevent infiltration.

The passive storage consists of 10 clear fiberglass tubes along the west wall. There is a 120-gallon, hot-water storage tank on the north wall which has a flap at the top of its insulated cover to let warm air circulate up and around the tank. Whenever the sauna stove is fired, hot water will thermosyphon into the tank. The stove will provide heat for the house and additional heat

Photo 9-18: *Attached-pit greenhouse. Clementsvale, Nova Scotia.*

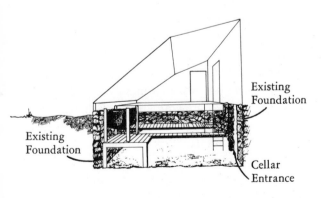

Figure 9-12: *Interior working platforms.*

for the greenhouse. There are plans to place a hot tub in the greenhouse which will serve a number of purposes. A person will be able to take a sauna, and the next night, use the water for a hot tub. The water is then allowed to cool, thus warming the greenhouse space. Then some of the water will be used to water the plants; the rest will be recycled.

David Kruschke and Karen Funk of Wild Rose, Wisconsin, have gone a step farther with the attached-greenhouse design by making it an intricate part of the biosphere of their home. In a sense, they live in the greenhouse which they

Photo 9-19: *Prince Edward Island Ark. New Alchemy Institute.*

Photo 9-20: *Interior of Ark.*

consider "not as the 'ideal home' but as a vehicle for personal growth."

They report that "our interior climate, which is typically both warm and moist, is moderated by our insulated cement floor, the Sheetrock on the walls, and out-insulated masses of earth and rock that serve as growing areas. We have 275 square feet of growing area. Our lower growing area is a long, insulated pit that has 168 square feet. This is at ground level next to the glazing and has a mass weighing 39,900 pounds. Next to this growing area, we have an elevated space (which is really a large planter). Here, rocks

Photo 9-21: *Integrated greenhouse. Occidental, California.*

	Comparison of High and Low Temperatures for Attached Solar Greenhouse in Northern New Mexico Altitude: 6,900 Feet					
	Average Inside High Temp.	Average Outside High Temp.	Average Difference	Average Inside Low Temp.	Average Outside Low Temp.	Average Difference
1/21–31/77	82°F.	38°F.	44°F.	38°F.	13°F.	25°F.
2/1–28/77	90	45	45	42	17	25
3/1–12/77	90	41	49	41	17	24

and wet earth are contained on four sides by solid cement-block walls. The south faces of the walls are painted flat black to increase solar absorption. The upper growing area has plants, stores solar heat, and conducts some heat to the cement floor and the lower growing pit. The cement floor weighs 18,900 pounds and the Sheetrock paneling on the walls and ceiling weighs 6,300 pounds. Our total cement, earth, and rock mass weighs 91,600 pounds. It is this mass that stores extra solar heat that otherwise would have to be ventilated out in order to maintain comfortable daytime temperatures.''

Attached Greenhouse as a Heat Source

David Kruschke and Karen Funk estimate nearly 60 percent of their heat requirements is provided by the solar greenhouse—which is a substantial contribution. And the following temperature data provided by David and Ann McDaniels of El Rito, New Mexico, confirms that an attached greenhouse is a significant heat source.

During the 51-day period from January 21, 1977, to March 12, 1977, the following temperature data was recorded:

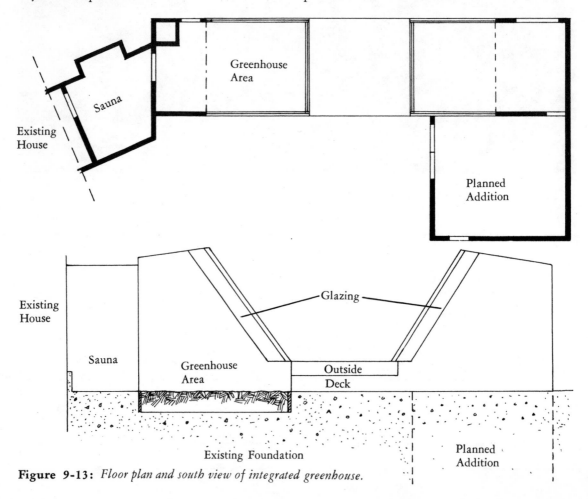

Figure 9-13: *Floor plan and south view of integrated greenhouse.*

Photo 9-22: *Integrated greenhouse. Wild Rose, Wisconsin.*

Unfortunately, they didn't begin recording the high and low temperatures until the coldest part of the winter had passed (mid-December to mid-January). Nonetheless, the above data indicates that you can get a truly impressive amount of winter heat from an attached solar greenhouse.

The temperature extremes were as follows:

Lowest ouside
temperature: 4°F., January 26, 1977

Lowest inside
temperature: 33°F., January 26, 1977
Highest outside
temperature: 58°F., February 17, 1977
Highest inside
temperature: 109°F., March 12, 1977

The reason for the high inside temperature on March 12 was due to the fact that the McDaniels were away on that date, and didn't ventilate the greenhouse. They report that the

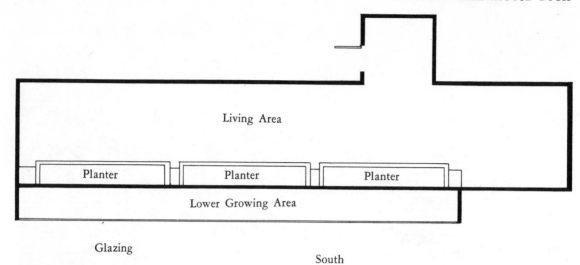

Figure 9-14: *Floor plan.*

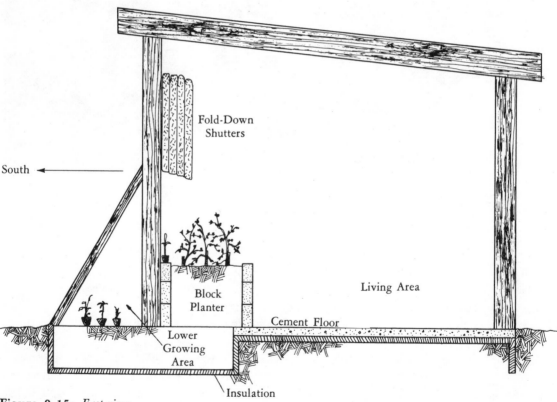

Figure 9-15: *East view.*

greenhouse provides most of the house heat during a sunny winter day. The McDaniels burn wood at night, using a cord or less during the winter heating season. Since the door between the home and the greenhouse is kept closed at night, the 33°F. low temperature shown above applies only to the greenhouse.

To add further weight to the argument that an attached greenhouse is probably the most cost-effective, solar-heating system available today, the responses to a questionnaire I sent to people in New Mexico, Arizona, and California, are quite illuminating. I asked, "If you have an attached greenhouse, can you estimate how much heat it provides for your house?" The following are typical responses:

"I can't really tell, but it is appreciable."
"It dropped my heat bill considerably."
"Heats up house pretty good."
"I would say well over 50 percent."
"I save $400 a year on propane."
"Greenhouse handles 80 percent of house-heating load."
The most enthusiastic answer was: "After nine months of living with this greenhouse we have come to the conclusion that it should be mandatory for every family to have a greenhouse (attached to their dwelling)."

Perhaps no one individual has worked harder to promote attached greenhouses than Bill Yanda of Santa Fe, New Mexico. Several years ago, Yanda received a small grant to build 11 attached greenhouses onto the homes of low- and middle-income residents throughout the state of New Mexico. This idea was to see just how effectively they would perform over a wide range of altitudes, climates, and growing seasons. The answer, of course, was that an efficiently designed and properly maintained attached greenhouse will work effectively almost anywhere.

Food Production in an Attached Greenhouse

In spite of its thermal efficiency, the *raison d'être* of an attached greenhouse is its potential for food production.

If we all lived at the equator, with its year-round growing season, forcing structures such as cold frames and greenhouses would be unnecessary. Here in New Mexico (and in many other parts of the country), however, at an altitude of 7,000 feet, with less than 12 inches of annual rainfall, and a growing season of only 90 days, a greenhouse is almost a necessity for anyone who strives to be independent of the supermarkets for their fresh vegetables. We've found that our effective greenhouse growing season is approximately 21 days before the vernal equinox to 21 days after the autumnal equinox—or roughly eight months. Recent work with highly experimental hydroponic window boxes in our home indicate that a year-round growing season for certain vegetables *may* be practical. We'll have to go through at least one more winter period to know for sure. Under ordinary circumstances, however, plant growth during the wintertime, in most sections of the country, will not result in enough edible tissue to justify the effort or expense. You can keep your tomato plants *alive* over the winter period, and you may harvest a salad or two from your lettuce plants, but food-production levels during the period of October 21 to February 21 will probably be but a pitiful fraction of what you'll harvest during the rest of the year.

To gather the experience of other Southwestern greenhouses owners, I sent out questionnaires to 27 different people in New Mexico, Arizona, and California. While the results of such a small sampling are probably not statistically valid (only 17 people returned the form), and the wording of the questions could have been better, the answers reflected a great deal of agreement on certain important points. Of the 17 replies to the question: "Approximately what percentage of your family's late-fall, early-spring food do you raise in your greenhouse?" only two people estimated their yield at 25 percent, and nine respondents estimated yields of less than 25 percent. Five replies either didn't answer the question, or stated that their greenhouse hadn't been in operation long enough to give a figure.

While one occasionally runs across over-enthusiastic claims for total food self-sufficiency from 160-square-foot greenhouses, a brief perusal of the responsible literature will quickly bring one's expectations in line with reality. Fred Lape, in the February 1977 issue of *Organic Gardening and Farming®,* states that:

> Most plant life goes quiescent below 50 degrees, and this means that although plants may stay in the sunpit without freezing, they will neither grow nor open their flowers until the February sun sends the temperature inside soaring.

After telling you that deep-winter greenhouse growing isn't worth the effort, I'm going to give you the experience of Bob Muson, a California greenhouse builder, who states in a letter appended to his questionnaire:

> Unfortunately, I couldn't answer question number 13 (relating to temperature

record) because we were too lazy to buy a (high-low thermometer). I am always amazed, though, at the germination period of three days for most seeds (including sunflowers), and that the growth rate is excellent in the dead of winter . . . towards spring, as the angle (of the sun) changes, the plants tend to 'freak out'. Lettuce begins to bolt, tomato vines grow to enormous lengths. Cucumber plants grow into the house area (Bob's greenhouse is attached to his dwelling), producing about seven cukes a day per plant. As summer hits and the sun swings directly overhead, no direct sunlight goes into the greenhouse and the plants calm down again. But all in all, plant growth is best in wintertime. Salads are leafy and tender and will not go to seed—producing huge leaves. I can just tell they enjoy that particular winter angle of the sun. Around spring they act as if the sun is too hot.

> I also find that growing plants inside is a different ball game from an outside garden. We planted vine tomatoes first and that turned out to be a mistake. The vines got wrist thick and overproduced leaves. I finally had to pull the monsters out before they took everything over. And the cucumbers went haywire—crawling out all over the floor. I coaxed them via pieces of string to grow along the roof beams. The pepper family was slow to start but, once up, they grew rapidly and the daily harvest was more than we could keep up with—excellent indoor plant.

> All of the plants grew differently indoors than I have known them to grow outdoors. It's as if everything was prehistoric in size. They raced up towards the glass and pressed

their leaves (against it). Thick stems, over-abundant leaves—but delicate-tasting fruits. Good root vegetables also, and very abundant.

The double-insulated glass, it seems, is the secret. Heat loss in the evening is *very* slow. The house will retain comfortable heat for at least two hours after the (winter) sun has set. Mornings are cold inside, but *nothing* compared to the blast of cold air when one walks outside. . . .

While Bob's growing experience seems to contradict that of other greenhouse vegetable gardeners, I'd be the last person to suggest that we dismiss it as either a fluke or an exaggeration. Too much of my own experience seems to directly contradict the pronouncements of the so-called experts and, while the winter growing season in my greenhouse has not resulted in yields like Bob's, I have managed to get excellent late-winter production from the experimental hydroponic windowboxes I mentioned earlier. A great deal of research remains to be done in this area, so don't rule out the possibility of good winter production from your solar greenhouse until you've experimented with winter growing for a few seasons. (This subject is treated in much greater detail in Chapters Twelve, Thirteen, and Fourteen.)

We could continue with other examples, but by now I think that the basic concepts of attached-greenhouse design and operation have been covered sufficiently to enable the reader to decide how best to integrate them with the requirements of his own situation. In a sense, no two greenhouses are exactly alike, for even though similar in design, each will mirror the personality of its owner. I have seen greenhouses which were used primarily as solar collectors, with hardly any plants at all, and I've seen others which were practically crawling with vegetation—where cucumber vines grew between four and six inches per day, and their owners were only half joking when they said they were afraid that the plants would soon take over the house. It sounds trite, but it's true—what you get out of one of these structures will be directly proportional to what you put into it.

It is extremely difficult to give meaningful cost figures for greenhouse construction, since the cost of materials varies from place to place, and in any case, would be modified by inflation between the time this is written and the time you read it. One figure given for attached greenhouses states that you should be able to build one for about $2.50 per square foot. Even this figure is elastic, however, since a good scavenger can often come up with enough free building materials to construct his greenhouse for little more than the cost of his time.

I am thoroughly convinced of one thing, however, and that is that the average attached greenhouse as described in these pages, will pay for itself very quickly in the food and heat it produces, not to mention in the satisfaction that you'll receive in having such a delightful addition to your life.

Chapter Ten

The Pit Greenhouse

James B. DeKorne

One of the simplest forms of a solar season-extender is the pit greenhouse, which has a long and fruitful history in this country. In fact, one of the country's first pit greenhouses, built in Waltham, Massachusetts, in the early 1880s, is still in existence.

The rationale for a pit greenhouse is very simple: a few inches below the frost line, the earth maintains a constant year-round temperature of about 50°F. If you put your greenhouse underground, you can take advantage of the insulating properties of the earth. It makes good sense: if the nighttime pit greenhouse temperature in early spring drops to 40°F. (unless well insulated, much of the previous day's gain will be lost through the glazing), it still will only have to gain 20° to reach the 60° optimum for our cool-season crops. An uninsulated, unheated freestanding greenhouse would probably drop to 30° or lower under the same circumstances, so the earth insulation of the pit greenhouse offers a definite advantage. (I am figuring an outside temperature of about 20°F.—my unheated pit greenhouse consistently maintains a nighttime temperature at least 20° warmer than the outside temperature. Thus, if the outside thermometer drops to 30°F. at night, the greenhouse will normally stay at 50°F. during the same period.)

I first became interested in greenhouses in general, and pit greenhouses in particular, when I read about the Lama Foundation's Growhole in *The Last Whole Earth Catalog*. Built around 1969 or 1970, the Lama Growhole was an experimental attempt to see if vegetables could be grown in wintertime at an elevation of 8,600 feet.

Construction of a Pit Greenhouse

Strongly influenced by the Lama prototype, I began construction of a pit greenhouse in the late summer of 1973. Lama's greenhouse is built into the side of a south-facing slope, but since I had no such feature on my property, I was obliged to improvise my own pit-greenhouse design. I started by hiring a backhoe to dig a 12-foot x 24-foot hole in the ground. The backhoe operator was instructed to pile most of the dirt from the hole on the north side—this was to make it easier for us to later berm the insulating dirt against the north wall of the greenhouse.

After the backhoe was finished, our next step was to pour a 12-inch-wide cement footing all around the inside perimeter of the hole. The footing served as the foundation for the concrete-block walls which we raised to a height of 8 feet on the north side and 4 feet on the south.

Photo 10-1: *Oldest Lyman greenhouse (exterior). Courtesy of the Society for the Preservation of New England Antiquities.*

Photo 10-2: *The original Lama Growhole. Albuquerque, New Mexico.*

Because I was afraid that the pressure of the earth might cause mortared walls to collapse, we filled every other hole in the blocks with concrete. The blocks themselves were laid up without mortar, relying on the poured-concrete "columns" to hold them in place. To add further strength, reinforcing rods were placed down the block holes about every four feet. The procedure we used during the construction was to lay up two tiers of blocks, pour the concrete down every other hole (tamping thoroughly to eliminate air pockets), wait a few hours for the cement to set, then lay two more tiers. The

Photo 10-3: *The Growhole as it looks today.*

reinforcing rods in the north wall were spliced together in two 4-foot lengths as the rows of blocks went up. (An 8-foot length of "rebar" would have been very difficult to worth with.) We don't feel that the splices weaken the wall in any way because the concrete holds it all firmly in place. Tightly wrapped baling wire holds the lengths of "rebar" together, with an overlap of about 18 inches.

This method of cement-block construction is very easy for the nonprofessional builder to master. Working leisurely in the described manner, another man and I raised the greenhouse walls in three days. When the last tier of blocks was laid, we inserted 6-inch-long, ½-inch-diameter bolts half their length into the wet cement every 4 feet or so. These, of course, were to provide tie-downs for the 2 x 8 wooden plates to which the rafters and other structural members are nailed.

The main roof beam consists of a 25-foot length of pine log which was obtained from the nearby national forest. Notched with a chain saw on either end and spiked in place, the log rests firmly on the wooden plates of the east and west walls. Three-inch pine poles, spaced every

material. (Note: Where I live, a rural area with a 400-year tradition of owner-built structures, the building inspector makes a definite distinction between dwellings and "outbuildings" which are used in conjunction with a farm or ranch. Codes for these latter aren't nearly so strict as for a domicile. For people worried about the 6-foot spacing of my rafters, let me state that they have withheld wet snow loads as deep as 18 inches without a hint of structural failure.)

A common and very effective method of storing heat in a solar greenhouse is the use of black 55-gallon drums filled with water and placed in strategic locations—generally along the north wall. When building my greenhouse I reasoned that, since the 20° roof angle left very little room on the south wall for growing space anyway, I could effectively wall-off a 4-foot section running the length of the building, plaster it over, and use the space as both a heat-storing water tank and a place to raise edible fish. As it turned out, wooden flats were placed across the top of the water tank to provide extra space for starting seedlings in the springtime, so I didn't really lose any growing space after all. Instead of cluttering up valuable space with 55-gallon drums, this feature provides all of the heat-gaining benefits of water storage as well as space to carry out some experiments with aquaculture. An added detail is a wind-electric system outside the greenhouse which provides power to pump the water through a small solar panel, thus providing further heat (see Photo 10-8). The result of these and other experiments are discussed in *The Survival Greenhouse*.

The main problem encountered in this method of water storage had more to do with my lack of building experience than with any real flaw in the concept itself. Even after plastering the cement-block tank with a fiberglass stucco, then

Photo 10-4: *Interior of Growhole.*

Photo 10-5: *Excavation for DeKorne pit greenhouse. El Rito, New Mexico.*

6 feet, serve as vertical rafters, and lengths of 1 x 4 roughsawn lumber, spaced at 4-foot horizontal intervals, provide nailing strips for the three rolls of 4-foot-by-25-foot fiberglass glazing

Photo 10-6: *Completed walls of DeKorne green-house.*

Photo 10-7: *Interior of pit greenhouse, showing water tank against south wall.*

Photo 10-8: *Completed greenhouse.*

Photo 10-9: *Interior. Tomatoes fed by hydro-*
ponic system.

Photo 10-10: *Interior. Onions, lettuce, and*
climbing peas.

several coatings of hot tar, it was a continually frustrating task to find and plug all of the leaks which developed. A much more effective water tank would be constructed entirely of poured concrete.

An important consideration in pit-greenhouse construction which I have never had to confront (aside from the leaking fish tank) is that of drainage. Flooding and high water tables are just not a problem where I live, but in some parts of the country they could make pit greenhouses totally unfeasible.

Thermal Efficiency

Another error I made in the construction of this pit greenhouse was in not insulating the *outside* face of the block wall from the surrounding earth. This could have easily been accomplished by placing pumice, or even Styrofoam panels, in the space between the wall and the edge of the hole before the loose dirt was replaced. Insulation like this would be particularly important around the water-tank portion of the wall, since a large percentage of the heat in the water is undoubtedly conducted through the wall and into the cooler earth which surrounds it.

In addition to the thermal advantage gained by putting the greenhouse underground and using the heat-storing capacity of water, there is another very important principle for trapping solar heat; that is, the concept of double-glazing. While the accompanying chart showing the percentage of transmission of solar energy through fiberglass panels indicates that substantially more energy can penetrate a single layer, the information is misleading because much of the heat portion of that energy can also be dissipated through the single layer after sunset. In other words, the slightly less efficient

Percentage Transmittance at Solar Noon through Fiberglass Panels Tilted at an Angle of Latitude Plus 35°		
	Double Layer	Single Layer
June 21	50%	72%
March/Sept. 21	71%	73%
December 21	77%	86%

Box 10-1: *Percentage Transmittance at Solar Noon Through Fiberglass Panels Tilted at an Angle of Latitude Plus 35°.*

transmittance of a double layer of glazing material is more than compensated for by its efficiency in retaining heat.

To avoid the higher expense of two layers of glass or fiberglass, most solar greenhouse owners use cheaper plastic sheeting for the inside surface. One brand which has been highly recommended is Monsanto 602, a plastic designed specifically for greenhouse use. This material is resistant to the destructive ultraviolet wavelengths of the solar spectrum, and will not turn yellow or become brittle as rapidly as the ordinary type of plastic sheeting. The effective life for this material is estimated to be from three to five years.

It is important that the space between the inner and outer layers not be too large, since heat loss can occur by air convection between the layers if the gap is wide enough to permit it. I have seen double-glazed greenhouses with insulating air gaps as wide as 4 inches, though most authorities state that a 1-inch gap would be more efficient.

One of the interesting features of the original Lama Growhole was that it was triple-glazed—the middle layer consisting of Aircap D-120—

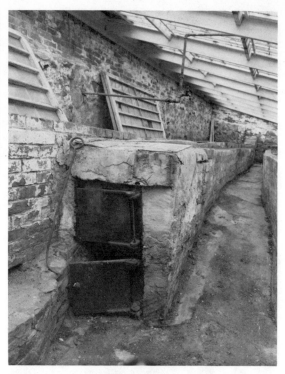

Photo 10-11: *Oldest Lyman greenhouse (interior). Courtesy of the Society for the Preservation of New England Antiquities.*

the plastic bubble sheeting commonly used as packing material for fragile merchandise. In theory, this interior layer of plastic bubbles should have provided tremendous insulating value, but in practice, I suspect that its index of transmittance, in conjunction with the two other layers of ordinary plastic, was too low for efficient crop production.

With any type of solar greenhouse it is important to consider a night curtain or shutter as an important design feature, since such an addition could cut nighttime heat loss by half (various insulating shutters are discussed in Chapter Three).

Equally important for a pit greenhouse is the

Photo 10-12: *Ventilators.*

Photo 10-13: *Taylor-Gregg pit greenhouse.*

use of a supplementary-heating system. A wood-burning heating system makes considerable sense. Modern thermostatically controlled wood stoves like the Ashley and Riteway, will keep a greenhouse warm through the coldest nights on a very small amount of fuel.

The original Waltham, Massachusetts, pit greenhouse made use of an ingenious heating system which insured that the soil temperature in the greenhouse was always adequate for the plants under cultivation. As I understand it, the plants grew in a raised bed which had a chim-ney flue running beneath it for its entire length. A firebox at one end of the flue was stoked with enough wood to last the night, thus maintaining enough heat in the greenhouse soil to raise tropical and semitropical plants through the cold Massachusetts winters. Reportedly, they even grew bananas in this fashion!) Obviously, these greenhouse gardeners of over a century ago were making use of the fact that high soil temperatures can compensate for low air temperatures.

Up to this point we have discussed the solar greenhouse in terms of its ability to admit and retain solar energy. During the cool-weather growing season this is particularly important, but on sunny days, even in the wintertime, the temperatures can get much hotter than we want them to. Obviously, our solar greenhouse must have a means of spilling this excess heat elsewhere, and it is for this reason that a ventilation system is mandatory.

It is a basic principle of physics that cool air sinks and warm air rises. We make use of this principle in solar-greenhouse design by providing a low vent from outside to admit cool air into the greenhouse, and a high vent from inside which expels the warm air out of the greenhouse. On a warm day, both vents are kept open, thus providing a continuous circulation of air. (Along with it, I might add, a fresh supply of carbon dioxide which is vital to the plants.)

For my pit greenhouse I have four 1-foot-by-6-foot ventilators placed along the top of the north wall to provide an exit for warm air. For the entrance of cool air, I just leave the door open. This system has always worked well for me, except on a few days each summer when the greenhouse temperature gets higher than I'd like, even with vents open. As I have noted elsewhere, however, I've never lost any plants to these high temperatures. A greenhouse shading system for hot days would go a long way toward solving the problem.

While doing research for *The Survival Greenhouse,* I came across a most interesting book which was first published back in the forties. Entitled *Winter Flowers in Greenhouse and Sunheated Pit,* this book describes the pit-greenhouse experiences of the authors, Kathryn Taylor and Edith Gregg. I consider it to be a definitive work on pit greenhouses, and I surely would have modified my own design had I known of this book's existence at the time of construction. Photo 10-13 shows the configuration of a typical Taylor-Gregg greenhouse.

Pit greenhouses have never gone completely out of style—in the February 1977 issue of *Organic Gardening and Farming®* magazine, Fred Lape, director of the George Landis Arboretum at Esperance, in central New York, defines what he calls his "sunpit":

Photo 10-15: *Interior of semi-pit.*

Photo 10-14: *Semi-pit greenhouse. New Mexico.*

A sunpit is basically nothing more than a hole in the ground covered by an inverted V roof, with glass windows on the southern side.

Essentially, Mr. Lape's sunpit is based on the same idea as the Taylor-Gregg design. This type of pit greenhouse might be called a "walk-in cold frame" since its primarily purpose is for the propagation of seedlings and cuttings to be transplanted outdoors at a later date.

Some friends of mine here in New Mexico

have constructed what can only be called a "semi-pit greenhouse." Built against the excavated side of a fairly gentle slope, the greenhouse is insulated by the earth on the north side (Photo 10-14). An "air-lock" vestibule is provided at the east side entrance, which is extremely effective in keeping out cold air. The greenhouse is caulked airtight everywhere—an often overlooked but extremely important method for retaining every last bit of solar heat. It was quite difficult to take the interior photograph shown here, since every time I entered the greenhouse from the vestibule, the humid 85°F. air would immediately fog my camera lens; out in the vestibule, the early April daytime temperature of 45° quickly cleared it. As you can see by the photograph, there are enough April salads growing in there to feed an army.

Chapter Eleven

Solar Cold Frames and Other Season Extenders

Leandre Poisson

Although freestanding solar greenhouses, as well as the attached and pit varieties, satisfy the requirements of many who wish to significantly extend their growing season, the solar cold frame which incorporates many of the essential features of the larger structures is most "appropriate" for year-round gardeners in many sections of the country.

The solar cold frame, which is actually a solar-efficient hotbed, had its origins centuries

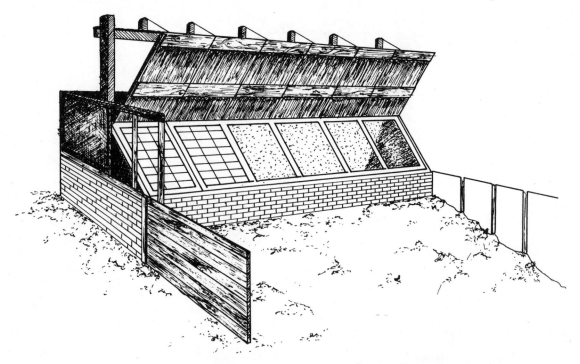

Figure 11-1: *"Solar" forcing frame (from* The Glass House, *John Hix, Phaidon, 1974).*

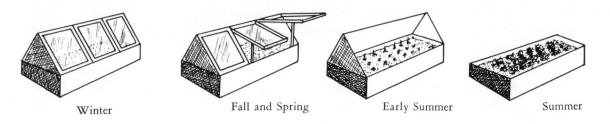

Winter   Fall and Spring   Early Summer   Summer

Figure 11-2: *Rooftop cold frames. University Settlement Community Centre, Montreal, Canada.*

ago. In *The Glass House* John Hix reports that "By the beginning of the eighteenth century, the Dutch had already developed forcing frames with sloped glass roof, producing oranges, pineapples and grapes. The slope-front forcing frame was engineered to control the environment. The back wall was always massive masonry that would absorb the sun's rays and retain the warmth into the night. Within the back wall or under the floor, heat and smoke from the furnace wound its way in a circuitous flue discharging at the top of the wall.

"The front south wall was constructed entirely of glass set in wooden frame, with hinges on the sides or the top. The frames were large enough to allow plants to be removed and replaced. The windows were often left open in the summer for maximum ventilation and the sun, but in the winter they were sealed against draughts and only opened to the air on a warm winter's day. Oil paper in frames was often fixed under the windows to act as double-glazing against the cold. One house shows a simple system of several canvas curtains in front of the windows, ensuring three layers of winter clothing against the cold. Another mechanized frame had a series of wood shutters hinged at the top to be let down by pulleys and ropes at the back

wall. This allowed the gardener to expose the glass on a sunny winter's day. There was also a sliding-wood panel perpendicular to the house that protected the whole device from the cold prevailing winds; but the panel could also be pushed back for ventilation, an early use of mechanized micro-climate."

From a historical perspective, the solar cold frame can be considered a versatile, efficient structure with applications in numerous situations where larger greenhouses are inappropriate or not desired. And, interestingly, there is renewed interest in this design. For example, 10 solar cold frames have been built on the rooftops at the University Settlement Community Centre in the Saint Louis district of Montreal, under the direction of Susan Alward, Ron Alward, and Witold Rybczynski, and in conjunction with McGill University.

Each structure has a south orientation, an opaque and insulated north-reflecting wall, removable glazing, and rear access for cultivation. The project coordinators report that "The north-sloping roof of each was insulated with a sandwich panel containing 2-inch-thick polystyrene insulation. East and west wall sections as well as all sides and floors or the soil boxes are similarly insulated. All interior exposed surfaces are covered with a glossy white paint in order to reflect incident solar radiation onto the plant canopy and soil. The roof frames are removable so that during late spring, summer, and early fall months, the beds can be converted to open-air gardens."

An interesting feature of the Montreal rooftop experiment is that "Three of the larger units have been fitted with a heating system, which uses waste heat, normally escaping up the chimney. In this system, a heat exchanger is placed at the point where the hot gases first enter the vertical chimney section. A circulating glycol

solution is heated by the rising gases and pumped up to the roof where it is fed in parallel into the three hotbeds. In each structure, the glycol solution passes in succession through a finned air-heat exchanger, a heating coil imbedded 25 centimeters deep in the soil, and a second finned air-heat exchanger. No storage of hot glycol solution is used; however, considerable heat storage is inherent in the system in the form of the heated soil. The glycol is used as a working fluid instead of water in order to eliminate the danger of freezing in the transfer pipes."

The Montreal rooftop experiences indicate

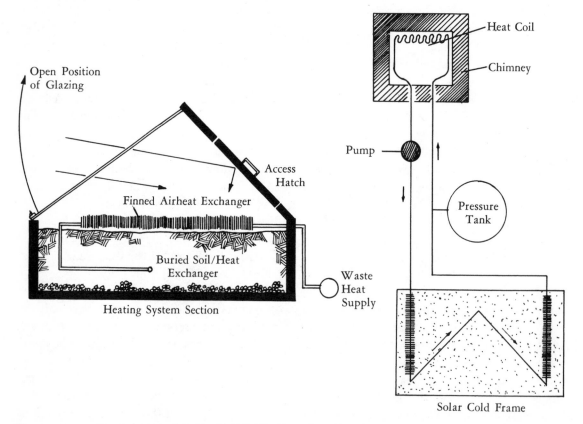

Figure 11-3: *Rooftop waste-heat distribution system.*

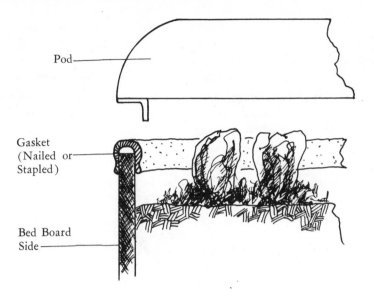

Figure 11-4: *Gasket detail.*

that solar cold frames are adaptable structures, perhaps with particular significance to urban areas or to other situations where small solar structures are called for.

At Solar Survival in New Hampshire, we have developed solar cold-frame devices which will permit year-round growing even in very harsh climates. The first device, called a solar pod, is a marked improvement over the traditional cold frame. The pod is double-glazed and, because of its domed shape, allows more light to enter. The original practitioners of the French-intensive method of gardening used straw mats over the glass to help insulate the plant beds. However, double-glazing serves as a more effective thermal barrier.

If desired, transparent fiberglass insulation can be placed between the two glazings. To accomplish this, you must enlarge the space between the glazings from ¾ inch to 2½ inches (see "Construction of the Solar Pod"). This

insulation will more than triple the insulating value of the pod.

Proper gasketing of the pod is essential to its thermal performance. We used discarded urethane-foam carpeting pad, gleaned from a carpet supply store, which is fastened to the edge of the bed wall (see Figure 11-4).

As a passive solar-heated device, the pod's effectiveness can be increased with the addition

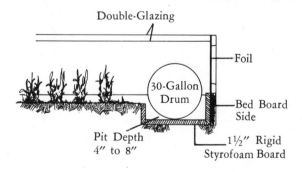

Figure 11-5: *Recessed drum and insulation.*

of extra thermal mass, which can be accomplished by adding a 30-gallon drum within the pod. The drum should be painted with flat black high-temperature paint. In effect, this makes the drum the solar collector as well as storage. For a storage medium we recommend used crankcase oil. While it won't store as much heat as water, crankcase oil does not present a freezing problem and it won't corrode the drum. And another important advantage is the thermal lag factor;

the oil will give off heat at a slower rate than water. On the other hand, if you choose to use water, make sure that you add sufficient antifreeze to prevent freeze-ups. If you want to extend the life of the container, you should include an anticorrosive additive.

The drum should be filled to 1½ inches from the top to allow for expansion. It is advisable to use pipe-joint compounds on the bungs to make sure they don't leak. The drum is recessed

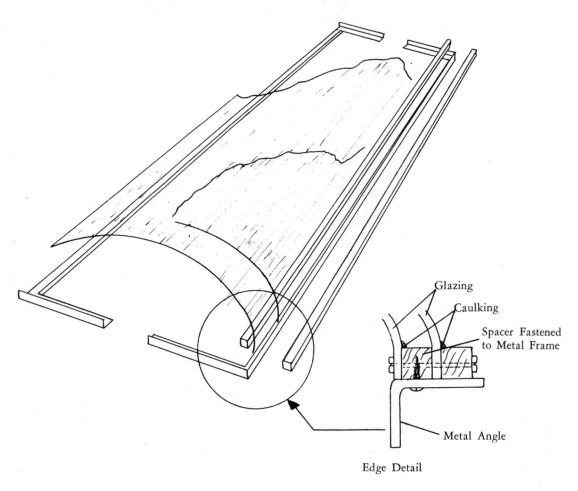

Glazing

Caulking

Spacer Fastened to Metal Frame

Metal Angle

Edge Detail

Figure 11-6: *Partial exploded view.*

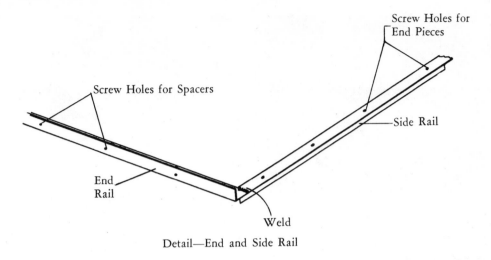

Detail—End and Side Rail

Figure 11-7: *Welded frame detail.*

into the ground for the following reasons. First, this procedure allows for more clearance between it and the inside of the pod so that the cold and warm air within the pod can "convect" more easily. Secondly, it allows for the coldest air to drop into a pit to be reheated rather than having it sit at the feet of the plants and taking heat from them.

To minimize heat loss to the ground we installed rigid foam (1½-inch Styrofoam board). To reflect more sunlight into the drum, the inside of the north end of the pod is covered with aluminum foil, the shiny side toward the drum. A piece of glazing plastic protects the foil.

Construction of the Solar Pod

The size of our pod was determined by the size of our beds, so don't hesitate to modify the concept. What is presented will hopefully serve as a guide.

The dimensions that we utilize in our French-intensive beds are 4 feet for the width of the bed and 2 feet between beds. We find these dimensions suit most people. The beds are 50 feet long and run on a north-south axis for maximum solar exposure. Like the original French-intensive appliances, our pods are interchangeable and can be utilized on all parts of the garden. The length of the pod was determined by the finished weight of the unit, and how manageable it was for two people to handle. We concluded that 6 feet to 8 feet are manageable sizes. The pod illustrated here (Figure 11-6) is 6 feet, 6 inches (the dimensions of bed frames found at the dump).

The side and end angles of the frame are welded together (Figure 11-7). The end-curve profile is determined by the width of the bed and the fact that the fiberglass sheet comes in 5-foot widths. If you need a wider span then you will have to make provisions for bringing two pieces of glazing together.

The end pieces of the pod are made of ¾-inch plywood and are painted to protect them from the weather. The hinged vent flap is 10 inches

Photo 11-1: *Drum placement.*

Photo 11-4: *Pod vent open.*

Photo 11-2: *Pod beds.*

in diameter. The ends of the metal frames are screwed to the plywood.

Before applying the fiberglass glazing, the mounting surface should have a small bead of caulking laid on it to make sure that the layers are well sealed. We used sheet-metal screws to fasten the glazing to the metal strip as well as on the wood sections.

The solar pod is an appropriate-technology device that will give you a net payback for many years if properly maintained. Its low, initial investment cost will pay itself back many times in fresh vegetables the whole year-round.

The Solar Frame

On the same scale as solar pod, we have developed a solar cold frame. This is a more elaborate and efficient solar device than the pod. It is permanently sited and has higher thermal efficiencies and capabilities. Because of the superior thermal performance of the solar frame, it is possible to grow plants in it that are not as cold-hardy as those in the pod. (See Chapters Thirteen and Fourteen.)

The solar cold frame is essentially a passive

Photo 11-3: *Gasket and frame detail.*

solar greenhouse that you cannot stand in. The size that we developed was determined by the dimensions of standard materials (i.e., 4-foot-by-8-foot plywood, 5-foot-wide fiberglass). It is possible for you, the designer/builder, to modify this concept by lengthening the solar frame or by adapting the "flip shutter" concept to a pit greenhouse. Accordingly, you can make this pit greenhouse a part of your home, therefore providing you with the extra benefit of supplemental heat.

Photo 11-5: *Insulation filling glazing.*

A. Configuration

The first thing we investigated was the ideal profile for the frame. We took the average yearly solar angles, for the colder parts of the country, and concluded that a face angle of 35° from the horizontal provided the solar frame with the most direct sunlight into it on a yearly basis. On December 21 at high noon, the sun casts a 12-inch shadow from the front edge, and on June 21 the shadow is 12 inches from the back wall. Another advantage of this angle is that it provides about 20-percent more growing surface area than the surface area of the glazing. (See Chapter Two for additional sun-angle information.)

Because plants prefer diffused light all around them to grow properly, we painted the interior of the frame a shiny white. Tests have shown that white works much better than silver at diffusing light.

Photo 11-6: *Raised shutter.*

B. The Glazed Shutter

The most difficult facet of a solar greenhouse is marrying an effective thermal shutter with the glazing. With a small solar device, it is even more difficult because of exterior access constraints. Also, as with most insulated shutters,

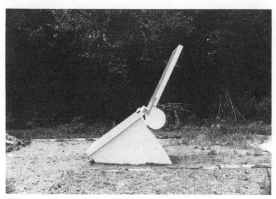

Photo 11-7: *Insulation returned to cavity.*

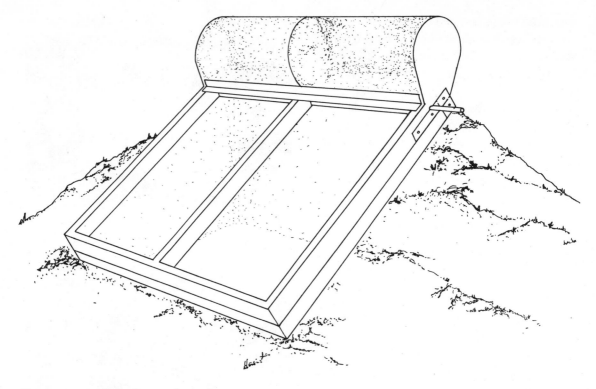

Figure 11-8: *Solar frame—bermed.*

Photo 11-8: *Thirty-gallon drums.*

the problem of an effective seal within close tolerances is almost impossible. Couple these two requirements with the need for simplicity and low cost and the problem seems insoluble.

The simplest and most direct way that we could develop is what we call the "flip shutter." This device permits the use of effective double-glazing and incorporates the shutter and its storage within it. In the morning the shutter is lifted up (Photo 11-5) and the insulation moves into the top cavity (Photo 11-6) of open lid. At the end of the solar day there is no need to reopen the lid and let valuable heat escape.

Simply turning the hand valve allows the insulation to fall into the glazing cavity where it functions as a thermal barrier overnight or longer. The 35° glazing angle and gravity permit the shutter to work satisfactorily.

The top edge of the frame has a 1-inch-thick-by-3-inch-wide, urethane-foam gasket, which makes for a good seal when the top lid is closed.

C. Insulating the Frame

In order to optimize the thermal performance of the solar frame it is essential that the outside of the frame be insulated. The simplest way to do this is to fasten 2-inch rigid urethane foam onto the plywood, then berm up the sides of the solar frame with dirt and sod (Figure 11-8). In this manner it is possible to utilize the earth to temper the unit. If the frame is only partially bermed or left freestanding, then the outside of the foam will have to be sheathed to protect it from the elements. This can be accomplished with either wood, metal, roofing paper, split shakes, or whatever there is at hand that does the job and looks presentable.

D. Thermal Mass

For successful solar-heating performance, it is mandatory that the solar frame have sufficient thermal mass. This is accomplished by adding two 30-gallon drums inside the unit (Photo 11-8).

The earth in the frame functions as thermal mass as well. The collector or window is 20 feet squared in area. That affords the frame 3 gallons of storage for every square foot of collector. This is a good ratio which is enhanced further by the mass of the earth. The drums should be recessed into the ground as was done for the solar pod. The drums need not be left in the

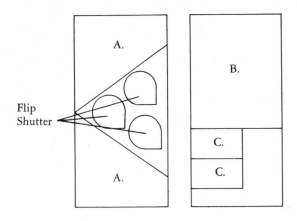

Figure 11-9: *Framing pattern.*

pod year-round. After the coldest season they can be removed to enlarge the growing area. But the weight of the containers makes removal difficult. And if you plan to salvage the liquid contents, it might take several people to do this.

E. Construction of the Solar Frame

The construction should start with the frame. You will need two sheets of 4-foot-by-8-foot-by-¾-inch exterior plywood. You will also need two 2 x 4 x 6 studs.

Before any of the pieces are cut they should be laid out on the plywood sheets. Figure 11-9 suggests a possible layout for most of the major solar-frame components.

Figure 11-10 is an assembly plan for wall sections. This unit will hold together well if all the sections are screwed and glued together. Where the 2 x 4s come together, they should be bolted with 4-inch hex-head lag bolts. If the unit has to be removed occasionally, the bolts and screws will greatly simplify matters.

After the separate panels are assembled (but

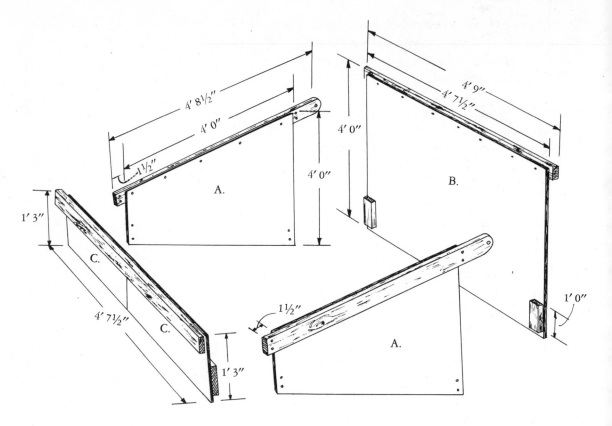

Figure 11-10: *Assemble plan for wall sections.*

before the total unit is bolted together), the panels should be primed and painted both inside and out. During the final assembly the edges should be made airtight, which can be achieved by either packing the joints with insulation or caulking them.

F. Constructing the Flip Shutter

For fabrication of some of the components for the flip shutter see Figure 11-9. For details of the rounded head of the flip shutter see Figure 11-11. For construction of the framing mem-

bers of the shutter see Figure 11-12. For assembling the framing members and the rounded head, see Figure 11-13.

In Figure 11-13, when joining piece A to B and C make sure that they are at right angles to each other, glue and clamp them together to be certain the pieces are aligned. Then screw them securely with 1½-inch flat-head screws.

Pieces B and C should be fastened to D with 3-inch flat-head screws. The A ends can be held in place by means of a temporary nailing strip laid across all three of the arms while the ends

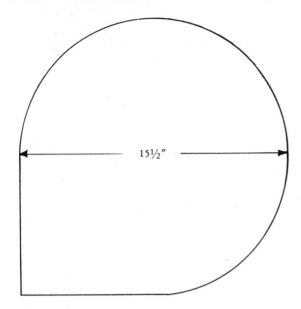

15½"

Figure 11-11: *Round head of flip shutter.*

lever tube is 2½ inches long. In the hinge pieces it is 1½ inches long.

The flap valve is located at the top, over the inside edge of the frame. The holes for the lever and the center hinge are drilled through the members. The short-end hinge hole is drilled to a 1-inch depth into the side member. It does not go all the way through. The lever and hinges are bolted through the flap valves with 1-inch-by-$\frac{3}{32}$-inch machine screws. The flap-valve system should be fitted to each cavity so that the unit turns easily. The tolerances need not be terribly close to affect a reasonable seal. There should be stops to prevent the valves from turning beyond the closed point. This can be achieved with small blocks of wood fastened to the side members, forward of the valve, and near the bottom. The final seal of the storage is achieved by the frame gasket pushing against the valves when the lid is closed. The gasket is fastened to the entire top edge of the frame, and should be at least 1 inch thick and 2 inches wide. This will assure an effective seal and prevent heat loss due to air infiltration.

The final step in the construction of the flip shutter is that of glazing. We glazed ours with 5-foot-wide, .040-inch-thick fiberglass sheet. A 12½-inch length is required to glaze the unit. The bottom of the panel should be done first and then continuing under and over the storage cavity. A small bead of caulking laid on the entire glazing mounting edge will seal the unit against air and moisture infiltration. The glazing is fastened to the frame with ¾-inch sheet-metal screws. It is possible to achieve the same results by utilizing a compression strip on the entire edge. The top layer of glazing is then fastened in the same manner. At this point the caulking is omitted until the unit is filled with insulation.

are being assembled. This will help keep the assembly square.

Next, notch the angle where A meets B and A meets C. This is done to the depth of the thickness of the 2-inch-by-2-inch-by-5-foot aluminum angle. Fasten the metal angle to the three arms. Predrill holes through the metal angle and recess them. Join the pieces with 1½-inch flathead screws.

The next step is to fabricate and install the flap valve. This is the part that keeps the insulation inside the storage compartment while the sun shines through the window (Figure 11-14). The flap valves can be made from heavy-gauge sheet metal, ¼-inch tempered Masonite, plywood, or Plexiglas. We used ¼-inch Plexiglas because there were a few scrap pieces on hand. The hinge and lever pieces are made from ¾-inch-diameter electrical tubing. The slot in the

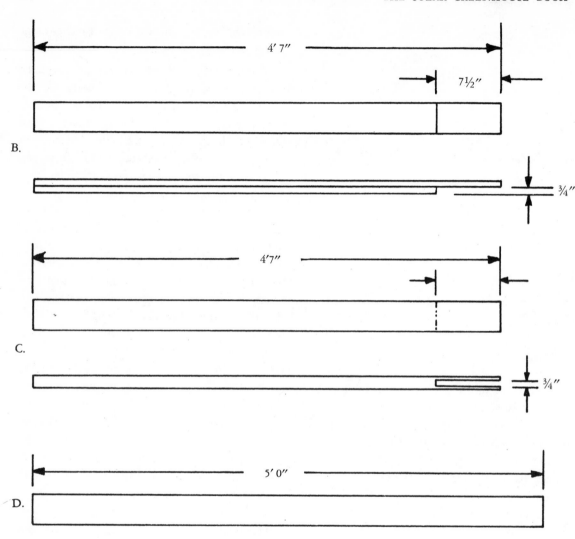

Figure 11-12: *Framing members of shutter.*

The unit should be filled after the hinges are mounted on the panel.

G. Hinging the Flip Shutter

The size of the shutter requires that the hinging mechanism be sufficiently sized to take the stresses imposed upon it, over extended use. The one we have devised meets these requirements and is simple to fabricate (Figure 11-15). We used 1½-inch-by-1½-inch steel angle for the arm and ³⁄₁₆-inch-by-3½-inch-by-5½-inch steel plate for the leg. The arm is made from an old

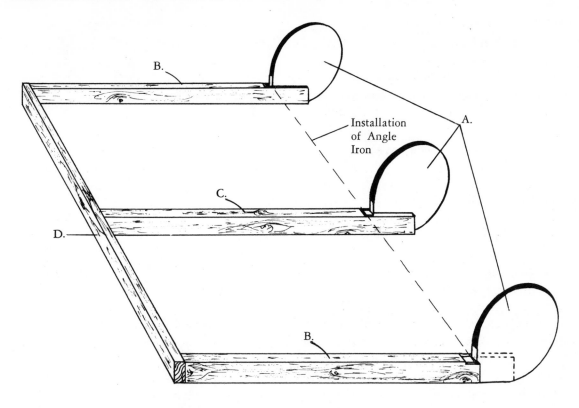

Figure 11-13: *Detail—assembling framing members and rounded head.*

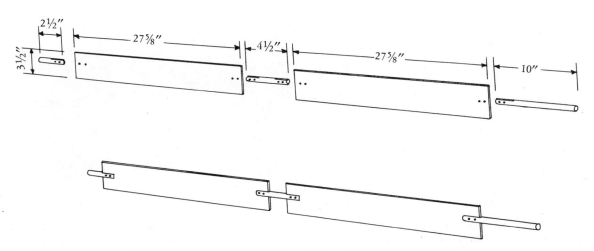

Figure 11-14: *Fabrication detail—flap value.*

bed frame. Weld the leg plate to the arm along
the top edge and inside on the bottom. The hole
in the leg plate should be ½ inch in diameter so
as to fit the ½-inch-diameter hinge bolt.

The hinge should be fastened to the side of
the frame with 1½-inch hex-head lag bolts and
to the bottom of the frame with 3-inch hex-head
lag bolts. The hinge should be painted before it
is mounted. Use a bright color. After your
hinges are mounted place the shutter on top of
the frame making sure the front and side edges
line up. Put ½-inch spacers between the frame
and the shutter. This should make the hinge
bolt hole line up in the middle of the 2 x 4
mounting. This space between the two sections is
essential for a uniform seal of the shutter with
the gasket. Remove the shutter and drill the ½-
inch hinge bolt holes through the mounting
frames. Mount the frame with ½-inch-diameter-
by-2½-inch bolts. For the open lid position, you
will have to fasten a stop block to the back of the
frame to prevent the lid from resting on the
plastic in the open position.

H. Insulating the Shutter

The final step is that of filling the shutter with
insulation. We utilized expanded Styrofoam
beads, about 7 pounds of them. It may be
possible to use dried sawdust or wood shavings,
but the beads will give a better insulating factor
than the other two. The beads are available
through plastic supply houses or insulation
suppliers. The "static cling" of the bead will
have to be eliminated. This is done by adding
about half-a-cup of Anstac 2-M to the beads and
mixing it all together making sure the beads are
well coated. It is also a good idea to wipe the
inside surface of the glazing with the same stuff.
The material is available from Chemical Devel-

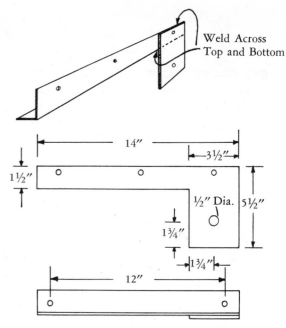

Figure 11-15: *Pattern—Hinge Fabrication.*

opment Corporation, Endicott Street, Danvers,
MA 01923. Check with plastics distributors for
they may have other sources.

Fill the reservoir. The beads compact about
20 percent when settling, so tap the storage

Photo 11-9: *Hinge in place.*

Photo 11-10: *Completed solar frame.*

reservoir to make sure that it is completely full. Fill it right to the flap valve and then turn it to the closed position. Tighten down the screws on the front glazing, close the lid, and open the valve. After the window is full there should be at least 15 to 20 percent left in the reservoir; run it back and forth several times to make sure that it works well and that you have sufficient insula-

tion. When that is done, loosen the top glazing sheet, put a small bead of caulking around the entire edge and tighten down the screws.

If your solar frame is in a windy area you may want to consider devising some sort of tie-down when the lid is in an open position. We have had no problems with wind opening the lid while it's been in a closed position.

Part III
Managing the Solar Greenhouse

Chapter Twelve

Growing Basics

John White

The solar greenhouse is designed to admit the maximum amount of light energy in the cool season. Ideally, energy is either absorbed and stored away or it is used for photosynthesis. Both functions are essential to plant growth in the greenhouse. The design and construction assures that the stage is set for gardening success. But even the finishing details inside—wall colors, location of growing areas, types of containers, and the arrangements of plants—can affect the health of the crops. An appreciation for a plant's basic requirements, particularly with reference to actual winter conditions in the greenhouse will be useful not only for setting up the planting environment, but also in choosing and caring for the plants.

Light Energy for Plant Growth

Photosynthesis is the process plants use to convert the raw products of light, carbon dioxide, and water into energy-rich plant foods. These along with water and elements from fertilizing materials, are used for growth. Plants are most responsive to visible light, and for photosynthesis, they use only its visible portion (see Chapter Two). Photosynthesis will occur quite well at light intensities as low as one-quarter of the maximum. Of course, various families of plants

---

Light Energy for Plant Growth

Thirty-seven percent of the energy in sunlight is within the wavelength (colors) useful for photosynthesis. Of the rest, 62.4 percent is infrared, or thermal energy, and .6 percent is ultraviolet.

One percent of the light that falls on a leaf powers photosynthesis. Ten percent of the light is reflected and 10 percent passes through. The leaf retains 80 percent and most of it is used for transpiration. Some is reradiated. The fraction that remains is available for building food from carbon dioxide and water.

Box 12-1: *Light Energy for Plant Growth*

---

require different intensities for most efficient photosynthesis.

It is the length of time adequate light is available that most determines the amount of food plants can make. The short days and low sun angles of winter are not conducive to rapid growth. Low sun angles make short days even shorter for photosynthesis, since afternoon and morning sunlight then travels through a thicker layer of the earth's filtering atmosphere. Because plants make less food on a winter day, they will take longer to grow. In some areas such as

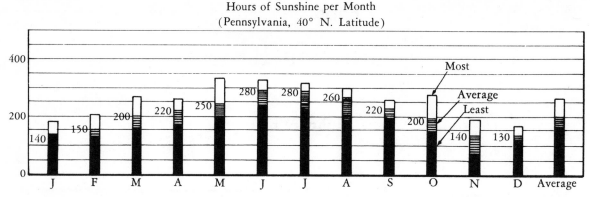

Hours of Sunshine per Month
(Pennsylvania, 40° N. Latitude)

This is a graphic comparison on the differences in available light between months and through the seasons. It combines the effects of day length and cloud cover. A chart like this can be made for any location to help plan cropping systems and planting dates.

Figure 12-1: *Hours of sunshine per month.*

the Pacific Northwest, the predominance of cloudy weather coupled with short days can mean extremely slow growth.

Other colors of light outside the visible range can affect certain growth processes. For instance, too much infrared light can make plants spindly and tall. While too much ultraviolet (produced by sun lamps) can kill plants, a little bit helps keep them stocky and straight. The glazing you choose should admit as much light as possible for the plant's sake. Because added thicknesses will cut out some light, consider carefully before going beyond two glazing layers (see Chapter Four). The glazing should not eliminate much of the visible reds and blues which the plant needs most.

Some plants such as spinach and lettuce will grow well with low-intensity, diffused light. Others like cucumbers need high-intensity, direct light for best growth and fruiting. Practically speaking, plants which tolerate medium intensities will do well nearer dark objects, and high-light intensity plants will grow best in full sun and in front of reflective surfaces. Not all vegetables will do well in all seasons. Plants that need plenty of high-intensity light will do best in spring inside the greenhouse; outside the days are getting long, though the air and ground may be still quite cool. For periods of marginal light, remember that root and fruit crops need to do a lot of growing before they produce any edible parts.

The simplest way to increase the amount of light for the plants is by painting the interior white or coating the walls and roof with aluminum foil. Research at the Brace Institute in Montreal suggests that this one improvement might increase the light by about one-third over what would be available in an all-glass house. In their comparative tests, plants in the house with reflectors on the north wall and roof matured more rapidly. White paint scatters more light, so a little more would pass out through the glass than if foil were used. The difference

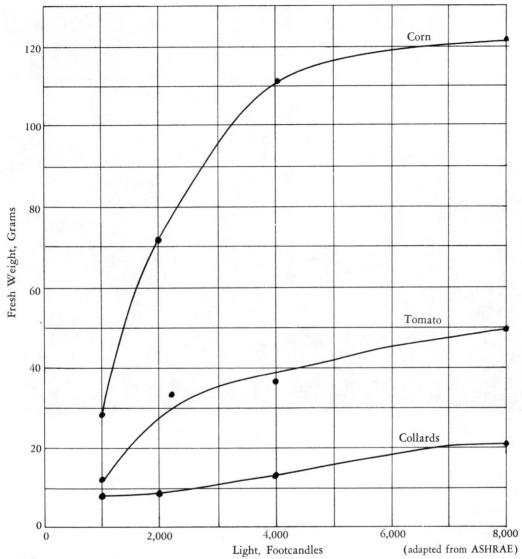

Light intensity at noon on a clear day is about 10,000 footcandles; on a cloudy day it is closer to 1,000. Good growth can occur with 2,500. Among other things, the data in the graph indicates that greens crops profit less from greater light intensity than fruiting crops.

Figure 12-2: *Effect of light intensity on plant growth.*

Photo 12-1: *Storage barrels, black to sun, white to plants.*

Photo 12-2: *Reflective coating, Pragtree Farm.*

is not large. All wooden beams and rafters should be white, too.

Supplemental lighting can be used to extend the duration of radiation which is strong enough for photosynthesis. This is most cost-effective on seedlings, since young plants are more efficient than older plants in using the extra light. And more plants can be raised under one light as seedlings. For example, when temperatures are too low to germinate a kind of vegetable seed in spring, supplemental light can be used instead of supplemental heat. Here is how. Simply wait a few weeks until the greenhouse

warms, then use lights at night to make up for lost time. For photosynthesis, cool, white fluorescent lamps with reflectors are as good as any. A light meter can be a valuable tool around the greenhouse. It will help you determine where the best spots in the house are and confirm your impressions about just when and which plants start growing faster.

Photoperiod refers to how the length of day or night affects plant growth, apart from the production of food via photosynthesis. Chrysanthemums will flower only when the days are short while spinach and radishes flower only

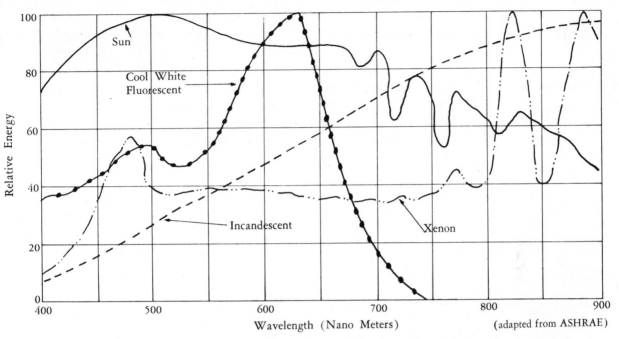

Plants use only the light wavelengths in the visible and near-visible colors, 360 to 760 nm. For photosynthesis, the most important light is blue (430 nm) and red (660 nm). Germination, flowering, and stem lengthening are influenced by red (660 nm) and far red (735 nm). Lamps which provide these colors are adequate for supplementation. Growth chambers often employ a combination of fluorescent light (70 percent of the installed wattage) and incandescent (30 percent).

Figure 12-3: *Spectral energy distribution of sunlight and fluorescent, incandescent, and xenon lamps.*

when the days are long. Besides increasing photosynthesis, some fluorescent lights may also be used to artificially initiate flowering in long-day plants. Incandescent lights will serve to lengthen the photoperiod, but are not good for increasing photosynthesis because they are inefficient in converting electricity to light. The length of night can be increased by using densely woven black cloth or black polyethylene over the plants.

Solar greenhouses, attached or freestanding, are designed so that they are shaded by the peak and opaque roof in the summer. In such tight, well-insulated buildings, this is essential to avoid overheating. Light intensities will still be ample for growth, though the duration of effective light will not equal conditions on the outside. According to reports, this has not interfered with the production of tomatoes, peppers, or cucumbers.

Temperature

Every growth process, whether it be movement

of water, minerals, and food in roots, stems, and leaves, or photosynthesis, or actual tissue expansion, is affected by the temperature. Temperature influences how fast plants will grow, not just whether or not they will live. Some plants, endive and kale, for example, can tolerate repeated freezing temperatures and continue to grow when conditions warm up. But very few of the life functions will occur below 40°F. For most vegetables, growth also declines when temperatures exceed the middle 80s. Plant families vary widely in the temperatures at which they grow best. Furthermore, for one plant there are different ideal temperatures for processes like germination, growth of cells, or photosynthesis.

Desirable temperatures depend on the crops

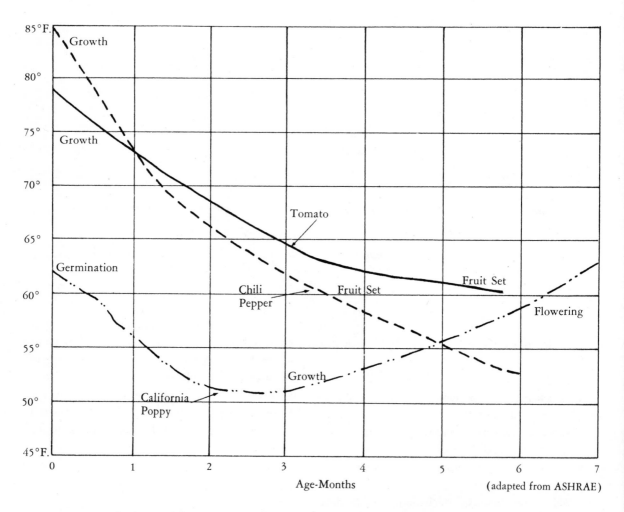

Figure 12-4: *Optimum night temperatures for growth and reproduction.*

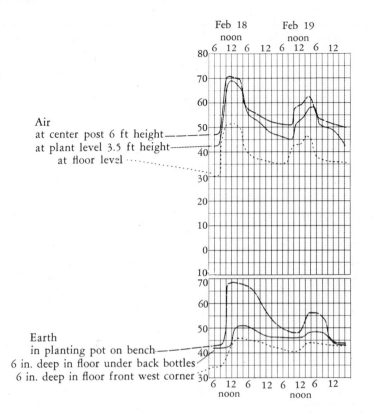

Figure 12-5: *The rate of daily temperature change in air, floor soil, and planting pots, sunny day followed by cloudy day. Maxatawny, Pennsylvania.*

that you intend to grow. If you stick mostly to cool-season crops, a temperature range of 40° to 60°F. is best. An occasional drop to 35° or increase to 90° will not hurt most of these crops. But prolonged lows will slow down growth, while prolonged highs will cause unwanted flower development and make the leaves tough and bitter tasting. If you are growing primarily warm-season crops, a temperature range of 60° to 80°F. is best. An occasional drop of 50° or increase to 100° will not hurt these crops. Prolonged lows will cause a loss of flowers and fruit, malformed fruit and a slowdown of growth, while prolonged high temperatures will

cause burning of fruit, wilted leaves, and a slowdown of growth.

In most solar greenhouses that we know of, daytime air temperatures even in the middle of winter are well within the desirable range for cool-weather crops. Air temperature rises rapidly with sunlight, so little useful light is wasted because the air is too cool for photosynthesis and growth then. Though air cools rapidly at night, temperatures will remain warm long enough to complete some growth, especially when only a small amount of food has been made during the day.

Cool soil temperatures during the day can

Cool Night Temperatures May Not Slow Growth

William Loefstedt and William Buzzard, horticulturists at the New Haven Park Department and the Connecticut Agricultural Experiment Station, respectively, have found that lowering the greenhouse temperature at night to 45°F. has no effect on the growth and quality of chrysanthemums and lilies. The crops in the cool house were compared to the same flowers grown at a constant night temperature of 60°F.

Dr. John Thorne, a plant physiologist associated with the horticulturists, explains the basis for this tolerance to cool temperatures: "During the first hours of darkness many plants complete their necessary metabolism, translocation, and utilization of products formed during the day." After those processes are complete, the plant is not affected if the temperature is lowered somewhat. Dr. Thorne suspects that certain crops like endive

and kale might be even more cold-tolerant. That is, some plants may complete their metabolic processes even faster than the ones tested. It is certain that some groups of plants and even certain varieties within a single group are different in this respect.

In this particular experiment, the heating system maintained 60°F. until 11:00 P.M. Between 11:00 P.M. and 6:00 A.M. the temperature was allowed to fall to 45°F. As the temperature was turned up in the morning, the plants were irrigated with 75°F. water to warm up the roots and soil.

The research indicates that the environment for plants in many solar greenhouses is better than might have been suspected. Furthermore, it suggests that growers should water in the morning with warm water if at all possible. A greywater system would be one way of doing this with little extra energy. It also suggests that if supplemental heat is required, the most effective time to use it is in the early evening.

Box 12-2: *Cool Night Temperatures May Not Slow Growth*

limit photosynthesis. When soil temperatures are very low, the membrane of the roots changes so that water is not admitted as readily. Especially early in the day when the leaves are warm (perhaps warmer than the air), wilting can occur even though the greenhouse isn't hot. Water, of course, is essential to photosynthesis. This was observed occasionally in the Maxatawny greenhouse. All other reactions associated with growth in the soil will be slower at cooler temperatures. Even for cool-weather crops, temperatures in the root zone below 50°F. will reduce growth.

The distinction between night and day, then, is not so clear cut in the soil. In a passive solar greenhouse in winter, the soil may be too cool

early in the day to take advantage of the climate in the air. On the other hand, late in the day it will retain warmth so that growth processes can continue for a while after dusk.

The great change between day and night temperatures in both soil and air in itself will not hurt the plant as long as its harmful temperature point is not reached or maintained for several days in succession. With respect to temperature, some growth is possible most days through the winter. Generally, there will be a period at night at which all growth ceases for a while.

You have control over several factors which can alter the temperature in the leaf and root zones. Temperatures can vary widely in different spots around the greenhouse, especially ver-

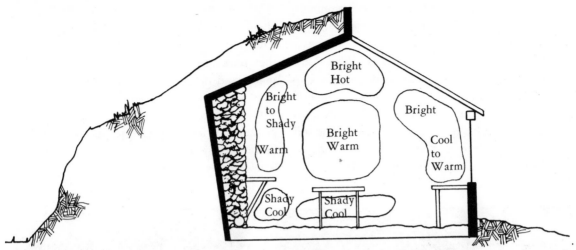

Microclimatic zones can occur in the passive greenhouse. They will change slightly with the seasons: the rear is shaded in the summer and the area near the glazing can become quite cold on winter nights. Circulating the air will reduce temperature differences between regions. Tall plants and hanging baskets will shade any plants behind them.

Figure 12-6: *Microclimate zones.*

tically. Uniformity of temperature within the commercial greenhouse is important only because crop uniformity is important. However, in solar-heated greenhouses, you can try to take advantage of natural interior temperature variations, essentially by placing warm crops nearer the roof and cool crops nearer the floor. The environment in these zones will also change from winter to summer. You will have to experiment to determine the best zones and seasons for each crop.

The growing containers, consequently, can be important for reaping the benefits of microclimates within the greenhouse. Pots hanging or on shelves are the obvious way to use the highest spots. Plants on trellises may have their tops basking while the roots are chilled, or vice versa, when trailing plants are trained to cascade from a high spot.

The choice which affects plant temperature most is whether to use benches or ground-level beds. Growing on benches puts the plants in a warmer air layer of the greenhouse. Whenever cold air enters the greenhouse, it immediately settles over the ground layer. Bench systems, however, usually mean the plants will be in pots of some kind. The accompanying graph (Figure 12-5) shows how closely the soil in a pot follows air temperature. The roots in a pot will be subject to great temperature fluctuations then, but will also heat up to growing temperatures fairly quickly. Note that at the Maxatawny greenhouse, soil temperatures in the pots could drop to freezing on occasion. In some cases, roots in pots tend to cluster around the outside of the soil ball and cool even faster. The soil in ground-level beds is one continuous mass and will change temperature much less radically.

Terracing is a good technique for combining the advantages of growing in an elevated spot and keeping the roots in a large soil mass buffered from stressful extremes. The New Alchemy Institute has incorporated terraces into their Cape Cod Ark and recorded soil temperatures averaging around 53°F. at noon in midwinter. Note that terracing puts some of the soil mass into a vertical position so the soil can absorb more solar heat that way as well.

A soil thermometer is a good tool for learning about these aspects of the soil environment. They come with stems of various lengths. Since they respond quite rapidly, you can easily check points and depths all over the greenhouse in a short time.

One way to find out how much the air temperature varies in your greenhouse is to use maximum-minimum thermometers. Record the temperatures each day in a notebook. Be sure to

Photo 12-3: *Hangers, shelves, benches. Noti, Oregon.*

Photo 12-4: *Terraces, Cape Cod Ark.*

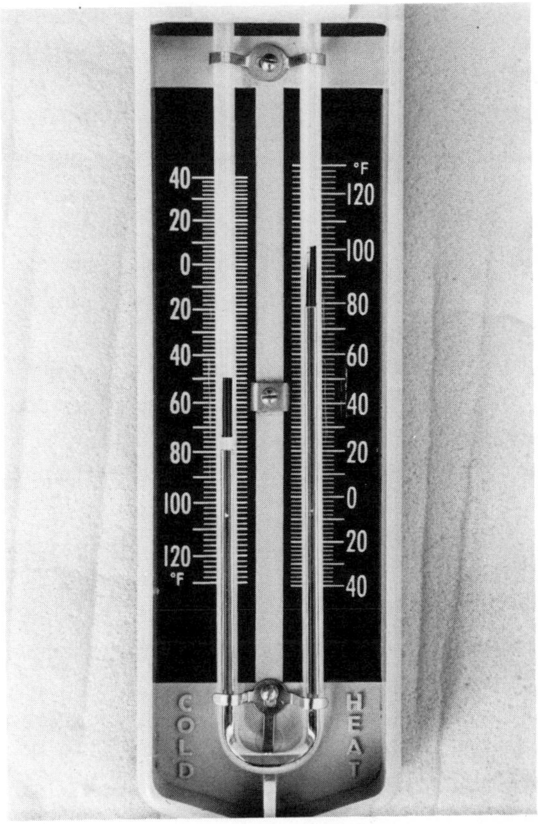

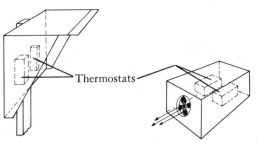

Photo 12-5: *Maximum—minimum thermometer.*

get an alcohol-filled rather than a mercury-filled thermometer. If you break a mercury-filled thermometer in a greenhouse, you may have to move out because the mercury fumes can be devastating to you and the plants. Be sure to shade the thermometer from direct sunlight and place it where the greatest mass of plants are, not just at a convenient eye level. You should realize that thermometers can be off several degrees when they first come from the factory, and therefore should be checked against water of a known temperature such as melting ice

Thermostats can be fan-ventilated when air temperature must be controlled precisely.

Figure 12-7: *Shading temperature control.*

(32°F. or 0°C.). Thermometers are slower to respond to temperature fluctuations caused by bright sun or cold air drafts than plant leaves because they have more mass per unit area. When a thermometer shows a maximum of 90°F. and a minimum of 50°F., the plant leaf may have fluctuated between 105°F. and 40°F. For most accurate temperature sensing, thermostats should be shaded or fan ventilated (Figure 12-7).

Record the temperatures each day in a notebook, along with the outside temperatures and weather notes. This will provide you with a good basis for developing your winter-gardening skill from year to year. If you are willing to check the greenhouse just before dawn each morning and again in early afternoon, you can get a good approximation of the daily high and low temperatures without a maximum-minimum thermometer.

You have several choices when temperatures fluctuate regularly into harmful extremes for the plants you are growing. At worst, you can close the place down for a while, either in the dead of winter or in the extreme heat of summer. Either time is good for roasting or freezing out insects and diseases, doing some general maintenance, or getting away on vacation. To date, however, experience has shown that there are some vegetables which can tolerate the coolest temperatures inside the solar greenhouse in most climates, though they may not be actively producing. These are the plants that will provide you with the earliest crops as the days begin to get longer at the end of winter.

Some people prefer to control temperature by supplementing energy (active system) and venting (active or passive system). The simplest is to use a fan to circulate air. This will make the air more uniformly warm between the top and bottom of the greenhouse. It will also put more heat into storage for night. Heaters can have a much more substantial effect. If the area is small, radiant heaters are the easiest way to concentrate the heat in one part of the greenhouse, for example, to charge the thermal mass. It is best

Percent Reduction in Fuel Use When Greenhouse Temperatures Are Lowered

	Present Greenhouse Temperature						
	65°F.			60°F.		55°F.	
	New Greenhouse Temperature						
Monthly Average Temp. (°F.)	60°F.	55°F.	50°F.	55°F.	50°F.	50°F.	45°F.
	Percent Reduction in Fuel Use						
20	11	22	33	12	24	14	28
24	12	24	36	14	28	16	32
28	13	26	39	16	32	19	38
32	15	30	45	18	36	22	44
36	17	34	51	21	42	26	52

Source: Harrison and Roberts. *Florist Notes*. Cook College, Rutgers University, December 1973.

Table 12-1: *Percent Reduction in Fuel Use When Greenhouse Temperatures Are Lowered.*

to have the supplemental heat controlled by a thermostat. Combustion heaters (wood, LP gas, oil, etc.) should be well vented to the outside to prevent buildup of pollutants. Plants are very sensitive to carbon monoxide, sulfur dioxide, PAN, and ethylene gases. Gas-fired heaters can be a significant source of ethylene. Tomatoes are very good indicators of even very low ethylene levels. Leaf edges cup down and the leaves become twisted at concentrations as low as 0.1 part gas per million parts air. Although the initial cost of electric heaters is usually less than gas heaters, the maintenance cost may be higher.

Most of all, choose varieties that suit the season and tolerate extremes. You can save considerably on your heating costs if you grow cool crops in the winter. The percent reduction in fuel use when greenhouse temperatures are lowered is shown in Table 12-1. If you are trying to grow in a passively heated greenhouse system with little or no fossil fuel, you will have to accept a greater fluctuation in temperature than when you have a backup heat source.

Atmosphere

The greenhouse atmosphere is composed of particles or moisture, carbon dioxide, other atmospheric gases (mainly nitrogen and oxygen), and perhaps some pollutants (gases or dusts). Moisture, which is expressed as relative humidity and carbon dioxide, have a profound effect on plant growth.

Normally, outside air contains .03 percent carbon dioxide, and for growth to be normal, plants need this minimum. Carbon dioxide from the air is a plant's only source of carbon, which makes up about half of its total dry weight. Actually, plants can use much more than the .03

percent which occurs naturally. Plants inside or outside will benefit from carbon-dioxide levels from .05 to .1 percent.

Besides sunlight and water, carbon dioxide is essential for photosynthesis. You have seen that adequate sunlight and water can be available inside a solar greenhouse in winter. However, if the greenhouse is tightly sealed on a cold, sunny day and it is filled with plants, then they may use up all available carbon dioxide within an hour or two of sunrise. Carbon dioxide must be supplied if the plants are to grow to their full potential.

There is another way to look at this. If the amount of carbon dioxide is doubled over normal levels, then photosynthesis during that time may be approximately doubled. In this sense, increasing carbon dioxide can offset partially the reduction of light in winter.

Scarcely any greenhouse will be absolutely airtight, so some carbon dioxide will come in with infiltering air. Still, an additional supply is essential. Attached greenhouses will have more carbon dioxide available due to greater infiltration from the home and from the breathing of the inhabitants. A half-dozen chickens were kept in the Maxatawny greenhouse. Though they certainly helped, the chickens probably did not bring the level of carbon dioxide up to the normal .03 percent. Carbon dioxide can also be supplied via dry ice, decaying organic matter, or ventilation.

Venting in midwinter brings much cold air into the greenhouse as well. To maintain normal carbon dioxide levels by venting, commercial greenhouses need a complete change of air at least every 10 minutes. During spring and fall when days are long, much more energy is available for plant growth and heat storage. Nights

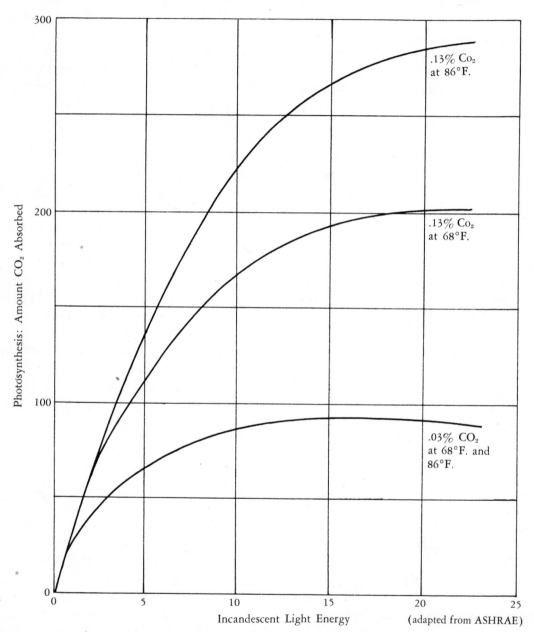

Figure 12-8: *Photosynthesis of cucumber leaf with CO_2 supplement.*

How Much CO₂ from Compost?

The amount cannot be predicted accurately because it will vary according to the materials used in each batch. But you can assume that the amount generated by a well-made pile will be substantial.

According to Clarence Golueke, a microbiologist at Berkeley who specializes in composting, the dry matter in a compost pile will lose one-third to one half of its weight over three weeks of active composting. Nearly all (95 percent) of that lost weight is carbon that has gone off as carbon-dioxide gas. Dry matter means that the weight of the water in the composting materials is ignored; typically the water accounts for 50 to 75 percent of the total weight of the usual manures and vegetable matter.

So if you have a bin that holds 200 pounds of wastes for compost, then roughly half that is water and the other hundred pounds is dry matter. That means that about 50 pounds of carbon will go into the air as carbon dioxide over three weeks if the composting is done properly. The process will also add heat and humidity to the environment.

The compost pile should be a fast one. It should be made of manures, vegetable waste, and hay, and turned every other day for ample aeration. If much woody material like straw or wood chips is used, the pile will need a richer source of nitrogen like extra manure. Even under the best circumstances, a pile with a lot of woody material in it will only give off one-third of its dry weight as carbon dioxide. If the materials are skillfully balanced, there should be very little nitrogen lost as gas. When a good pile has cooled down from 150° to around 100°F., then most of the rapid carbon-dioxide release is over.

Finished compost like this still has carbon in it, but it will break down very slowly. Used in potting mixes or soil for planting beds, however, soil microorganisms do continue to work on it and their digestion and respiration continue to provide an important source of carbon dioxide in the greenhouse.

Box 12-3: *How Much CO₂ From Compost?*

are not so severely cold. Under those conditions, venting can be a useful source of carbon dioxide and temperature control with no drain on the thermal performance of the greenhouse. Because venting touches on several important aspects of your greenhouse growing, it will be treated more fully later.

There is a considerable potential for carbon-dioxide supplementation through composting in the solar greenhouse. The pile should be kept active and be carefully made so that excess ammonia gas is not released into the air. This should not be a problem if manures and other high-nitrogen sources are balanced with ample dry matter like straw or hay. Compost temperatures should reach 140°F. to 160°F. which also will help the greenhouse stay warm.

The continual breakdown of organic matter in the soil by microorganisms is good reason for using plenty of finished compost in planting mixes. As the sun warms the soil, the activity of the microbes increases, another good use of solar energy. There is steady release of carbon dioxide from the growing media, though it is not nearly as high as from a composting pile. Bed plantings provide a great volume of soil organic matter slowly decomposing in the greenhouse. This is part of the reason for the bed-planting system at New Alchemy Institute and the CET

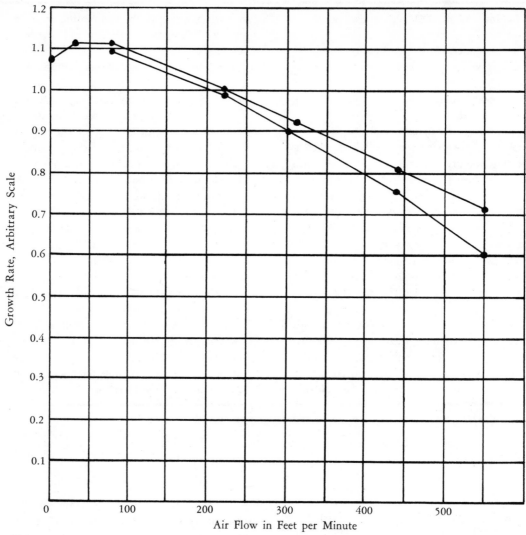

Slight air movement has a beneficial effect on growth probably because it enhances carbon dioxide exchange and transpiration. It also helps keep the leaves from overheating. Rapid agitation, however has a stunting effect.

Figure 12-9: *Effect of air movement on leaf growth.*

greenhouses. In the Maxatawny greenhouse, space under one of the benches holds a compost bin. See the CET greenhouse for details on how composting trenches may be arranged under-

neath catwalks. The pioneering work with composting by Dan Knapp is given special attention later in this section.

At least two experimenters have tried methane

digesters in the greenhouse. As for the compost pile, the greenhouse can give the digester the solar boost it needs in order to become active in winter. Carbon dioxide is one of the products. Jim Burgel built a greenhouse attached to the south side of a Minnesota dairy barn, and Ken Stauffer installed his in a small freestanding greenhouse near Boyertown, Pennsylvania. No information has come in yet about the true wintertime carbon-dioxide potential of digesters, but it is another tantalizing technique for future work. The carbon-dioxide problem must be solved if the solar greenhouse is to provide maximum plant growth.

Through tiny pores in the leaf, carbon dioxide enters from the air. When the air is quite still as in a passive greenhouse, there can be a film of air which is depleted of carbon dioxide around each leaf. A fan operated at the hours of maximum photosynthesis will break these films and distribute the available carbon dioxide through the greenhouse.

Most plant species grow best when the relative humidity of the air is between 30 and 70 percent. Below 30 percent, plant tissues, except in cacti and succulents, become dessicated. Above 70 percent, disease organisms are more likely to be a problem. A combination of high relative humidity and high temperatures can be especially harmful. A dog pants when it is hot; moisture evaporated from its tongue has a cooling effect. Similarly, a plant must lose moisture by transpiration to keep from overheating. A high relative humidity makes it harder for the plant to give water off to the air.

Because the solar greenhouse is kept tightly sealed in winter to prevent heat losses, high humidity can be a problem. An 80-percent humidity may be acceptable, but close attention must then be given to preventing diseases. Germinating seeds and unrooted cuttings need humidity near 100 percent. After the seedlings develop true leaves or roots have formed on cuttings, the humidity should be gradually reduced.

Ventilation is the best way to reduce the relative humidity when it is too high. As mentioned earlier, this will be no problem in much of the spring and the fall. During the summer in areas like the Southwest, venting for heat sometimes needs to be limited so that the greenhouse doesn't become too dry. In winter, venting should be avoided in all cold climates. Not only does it bring in cool air, but that air is also drier. Once in the greenhouse, it begins to absorb more moisture which has the effect of further cooling the greenhouse. Consider that when a pound of water (one pint) evaporates at 60°F., it absorbs more than 1,000 Btu's. But when the air becomes extremely humid, causing disease and overheating, some compromise will have to be made between energy conservation and humidity control.

For this reason, it is very important to water sparingly in winter. Excess water in the soil and spilled onto the floor will be evaporated as the sun's rays strike it and warm it. It is best to provide a way to collect excess water. Whenever possible, water-storage containers should be sealed. Bill and Marsha Mackie note that the warmth of their greywater makes for higher evaporation from the tank. It would help to cover it since there are no fish. CET has developed an effective drainage trap for large beds.

The relative humidity can vary greatly over 24 hours in a solar greenhouse. As the air warms in the morning, its moisture capacity increases. At the same time, sunlight and warmer temperatures

Relative Humidity

Relative humidity shows the change of seasons in the greenhouse clearly. The curves for Maxatawny are very similar through a week of varying weather outside, but weeks in early winter, late winter, and late spring are each distinct. Two forces are at work. Sunlight evaporates water and causes the plants to transpire, and warm air holds more water creating a lower relative humidity. The evaporation and transpiration effects dominate the mornings; maximum relative humidity generally occurs around 10:00 A.M. After that, the heating of the air takes over and causes the percent moisture in the air to drop until about 2:00 P.M. Then the cooling of the air lowers its capacity for moisture, and the relative humidity rises steadily till the lowest temperature occurs near dawn. The sharp drop in humidity before noon may possibly be influenced by a slowing of transpiration associated with photosynthesis due to a carbon-dioxide shortage.

The effects are the same in early winter and late winter, but have greater force during the longer days in March, as the curve shows dramatically. At warmer temperatures, evaporation and transpiration are much faster, and the sun makes the greenhouse hotter at noon. At the end of the week in March the greenhouse has become warm enough through 24 hours to force a lot of evaporation, but it does not heat enough during the day to drop the humidity. The week in May shows the effect of daily venting.

Box 12-4: *Relative Humidity*

increase evaporation from soil. The leaves transpire water into the air while photosynthesis

takes place. When the sun is gone, these activities cease, but the temperature drops as well. At a lower temperature, the air can hold less moisture, so the relative humidity rises. The accompanying humidity charts from the Maxatawny solar greenhouse show what actually happened and some of the variations between long and short days.

Humidity in attached greenhouses can be a boon in the wintertime, since most homes are much too dry. Proper ventilation will benefit both plants and people then. In warmer seasons, high humidity from the greenhouse could make the home uncomfortable and encourage mildew on furnishings.

Ventilation

Ventilation, as you have seen, cools the greenhouse, adds carbon dioxide, reduces the relative humidity, and mixes the air. In winter, you should manage your greenhouse so that the need to vent and lose heat is minimized. If an attached greenhouse seems to need winter venting, the amount of heat storage should be increased, and perhaps the vents into the home should be redesigned or supplemented with a fan. In a freestanding house, it may be necessary to vent any day of the year.

In spring, fall, and summer, adequate provisions for venting can make the very favorable environment in the solar greenhouse even better. Then, there is ample sunlight for good growth. Maintaining production temperatures at night is less of a problem for the heat-storage system. Ventilation can assure ample carbon dioxide and air mixing. In all but very arid climates, humidity can be controlled. David MacKinnon reports that in Flagstaff, the greenhouse can dry out very quickly if left wide open in summer.

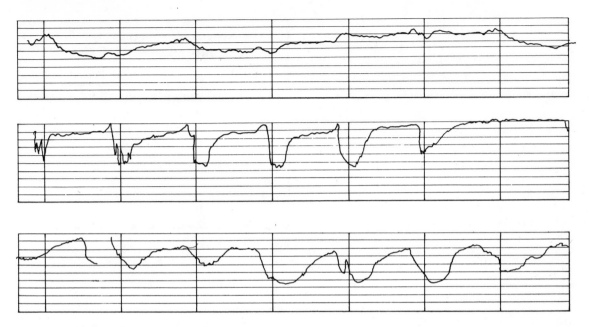

Figure 12-10: *Relative humidity.*

All solar greenhouse designs should be self-shading to reduce the tendency to overheat so that summertime venting can be accomplished with a minimum number of well-designed vents. Since cracks around vents are prime heat-loss areas, the venting system should use the least number of openings and be well-designed. Self-shading greenhouses will admit plenty of light in summer for growth, since the intensity of light is ample, except in extremely cloudy areas, and days are much longer.

If the heat becomes excessive, it can be reduced by shading all or part of the glazed area. Lath or Saran netting will partially block out the sun's heat. They are easy to remove. For attached greenhouses, a screen of plants like sunflowers or morning glories on a trellis seems to be

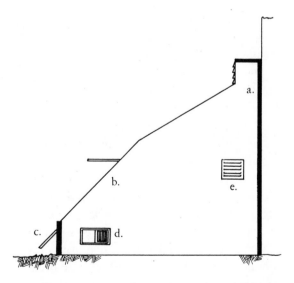

Figure 12-11: *Vent Locations: a. louvered stack; b. hinged vent; c. hinged and d. sliding to augment high, passive vents; e. fan.*

popular. They can do a fine job of keeping the greenhouse cool and at the same time are beautiful whether you are inside the greenhouse or out. Shading compounds, which are sprayed on the roof, are also available. When I was young and working in a greenhouse in Oklahoma, I made a weak solution with clay soil and spread it on with a broom. It didn't rain much, but after it did I would just put on another coat.

Irrigation

Watering plants grown in containers is more an art than a science. It is difficult to teach someone when to irrigate and how much water to use. Experience is the best teacher. The plant's moisture needs, the time of year, and kind of day affect how rapidly water is used up. The most critical periods for sufficient moisture in the life cycle of certain vegetables is given in column 2 of Box 12-5. Using a uniform soil mixture and the same type of pot for most of your plants will greatly simplify the learning process.

More plants are overwatered, in the name of "playing it safe." But when the soil or medium is too wet, a lack of oxygen causes parts of the root system to die. The dead cells provide an easier path of entry to the plant for disease organisms than live tissue does.

A well-prepared medium will greatly promote proper drainage. The mixes given in the following section should provide sufficient pore space so that they will not be overwatered easily.

Container size and composition have a significant effect on how often you will need to irrigate. The soil pores at the bottom will be filled with water regardless of the container's depth. The deeper the container, the longer the column of pores which are filled with air after

Life Stages of Vegetables When Adequate Water Is Critical	
Vegetable	**Critical Period**
Bean	Pollination and pod development
Beet	Root enlargement
Broccoli	Head development
Cauliflower	Head development
Cucumber	Flowering and fruit development
Eggplant	Flowering and fruit development
Lettuce	Head development
Onion	Bulb enlargement

Box 12-5: *Life Stages of Vegetables when Adequate Water is Critical*

the excess water drains away. The effect is that a shallow container holds less total available water, but is more easily overwatered than a deep container of the same volume. Therefore, a large plant growing in a shallow container requires frequent irrigation but must have a well-drained soil mix to avoid overwatering.

Plants grown in clay containers, which are porous, require more frequent irrigation than plants grown in plastic or metal containers. Some growers tap the side of a clay pot and irrigate when there is a hollow ring rather than a dull thud sound. The hollow ring indicates that the soil mix has shrunk away from the sides of the clay pot. Since it is not feasible to do the sound test with a plastic pot, you may feel the soil surface or pick up the pot and test its weight to determine wetness. A hard soil surface, lighter colored soil, or lighter weight all indicate a reduced moisture content.

Watering beds in the greenhouse will be different than pots in several respects. If the bed is completely contained, be sure to make provisions for drainage. Drainage in beds will be much slower; the sides may tend to dry sooner

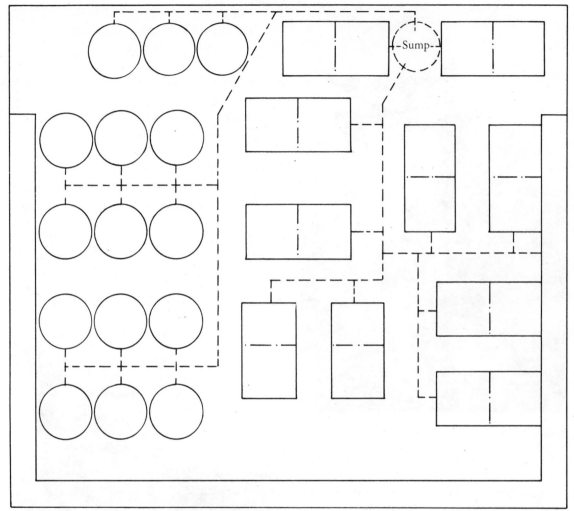

This is one scheme for providing drainage and collection of excess water. Tubing runs from the bottom of growing beds and tubs to a collection sump. All tubing should be recessed into the floor and sloped slightly into the sump. See the CET greenhouse in "The Freestanding Greenhouse" chapter for a drainage system suitable for large beds.

Figure 12-12: *Drainage system.*

than the center. If the greenhouse encloses the original ground so that it can be used for planting, there will be natural percolation. The sides of the foundation, however, will be fairly waterproof. If the soil outside is saturated or frozen, drainage in the greenhouse may be slower than expected.

The most important step in watering is to be thorough. Unused fertilizers migrate to the soil surface with the evaporating water. Unless the

Photo 12-6: *Irrigation, Farrallones Institute.*

as a conductivity meter. They measure the flow of electricity (conductance) in a salt solution. Since fertilizers are salts, the dissolved fertilizers carry a current of electricity. The more fertilizer in solution, the more current is conducted. So in a cup of distilled water, most of them will register dry. Add a very small pinch of salt and the meter will move toward the wet side of the dial. As a soil mix becomes drier, the fertilizers in solution become more concentrated and the meter reads drier. If all of your media have the same concentration of fertilizer, the meter will

Photo 12-7: *Ground-level beds and higher benches, Cape Cod Ark.*

soil is watered thoroughly, the migrating salts accumulate and may injure plant roots.

When soil dries, it may shrink away from the sides of the container. To make sure that some excess water flows through the soil mass, it may be necessary to double-water. The first watering expands the soil mass, filling the voids between the medium and containers. The second irrigation leaches out the unused salts and wets the whole soil mass.

Commercial irrigation meters may help you determine when to water, but you should be aware that they may not be consistently accurate. These meters all work on the same principle—

indicate relatively similar moisture for that salt condition. But, if the fertilizer concentration varies from pot to pot, the meter reading could be indicating dryness when in fact the soil was wet but the fertilizers were more concentrated.

Containers

Greenhouse crops can be grown directly in ground beds if the soil has been prepared properly and adequate drainage provided. Beds permit roots to range wide for nutrients. Most crops are grown in some type of container, either raised beds or pots. Large plants with deep roots need a substantial volume of soil for adequate development. A mature tomato, cucumber, or plant of like size will need a soil volume equal to a gallon container. Seeds can be sown and seedlings grown in containers two to three inches deep.

Almost any material is fine, as long as you create some drainage. Egg cartons, milk cartons, or other shallow plastic containers left over from kitchen use can be used for seed starting or for transplanting seedlings or cuttings. Quart-size cottage cheese or ice cream containers can be used for growing herbs, lettuce, cabbage, spinach, radishes, or strawberries to maturity. Half-gallon bleach bottles or ice cream cartons are suitable for mature dwarf tomatoes, green peppers, eggplants, onions, carrots, beets, chard, or rhubarb. Gallon tubs or large fruit baskets lined with plastic are needed for squash, cucumbers, potatoes, and standard-sized tomatoes. Drainage holes should be made in the bottom of all containers and additional holes in the lower sides of large containers.

For most efficient use of space, start seedlings together in containers and plan to transplant just

Photo 12-8: *Started in flats, transplanted to cans. Circle, Montana.*

the number you need as they get larger. Putting small plants into big containers will result in much unused space. Beds use the planting area well since there is open soil between large plants which can accommodate succession transplants.

Growing Media

Greenhouse crops will grow in a wide range of substrates. Especially in such a small, artificial environment, the growing medium you start with should be free of insects, nematodes, weed seed, and disease-causing organisms. Good drainage and porosity are particularly important for pot-grown crops. Remember, the smaller and the more shallow the container, the more critical it is to provide good drainage and porosity.

Soil-borne pests such as insects, nematodes, weed seed, and disease-causing organisms are best killed by pasteurization, heating the medium to 140° to 180°F. for 30 minutes. Sterilization means killing all organisms while pasteurization means killing only harmful organisms. The following temperatures, used for 30 minutes, are effective in controlling various soil pests:

Pests	Temperatures (°F.)
Nematodes	120
Damping-off and soft rots	130
Pathogenic bacteria and fungi	150
Soil insects and most viruses	160
Most weed seeds	170
Beneficial bacteria and some viruses	180+

Aerated steam is best for pasteurization; few people have equipment for this process, however. Oven cooking is the next best method. Be careful not to cook the medium too long or at too high temperatures. The reasons for not using 212°F. heat (boiling) and long periods of time is that this high temperature kills the necessary beneficial bacteria that are essential for the conversion of organic nitrogen to usable nitrate forms. In some soils, the higher the temperature and the longer the soil is heated, the more potentially toxic chemicals are released. Manganese and ammonium are among the most

likely chemicals to be released at high temperatures. Additions of gypsum to the medium before planting, followed by leaching (thorough irrigation), will usually remove much of the potentially toxic ammonium and other salts.

For most effective pasteurization, the soil should be moist and have no large clods. By keeping the soil moist for a few days before heating, weed seeds start germinating and thus are easier to kill. The smaller the soil particles, the quicker the heat can penetrate. That doesn't mean you should make the soil into dust, but you should break up the larger clods.

Well-made compost should not need artificial pasteurization. First of all, the heat of composting may reach pasteurization temperatures (140° to 160°F.). Unless all parts of the pile reach this temperature, pest control will not be absolute, but it will be good. Second, pasteurization can cause loss of nitrogen, an essential nutrient. Tend the pile carefully, let it cure well, and compost should not be a cause of insect or disease problems. Compost can be a valuable source for reintroducing many kinds of valuable beneficial organisms to soil that you have pasteurized.

Perlite and vermiculite, which are used as coarse aggregate amendments, should be sterile in the bag, because these minerals are expanded at high temperatures. However, once the bag is opened, they can become contaminated. Coarse sand is a commonly used aggregate amendment, but it is heavy. In large containers, it will be hard to work with and may hasten compaction.

Do not assume that bagged or baled peat is free of harmful organisms. Although the low pH (3.0 to 4.0) of sphagnum moss usually reduces the chances that it contains harmful

---

Test for Weed Killers

If you have to buy soil or get some from your neighbor's lot, and you suspect there may be some residue in the soil, you can test it to see if weed killer is still present. Prepare two flats of soil and mix 1 tablespoon of activated charcoal throughly into one of the flats. Plant some oats, 10 to 15 seeds, in each flat, with the germ end down. Water both and observe the growth. After the oats are up, reduce watering to induce stress on the plant. If both flats of oats look the same after 14 days, you can be reasonably sure that weed killers haven't contaminated the soil. If, however, the oats in the soil without charcoal become yellow and the tips turn grey or twist, then suspect an herbicide. Do not use this soil. For a more complete test, divide the flat, sow tomato seeds in half of it, and proceed as with oats. Tomato seed takes longer to germinate but it is even more sensitive to weed killer residue than oats.

(From *Organic Gardening Under Glass*, George and Katy Abraham)

Box 12-6: *Test for Weed Killers*

bacteria, or fungi, it does not eliminate insects or weed seed. Native humus peats also may contain harmful agents.

Loamy field soil should be used when possible. If you don't know the land where you get it, be wary of possible contamination with herbicides often used on farms and along roadbanks.

Greenhouse growing media are usually made from combinations of field soil, organic matter (compost and peat), and coarse aggregates (vermiculite, perlite, sand). The heavier the soil, the more organic matter should be added.

Some typical mixtures are:

1 part clay loam soil
2 parts organic matter
2 parts coarse aggregate

1 part loam soil
1 part organic matter
1 part coarse aggregate

2 parts sandy loam soil
2 parts organic matter

These mixtures should be blended carefully without breaking down the larger particles which supply the pore space.

Essential Mineral Nutrients

Plants require minute to large quantities of 16 essential elements. When I was a student, only nine were considered essential, but in the past 30 years, seven more minerals have been proven essential. Perhaps others will be added in the future as we learn more about the chemistry of plants—all the more reason to use organic materials made by plants from all the things they need, instead of artificial preparations which contain only the things a man has put into them.

The essential elements are boron (B), carbon (C), calcium (Ca), chlorine (Cl), copper (Cu), iron (Fe), hydrogen (H), potassium (K), magnesium (Mg), manganese (Mn), molybdenum (Mo), nitrogen (N), oxygen (O), phosphorus (P), sulfur (S), and zinc (Zn). To determine the quantities of nutrients to add to your growing medium, you should have the soil tested. The test will refer to these

Photo 12-9: *Hydroponic Beds. Washington, D.C.*

trace elements such as boron, molybdenum, copper, manganese, zinc, or iron. Deep-rooted plants absorb these elements and incorporate them in their stems and leaves. When these decompose, they release very small (trace) quantities of the elements slowly back into the soil solution in the range of shallow-rooted plants. Part of the growing medium should be composed of leaf mold or compost to provide a source of the microelements.

Plants need larger quantities of phosphorus, potassium, sulfur, calcium, and magnesium than can easily be supplied by decomposing organic matter alone. These chemicals are called macronutrients. Greenhouse crops have difficulty getting sufficient macronutrients because their roots cannot extend out over large areas as they might when planted outdoors. Since the greenhouse crop is grown in a limited volume of medium, it removes the available moisture faster and must be irrigated more often. The more frequent irrigations leach out some of the macroelements. Consequently, more concentrated organic supplements will stimulate greater vigor and growth. These can be incorporated into the soil before planting or surface-applied (dry or in solution) after planting. Some of the sources of macroelements include:

A. *Nitrogen*

Manure teas will add nitrogen, potassium, some phosphorus, and trace minerals. Fish emulsion, blood meal, and seaweed concentrates also make fine solutions (or tea) for supplementing nitrogen. Blood meal, fish meal, soybean meal, and similar concentrates along with dried manures can also be incorporated into the soil mix prior to planting. The amount of each nutrient these materials contain will be

basic elements by their abbreviated names. It will also tell the pH of the soil, that is, its acidity (sourness) or alkalinity (sweetness).

The carbon and some oxygen come from carbon dioxide (CO_2). The hydrogen and some oxygen come from water (H_2O). Nitrogen can come from the atmosphere, being fixed in the soil by legumes, or from decaying organic matter like hay, blood meal, or manure. The other elements are naturally occurring minerals in the soil.

Decomposing organic matter is also one of the best balanced sources of micronutrients or

Organic Hydroponics

Organic hydroponics has some application in most solar greenhouses. By hydroponics is meant any plant feeding that uses formulated nutrient solution rather than just fertile soil and water. For the urban gardener, a completely hydroponic system may be the best way to set up a growing area.

One reason is that container-grown plants will have less soil in which to forage for the nutrients they need. Putting organic forms of these elements into an irrigation solution is a fine way to supplement controlled amounts of the essential elements.

In the city, enough good soil to stock a rooftop greenhouse is hard to come by. It will be far easier to carry the amount of vermiculite and perlite needed to fill beds and pots up to the roof than a like amount of soil. The weight of an artificial medium will be much less strain on the roof structure.

There are many ways to blend nutrients. Manure and compost teas are routinely used by all gardeners and certainly will do as well for greenhouse hydroponics. Know the com-

position of the starting materials to get the right balance of nutrients for the plants you have. Watch the pH too.

At rooftop gardening projects in Montreal and at the Institute for Local Self-Reliance in Washington, D.C., organic gardeners have done well using a nutrient solution made of 1 tablespoon each of liquid seaweed and fish emulsion and 1 teaspoon of blood meal in each gallon of water. Both those experiments also report good results with a medium of half perlite and half vermiculite to support the roots. In the ILSR greenhouse, the medium is a little more than a foot deep and contained in large plywood beds.

Hydroponic containers should be waterproofed and well drained. There should be some provisions for collecting excess nutrient solution. If light materials like the expanded minerals are used, the surface should be contained in some way, for example, with a fabric or wire mesh to keep water drops or spray from dislodging particles of medium and disturbing the plants. Drip irrigation methods are commonly used to feed plants in commercial hydroponic systems.

Box 12-7: *Organic Hydroponics*

stated on the package, if they are sold as fertilizer. Note that fish emulsion makes an alkaline solution.

B. *Phosphorus*

Bone meal, raw or steamed, is a source of a little nitrogen and 20- to 30-percent phosphoric acid. Ground phosphate rock and colloidal phosphate respectively contain 30- to 50- and 18- to 30-percent phosphoric acid.

C. *Potassium*

Wood ashes are a good, though variable,

source of potassium containing 3- to 7-percent potash and 1- to 2-percent phosphorus. Granite dust and greensand provide 3- to 5- and 6- to 7-percent potassium, respectively. Superior greensand deposits also contain iron, magnesium, calcium, and phosphorus.

D. *Sulfur*

Sulfur can be fixed in the soil from the atmosphere by certain bacteria. Industrial air pollutants often add sulfur to fields. Gypsum (calcium sulfate) is a natural soil conditioner and a source of both calcium and sulfur.

E. *Calcium*

Ground limestone is the main natural source of calcium. The finer it is ground, the more readily available the calcium. For greenhouse crops, 80 percent of the limestone should pass a 100-mesh screen and 50 percent should pass through a 200-mesh screen. Limestone additions should be based on pH measurements of the soil because it will make the soil more alkaline. Each crop has a particular soil pH range which produces maximum yield and quality.

F. *Magnesium*

Ground dolomitic limestone is a natural source of both calcium and magnesium. You must specify high magnesium or dolomitic limestone to get the higher magnesium balance. Vermiculite is a source of small quantities of magnesium and potassium.

Insects and Disease

These are an accepted part of greenhouse maintenance. The more you can do to prevent pests from getting started, the further ahead you will be. The first step in control is to be a good observer and identify the pests properly. Get a good 10× magnifying glass and carry it with you when you go into the greenhouse. Inspect the plants each day. You should take a close look at both tops and bottoms of leaves, the stems, and roots at least once a week. Many times you can eliminate pests if you find and manually kill the first few invaders before they get a foothold.

Sanitation and cleanliness—kitchen clean— go a long way toward prevention. Besides using resistant varieties and rotating crops, it's about your only real defense against disease. Insects and previously infected plants are often the carriers of disease, especially viruses. Here are a few reminders:

1. Clean up trash in and around the greenhouse. Slugs, snails, and other pests like to hide in trash. That holds for weeds, too. Many insects and diseases live on the weeds which can be a continuous source of these pests.
2. Pick off dead leaves and discard infected plant parts. If severely infected, discard whole plants rather than risk contaminating the whole greenhouse.
3. Keep the air circulating. Stagnant air can promote and be a source of disease organisms. Keep plants well spaced for good air circulation.
4. Use only disease-resistant plant varieties.
5. Isolate new plants for observation before bringing them into the greenhouse.
6. Use only sterile containers and pasteurized soil mixes. Before reusing pots, clean off all soil particles. Then boil or soak them in a solution of 1 part Clorox to 10 parts water for 30 minutes. Sterilize tools after working with any suspected diseased plant.
7. Hang up the watering hose to keep from spreading diseases which might be picked up on the end of the hose nozzle.
8. Wash hands and use washable aprons for the same reason.
9. Do not smoke in the greenhouse. Viruses are spread from tobacco to other plants, especially tomatoes.

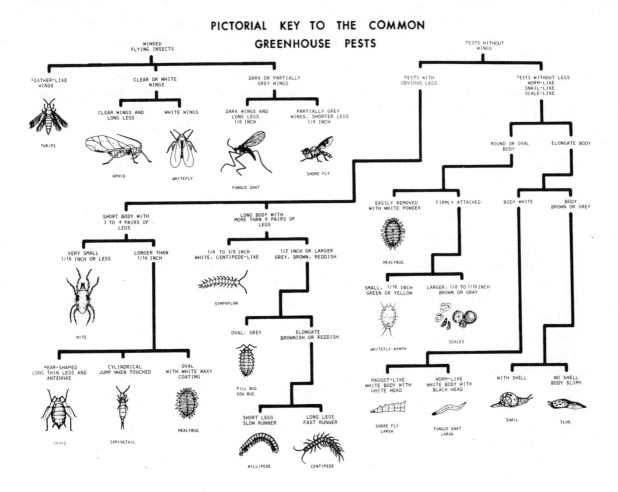

PICTORIAL KEY TO THE COMMON GREENHOUSE PESTS

Figure 12-13: *Insect pest profiles.*

Identification and Control of Insects and Animals

Aphids (plant lice) suck plant juices and excrete honeydew on which may grow a black fungus. Aphids give birth to living young. Ants use aphids as we use cows and will carry them from one plant to another. Aluminum foil around a plant will not only reflect more sunlight onto a plant, but also confuse some insects. Aphids fly into the foil, land upside down, and are not able to fly away. Some think the aphids see the foil as the sky and try to fly towards it. Ladybugs are predators of aphids. Nicotine spray is a good natural chemical control. Don't use tobacco juice on tomatoes.

Gnats (fungus or root gnats) are small black-flies, the larvae of which feed on plant roots. Tobacco juice (nicotine) and vinegar have been used as soil drenches for suppression of the larvae. Starting with pest-free soil is the best control.

Mealybugs are white, cottony-like small insects which suck out plant sap and secrete a honeydew. Spray with nicotine, pyrethrum, Naphtha soap, or touch each insect with a cotton swab soaked in rubbing alcohol.

Spider mites (two-spotted or red spider) are microscopic-sized mites (not spiders because they have six legs) which suck out plant juices. Mites do not like water or low temperatures. Syringing the undersides of leaves with a strong stream of water will dislodge them. Adding soap or detergent to the water will help water penetrate their webs and the trichomes (hairs) of some plant leaves. Try 1 ounce of detergent to 10 ounces of water.

Nematodes (eelworms) are microscopic, transparent worms that invade plant roots and cause knots on the roots. Pasteurization of the soil and clean plants are the best methods of prevention. Destroy infected plants and throw out the soil surrounding their roots.

Slugs are slimy, greyish animals. As they crawl, they leave a glistening trail which is easily seen by flashlight. Slugs eat plant leaves, roots, and flowers. Yeast cakes, rubbing alcohol, and beer are favored foods and so make good baits. Put a layer of table salt in a can or jar lid, and add yeast or alcohol. Slugs will also crawl into lids full of beer and drown.

Thrips are tiny, white, transparent jumping insects that are hard to catch. They rasp off the top layers of plant cells causing damage and providing points for disease invasion. They usually don't stay around very long but can be very damaging in a short period of time. Pyrethrum and rotenone may scare them away.

White flies are small flies that look like a miniature snowstorm when present in large populations. They hide on the underside of leaves where they lay eggs. Try attracting them with pieces of yellow paper or cloth, then sweep them up with a vacuum cleaner or paint the yellow surface with a sticky substance such as Ced-O-Flora oil. Also consider trying a parasite called *Encarsia formosa.*

Worms or caterpillars can be controlled with *Bacillus thuringiensis,* a bacterial disease specifically harmful to certain caterpillers. Strains are available under the names Biotrol, Dipel, and Thuricide. This bacteria is believed to be non-toxic to humans, animals, fish, or birds.

General Control Methods

Once a population of insects gets hold in the greenhouse, it will be much harder to eliminate them than killing individuals. They will be present in all stages of growth from egg through mature adults, and some of the stages will be almost impossible to find. More active controls, probably a combination of them, will be necessary to control an epidemic. Though they may never be eliminated until you close the greenhouse down to freeze, cook, or starve them out, constant attention can reduce their numbers to levels your crops can tolerate.

Predators include ladybugs, praying mantis, braconid wasps, green lacewings, trichogramma wasps, frogs, toads, and salamanders. Some will eat only one type of pest insect. There must always be a supply of the prey for them to live in the greenhouse. Predators are not cheap nor are they always easy to get.

Devise traps for the insects. A few have been mentioned. Observe the pest's habits and give the problem some thought. Sometimes, for example, they will show great preference for one kind of plant. If these are brought into the greenhouse, the pests will gradually move off crops and onto their favorite. Periodically discard trap plants as they fill up with pests.

Natural plant chemicals are biodegradable, that is, they break down quickly. The application must be repeated often. The best of these are rotenone, nicotine, and pyrethrum.

Marigolds, garlic, chives, various herbs, and other companion plants may repel certain insects. The best way to learn which to use is trial and error.

Chapter Thirteen

Crops for the Solar Greenhouse

John White

As you plan a planting schedule, keep in mind that no matter what the region, you have two distinct crops in the solar greenhouse. First are the plants that you will grow for harvest in the greenhouse, and there may be some of these all year long. Then there are the transplants you start for the garden outside. You must reserve space or be ready to make plenty of room for these. In warmer climates, the solar greenhouse may be cleared out in the summer months, except perhaps for rooting cuttings, because it gets so hot and the outdoor season is long enough that it isn't needed for food then. In the North, the greenhouse may stay chock-full all year. Juggling the space for the cropping cycles may require several seasons before you feel comfortable with a system. In any case, a solar greenhouse is likely to mean more intense gardening activity over a much longer season rather than quiet puttering on a January evening.

For the kitchen, the greenhouse will bring in a longer harvest of your favorite vegetables. It can be managed like a storehouse of living food if the vegetables planted to mature in late summer and picked into early winter. Almost every region can count on salads and some greens through the winter, from the reports we have received. In spring, the variety of food will start again in the greenhouse and continue from the

Photo 13-1: *Mature crops and garden seedlings.*

large transplants you can produce for the outdoor garden.

264

Photo 13-2: *Late-summer planted kale, spinach, and lettuce in early spring.*

Photo 13-3: *Lettuce in solar pod.*

Begin with those crops you and your family enjoy eating as you plan what to grow. It may be easy to grow radishes in winter, but why plant a lot of radishes if you don't particularly like them? Some crops fill too much space with leaves for the amount of fruit they produce. Except for an occasional treat—cantalopes or green soybeans in the far North—leave crops of pumpkins, squash, corn, potatoes, lima beans, and fennel to the outdoor garden.

Though all this planting and transplanting might sound slightly mysterious, it isn't. Any kind of gardening which involves a wide variety of plants simply requires some experience. Start with a cold frame, and learn how to winter garden. The scale can be small or large with cold frames. Use one or several bed-sized frames. Work your way into a walk-in sized frame. The cold frame can provide you with a substantial amount of food—that is determined only by its size. Crops like kale, collards, endive, lettuce, parsley, and chives will thrive well past the first freezing weather and begin to produce again in the first days of spring inside a cold frame. The experience will teach you which cold-hardy crops you like, as well as timing for both winter gardening and starting you own garden plants from seed. Leandre and Gretchen Poisson have picked lettuce all through New Hampshire's winter from a solar cold frame. They also report that tomatoes, peppers (heat-loving plants), and leeks sown directly into the ground under a cold frame germinated and grew into fine plants for the garden. Depending on your climate and preferences in vegetables, some kind of cold-frame system may be all you need. A cold frame is also a useful tool for hardening plants for the garden as they are ready to move out of the solar greenhouse.

Accept the natural rhythm of seasonal change and plant growth response to the changes. Passively heated solar greenhouses have greater temperature variations than those with back-up heat sources and automatic ventilators. The vegetables you grow must tolerate these extremes. Although some crops may grow well in areas with more winter sun, growth will still be slower than in spring or fall because of shorter days. Growth will slow down in mid-

Photo 13-4: *Chinese cabbage and parsley (CET).*

summer too, if there is heat stress. A cool-season crop is more than one that grows best with cool temperatures. The flavor of many of these crops is significantly improved if they mature when it's cool.

The length of day has a major effect on the growth habits of some vegetables. Chinese cabbage and some varieties of spinach or radish "bolt" (set flowers) when the days are longer than 12 hours. These crops do well when planted so that most of the growth occurs as the days are getting shorter. Some of the newer

nonbolting radish varieties can be grown in the spring and summer.

For vegetables grown to harvest in the greenhouse, the early-spring crop is the most productive in any region because days are lengthening as the crop matures. Plants seem to start growing faster after about the 21th of February, as the days approach 12 hours of light and the nights begin to warm slowly. So these crops should be ready to transplant into individual containers around the end of February. This means sowing the seed a month earlier, perhaps under fluorescent lights if the days are heavily overcast.

Transplants for the garden, of course, should be started in accord with the date of your last average frost. Seedlings transplanted into containers can be grown quite large inside before transplanting with little shock. However, growth won't be rapid until outside soil temperatures warm to the plant's liking. Be sure to harden the plants off before moving them into the garden (See Box 13-1).

The fall and winter food crops in the greenhouse should be started early enough so that plants are well established and fairly large before October 21. After October 21, the days are much shorter than the nights, the greenhouse admits more direct light, and the night temperatures are harder to maintain. Most of the fall crop should either be sown in August or moved in from the outdoor garden before the night or soil temperatures fall below each plant's desired minimum. The biggest problem with bringing crops in from the patio or garden is the risk of bringing insects and disease, too. Check them carefully.

Some of the winter crop can be started in the fall. These two crops tend to overlap. Long-

Planting Chart for Greenhouse Vegetables

Vegetables	Best pH	Depth to plant seed (inches)	No. of seeds to sow per gallon container	Distance between plants (inches)	No. of days to germination	Weeks needed to grow to transplant size	Days to maturity	Temperature range for germination (degrees Fahrenheit)
Beans: bush snap	6.8	1½–2	6–8	2–3	6–14	NT	45–65	70–80
pole snap	6.8	1½–2	4–6	4–6	6–14	NT	60–70	70–80
bush lima	6.0	1½–2	5–8	3–6	7–12	NT	60–80	70–80
pole lima	6.0	1½–2	4–5	6–10	7–12	NT	85–90	70–80
Windsor bean	6.2	2½	5–8	3–4	7–14	NT	80–90	70–80
Beets	6.5	½–1	10–15	2	7–10	NT	55–65	65–75
Broccoli, sprouting	6.5	½	10–15	14–18	3–10	5–7	60–80T	60–75
Brussels sprouts	6.2	½	10–15	12–18	3–10	4–6	80–90T	65–80
Cabbage	6.5	½	8–10	12–20	4–10	5–7	65–95T	65–80
Cabbage, Chinese	6.2	½	8–16	10–12	4–10	4–6	80–90	65–75
Carrot	6.0	¼	15–20	1–2	10–17	NT	60–80	60–80
Cauliflower	6.5	½	8–10	18	4–10	5–7	55–65T	65–80
Chard, Swiss	6.5	1	6–10	4–8	7–10	NT	55–65	65–75
Chives	6.0	½	8–10	8	8–12	NT	80–90	60–70
Collards	6.5	¼	10–12	10–15	4–10	4–6	65–85T	70–80
Cress, garden	6.0	¼	10–12	2–3	4–10	NT	25–45	60–70
Cucumber	7.0	1	3–5	12	6–10	4	55–65	70–90
Eggplant	5.5	¼–½	8–12	18	7–14	6–9	75–95T	70–90
Fennel, Florence	6.2	½	8–12	6	6–17	NT	120	60–75
Kale	6.5	½	8–12	8–12	3–10	4–6	55–80	60–75
Kohlrabi	6.5	½	8–12	3–4	3–10	4–6	60–70	65–75
Lettuce: head	7.0	¼–½	4–8	12–14	4–10	3–5	55–80	60–75
leaf	7.0	¼–½	8–12	4–6	4–10	3–5	45–60	60–75
Muskmelon	6.0	1	3–6	12	4–8	3–4	75–100	75–95
Onions: sets	6.0	1–2	DA	2–3	DA	DA	95–120	DA
plants	6.0	2–3	DA	2–3	DA	DA	95–120T	DA
seed	6.0	½	75	½	7–12	8	100–165	60–75
Parsley	6.0	¼–½	10–15	3–6	14–28	8	85–90	55–75
Peas	7.0	2	6–7	2–3	6–15	NT	65–85	50–70
Peppers	6.5	¼	6–8	18–24	10–20	6–8	60–80T	70–85
Radish	7.0	½	14–16	1–2	3–10	NT	20–50	60–80
Spinach	6.5	½	10–12	2–4	6–14	NT	40–65	60–80
Malabar	ND	½	4–6	12	10	NT	70	60–80
New Zealand	ND	1½	4–6	18	5–10	NT	70–80	60–80
tampala	ND	¼–½	6–10	4–6	ND	NT	21–42	60–80
Tomato	6.0	½	6	18–36	6–14	5–7	55–90T	65–80

T Number of days from setting out transplants
NT Not normally transplanted
ND No data
DA Does not apply

Box 13-1: *Planting Chart for Greenhouse Vegetables*

Photo 13-5: *Spinach for salads. Maxatawny, Pennsylvania.*

term vegetables like tomatoes, peppers, onions, and Brussels sprouts are best started in mid-summer so they can reach maturity in fall. Cold-tolerant plants such as the cole crops, lettuce, endive, parsnips, artichokes, and spinach can be started later for reaching maturity either in fall or in late winter. The cold-tolerant vegetables grow slowly but are not harmed by the low light and occasional cold nights in midwinter. Brought to maturity in mid-autumn, the food will remain fresh (though growing little) until you need it.

In some parts of the country in the summer the solar greenhouse might not be used except for root cuttings or tropical house plants. However, there are special situations or regions where the greenhouse may be necessary for certain summer vegetables. At higher elevations or wherever the temperatures drop into the 50s at night, some crops will not develop properly. In these cases you may want to try growing melons of all kinds, sweet corn, cucumbers, okra, squash, peppers, eggplant, and tomatoes in the green-house. Be sure to open the house up during the day for cooling and for allowing insects and wind to pollinate these crops.

When the greenhouse is closed tight, crops such as squash, cucumbers, tomatoes, and straw-berries can be hand-pollinated. Tomatoes and strawberries need only be flicked lightly with your finger. Squash or melons require the trans-fer of pollen from the male flower to the female flower. Some people use a fine-bristled paint-brush and others use a chicken feather as a pollinator. Cucumbers also have male and fe-male flowers, but many of the newer European varieties will grow fruit without fertilization. Some plants do not set fruit even though they have been properly pollinated. Factors which affect pollination and early fruit development are the variety, temperatures high (above 90°F.) or low (below 50°F.), relative humidity, and soil-related stresses. For best fertilization and fruit set of peppers, tomatoes, eggplants, and some beans, keep the air temperature between 60° and 80°F., the soil moist, and relative hu-midity between 40 and 60 percent, and avoid adding too much fertilizer in the soil.

Here is a scheme for planting seed of selected popular vegetables in a solar greenhouse for year-round cropping.

Seasonal Effects of Light and Temperature on Rate of Growth in Solar Greenhouse

Recommended Crop
Temperature (°F. at night)

	45	Actual Average Temperatures (°F. at night) 55	65
		Midwinter (low light) *Added Time from Sowing to Maturity (%)*	
65	100	50*	25
55	50**	25	0*
45	25	0*	0*
		Spring or Fall (good light) *Added Time from Sowing to Maturity (%)*	
65	50**	25	0
55	25	0	0*
45	0	0*	0*

*Cropping time may not be lost when higher than normal temperatures are used, but quality may be reduced or the crop may not mature properly.

**If a crop is supposed to mature in 25 days, 50-percent added time means it will take about 37 days to reach the same stage of maturity with the lower temperature or light conditions.

Box 13-2: *Seasonal Effects of Light and Temperature on Rate of Growth in Solar Greenhouse*

Summer

Seed in July
tomato (for continuous harvest)
pepper
eggplant
Brussels sprouts

Seed in August
cabbage (for continuous harvest)
broccoli
kale
kohlrabi
lettuce
parsley
spinach (for early-winter harvest)

Fall

Seed in September
Chinese cabbage (for late-winter harvest)
celery

Seed in October
lettuce (for continuous harvest)
fall radishes
dandelion
herbs (for garden transplants)
onions, leeks

Winter

Seed in February
beans (for spring harvest)

spinach
cauliflower (for spring harvest or garden trans-
    plants)
chives
chard
tomatoes
peppers
eggplant
broccoli

Spring

Seed in May
cucumbers (for transplants to the garden or
    summer greenhouse harvest)
squash
melons
eggplant
pepper
pumpkin
corn

Of course, there will be overlaps in the planting and harvesting season, as outlined, depending on the climate in your region. Optimum
planting dates may be earlier or later. For some
vegetables, successive sowings may produce the
best results.

The plan Pragtree Farm is following is an
interesting example of what the greenhouse
might do for gardeners on the mild but extremely cloudy Northwest coast. The gardeners
at the farm plan two distinct crops. Cold-hardy
vegetables such as lettuce, spinach, and Chinese
cabbage are established in the fall for harvest beginning in late winter. Heat-loving vegetables including melon, cucumbers, tomatoes, and the like,
are barely productive in outside gardens around
Seattle. Melons usually won't mature without

Photo 13-6: *Beets, lettuce, turnips. Flagstaff,
Arizona.*

great pains to shelter them from both early and
late frosts. Cucumbers are set into the greenhouse at the end of April, and melons started
some time near the end of May. Eggplants,
tomatoes, and peppers are usually killed by frosts
right in the middle of fruit ripening. In the
solar greenhouse, they are planted in June just
as soon as the large crops of late-spring greens
are harvested. Fruit can continue to ripen until
December.

Here are details for growing some of the most
popular vegetables in a solar greenhouse, with
with emphasis on winter conditions. Whenever
possible, the experiences of gardeners who have
tried them are included.

Bean

Beans need at least 60°F. soil temperature for
germination. Beans are quite productive for
the space they require. At least 10 plants are
needed for three or four servings for a family
of four. A 10-foot row will produce about 5
pounds of pods or 1½ pounds of shelled beans.
An intercrop of lettuce or radishes can be used

between rows of beans. Bush beans, either snap or lima, are best for container culture. Climbing beans grown on strings do well against a white wall. Sow seed directly in a small pot for transplanting later.

CET tried a late-winter sowing of beans, but they failed to germinate. In cold areas, no kind of beans will do well. They need to flower to fruit and so low light may be a problem with some types. An early-spring sowing should set pods well as days lengthen. The solar greenhouse can also produce long-season beans like soya and lima where the outside season is too short.

Beet

Beets are an easily grown cool-season crop which should be sown directly in the container. The container should be at least 8 inches deep to produce full-size roots. Sow thick and eat the thinnings. Both leaves and roots are edible and are best while young. Yellow beets are often sweeter than the red and they don't bleed.

Beets need sweet (alkaline) soil, but if you use too much limestone, essential boron may be tied up. Beets do well in soils high in organic matter, even straight sphagnum moss peat if it's properly limed. A 10-foot row at 4-inch spacing should produce about 10 pounds of beet roots.

To date, beets have been a popular choice for solar-greenhouse gardeners because they do well in cool weather. However, beets have produced greens rather than roots during the coolest months. The leaves tend to be thin and grow slowly. They are excellent for salads, but won't make many meals as potherbs. In the Maxatawny greenhouse, three-month-old beets yielded roots the size of golf balls in early April.

Photo 13-7: *Healthy chard, heat storage, maximum use of space. Cape Cod Ark.*

Carrot

They are a cool-season crop which should be sown directly in the container. Carrots grow well in soil-less media such as sphagnum moss peat. A 10-foot row will produce about 10 pounds of mature carrots. If carrot fly is a problem, try intercropping with sage plants. Hot weather and dry soil will retard growth and cause a strong flavor. Sow thick; thin to one plant every 2 inches.

If you have room outside and carrots grow in

your climate, they are best planted so that they mature before the first frost, and should be left in the ground. Covered with hay to prevent freezing, carrots of excellent quality can be dug as long as the ground is soft. In short seasons, carrots will do well started early in a bed covered by a cold frame.

Chard

Chard is a member of the beet family which is grown only for its leaves. It's an easy crop to grow most of the year. The leaves can be picked continuously, but seem to be at their best when nights are cool and days sunny. It can be used as a potherb or in salads. Ruby or rhubarb chard make beautiful centerpieces when grown in an attractive 6- to 8-inch pot. Grow it just like beets.

Chard has proven quite popular so far among solar-greenhouse gardeners. Large plants brought in from the garden continue to produce leaves regularly. Growth will slow when the sunlight is lowest. New Alchemist Kathy Ryan observed that chard seedlings started for the greenhouse in early fall appeared more vigorous than the mature plants that were transplanted from the garden.

Cole Crop (*Brassica* Species or Cabbage Family)

For true winter growing, the cole crops are king in solar greenhouses. The group includes broccoli, Brussels sprouts, cabbage, cauliflower, Chinese cabbage, collards, kale, kohlrabi, and mustard which are all members of the cabbage family. All tolerate cold weather and can be stored after harvest for long periods in the

Photo 13-8: *Cole crops. Maxatawny, Pennsylvania.*

refrigerator. Sow the seed about six weeks prior to transplanting them into the final location. Most members of the cole family are susceptible to a slime mold called club root. Large growths on the roots cause the leaves to turn yellow. The disease organisms can persist in the soil for several years and for this reason, cole crops should always be planted in virgin soil. Chinese cabbage, collards, kale, and mustard will produce the most food for the size of the plant. Kale and mustard will last well into freezing weather in a cold frame and will begin producing again quite early in spring.

Broccoli can be harvested over a long period. After the center cluster is cut, the side shoots develop clusters for a month or more. They tend to get tough and stringy during hot weather, so early-spring and fall crops are better than midsummer. Each plant will yield about 10 pounds.

In the greenhouse, the Brussels sprout is almost a perennial. Twist the leaves off from beneath each sprout as it reaches maturity. The fruit matures in sequence from the bottom up as long as the plants don't freeze, so they should produce well in the solar greenhouse. Ten plants should yield at least 10 pounds of sprouts. Start plants in midsummer.

Cabbage are heavy users of nitrogen fertilizer so keep them well mulched with manure. Cabbage heads tend to split open when they mature in warm weather. To reduce splitting, hold back on water near maturity. A cabbage head will range from 2 to 6 pounds in weight. Bolting (producing flowers) can occur if young plants are exposed to 50°F. or less for two or more weeks.

Cauliflower is more demanding in temperature control than cabbage or broccoli. They will not head properly in hot weather nor tolerate as much cold. For uniform heads, use a soil high in humus and keep them moist at all times because the heads are about 95-percent water. Most cauliflowers need to be blanched by shielding the heads from the sun. This is done by tying the outer leaves over the head with a string. A well-grown cauliflower head will weigh about one pound. Radishes, lettuce, or bush beans can be intercropped with cauliflower. Start with radish or lettuce, then cauliflower, and follow with beans. CET reports great success with cauliflower, harvesting 8-inch heads in mid-April, 3½ months from seed.

The term Chinese cabbage refers to a number of different greens. They all tend to form flowers during long days and warm weather. It is best grown as a fall-winter crop. Pragtree Farm harvested a fine fall planting by the end of February.

Some people think of collards, kale, and mustard as hog food, but where I grew up in southeastern Oklahoma, they were mouthwatering, early-spring or late-fall vegetables cooked with ham hock. They were served with their vitamin-rich juices poured over cornbread. Collards will tolerate more hot weather than kale and more

Photo 13-9: *Climbing cucumbers. Penn State.*

cold than cabbage. The flavor of kale is improved by a light frost. Each plant yields about ½ to 1 pound of leaves. The leaves of some kale are ornamental, curled or fringed and ranging from dark green to bluish purple.

Kohlrabi, although turnip shaped, is not a root crop and has a far more delicate flavor. I saw a purple kohlrabi in a solar-heated greenhouse in Los Alamos, New Mexico, that was at least six months old. It was about two feet high, very attractive, and had dozens of small rabi sprouts coming off of the main stem. I believe it could be considered essentially a perennial in the greenhouse. Although the average yield is about ½ pound per plant, the one in Los Alamos must have weighed 5 pounds or more.

Cucumber

Cucumber plants need warmth, high humidity, sunlight, and high soil moisture. The solar-heated greenhouse in late spring, summer, and early fall is nearly ideal for growing cukes. Start cucumber seed in peat pots and transplant in about four weeks to at least a gallon container. They can trail on the ground, but grow best if given something to climb. The older varieties of cukes require insect or hand-pollination and their acidity causes burping. Some newer varieties will develop without pollination and are burpless.

Keep cukes well watered and well fertilized because they grow fast and produce large leaves. Cold water may cause wilting, while hot water can burn the roots. Well water may be too cold, while water laying in a hose exposed to direct sunlight might be overheated.

Cukes are susceptible to mildew. Syringing the leaves in the morning will help to control mildew by washing off the mildew spores. Do not syringe in the afternoon or evening when moisture will remain on the leaves overnight. Select varieties which are virus resistant and control the virus transmitting aphid and striped cucumber beetle. Syringing the underside of the leaves helps control two-spotted or red spider mite. Pull off the leaves below the fruit as it is picked.

Don't worry about the first flowers not setting fruit. The male flowers open first and fall off,

then female flowers develop. There are usually 10 to 20 male flowers for each female flower.

A cucumber plant should produce about 10 pounds of fruit per season except Zeppelin, which may produce several 10-pound fruit.

The solar greenhouse will be an excellent source of both early and late cucumbers. In extreme northern climates, you may get an abundance of cucumbers for the first time this way. The same holds true for certain squash and melons, like cantalopes. The culture of these is nearly identical to cukes, except they may not climb as readily. Look for early and bush varieties.

Eggplant

Eggplants must have warmth and moist humus soils. The seed won't germinate at less than 75° and do best when kept at 80° to 90°F. At the least, a solar greenhouse will bring an eggplant crop in much earlier and extend it greatly. Pragtree Farm (48° north latitude) harvested eggplant in November in a double-glazed but uninsulated dome much like a large cold frame. Sow in peat pots and handle carefully when transplanting. Fertilize with fish emulsion monthly. Harvest the fruit before it loses its shine; picking before seeds mature will encourage steady production. Two or three healthy plants will supply a family's needs. Eggplants grow slowly, so radishes and lettuces can be grown in the space around them when they are young.

Lettuce

A solar greenhouse can provide lettuce through the winter in most regions that we have heard from. In far northern latitudes and areas with

Photo 13-10: *Eggplant and peppers. Pragtree Farm.*

Photo 13-11: *Butterhead lettuce. Cape Cod Ark.*

heavy cloud cover, supplemental lighting may be necessary for a month or two. Truly fresh lettuce in the middle of winter is a treat you must grow yourself to enjoy. Many of the finest varieties are just too perishable to be seen in the grocery store. All of the lettuces prefer cool temperatures and need partial shade in the summer. You can grow four types: Crisphead (Iceberg), Butterhead, Leaf (Bunching), or Cos (Romaine). A midwinter (October-sown) crop may take twice as long to reach maturity as a spring

Photo 13-12: *Lettuce Trials. Cape Cod Ark.*

(March-sown) crop (see Box 13-2). Yields average up to ½ pounds for leaf types and up to 2 pounds for head types. Endive can be used as a lettuce substitute.

The leaf lettuces grow fast. You can eat the thinnings and then the outer leaves as they develop. Leave plenty of space between the heading types or you will get small heads. One plant per gallon container is enough for final spacing of the head type. Water is most critical as the inner heads begin to swell and even one day of dry soil can make the leaves tough and bitter tasting. The variety Anita is fairly resistant to mildew, tip burn, rot, and bolting which are the most common problems.

In the Cape Cod Ark, New Alchemist Kathy Ryan has given special attention to eight lettuce varieties to see if there is much difference for winter gardening. On the results so far, she recommends Ruby and Bibb.

In Flagstaff, Dave MacKinnon picked about 6 pounds of leaf lettuce beginning at Christmas and continuing steadily through January from a space just 10 feet square.

Onion

Onions grow tops during the cool, short days and bulbs during warm, long days. Varieties are classified by their day-length response. Northern varieties usually form bulbs with 14- to 16-hour days, while southern varieties form bulbs with 12-hour days. To get the small pearl or pickling type grow Eclipse in the North with an April planting. Though you can't grow bulbs in winter, some varieties will make green onions or scallions. Tender tops of onions, shallots, and chives are very useful for salads.

Onions grow best in a soil high in organic matter and, in fact, I have had best results growing them in straight humus. You can grow them from sets (easiest), seeds, or transplants (bunching type). The greenhouse is a good place to get the early start you need in the North for onions, leeks, and other members of the family from seed. Sets are just small bulbs of onions started from seed the previous year. Make successive plantings each month all year. Keep onions well watered to keep them growing fast and sweet tasting.

Peas

Peas thrive in cool weather and in moist cool air. Peas must be sown about two inches deep directly where they will mature. Plant 45 seeds (15 seeds per gallon container) every 5 to 10 days for a continuous crop. They perform best if given a chicken-wire fence or trellis on which to grow. Peas are available as bush and vine. The edible-pod type (snow or sugar peas) yield more food because there is less waste.

Do not use a nitrogen-rich soil or the plant will make mostly leaves. Instead, treat the seed with a garden-legume inoculant. To start peas producing fruit, pinch back the growing points and remove one-quarter of the leaves. Peas need lots of water when they start flowering. Keep the peas picked off to keep them producing. Morning harvesting seems to help preserve the sweet flavor. A good plant should produce about one pound of peas in the pod.

Pepper

Peppers need warm air, soil, and plenty of light. Both sweet and hot peppers grow well in the greenhouse under those conditions. Fruit set occurs only between 60° and 90°F. Small-fruited types tolerate higher temperatures than large-fruited types. Within the correct temperature range, peppers set and develop fruit continuously. For a variety of colors and shapes, grow a plant each of California Wonder (green), Burpee Fordhook (red), and Sweet Banana (yellow). Keep well watered and fertilize with fish emulsion at the time the first blossoms open. Each plant should yield one to two pounds of fruit.

Radish

If you like radishes, you are in luck because they are about the easiest and fastest growing year-round greenhouse crop. Red or white, round or long, all are at their best as a cool-season crop, but will produce in any season. Double the number of days from seed sowing to harvest for the October through January sowings. Radishes should be directly sown in a soil rich in organic matter. Sow four seeds per square inch and thin to one. If the plants seem to be mostly leaves with few enlarged roots, try incandescent lights for four hours in the middle of the night, or try providing more space between plants (one plant every two square inches). Yield is usually one to two ounces per plant.

Spinach

True spinach grows only in cool weather, requiring 45° to 50°F. night temperatures. Despite that, it has not done well in the middle of winter in solar greenhouses. Gardeners have tried it from Massachusetts to Arizona and have been disappointed. Plants look spindly and small. On the other hand, late-winter sowings at Maxatawny and Pragtree Farm produced well.

Photo 13-13: *Spinach and lettuce intercrop. Flag-staff, Ariozna.*

Spinach is a fine crop for growing in a cold frame. Sown in late summer, it will grow a little in fall, then in early spring it flourishes. Winter Bloomsdale tolerates cold better than most varieties and is blight resistant as a bonus.

Direct seed or transplant one plant per gallon container. Thinnings are excellent in salads. Spinach has a high nitrogen requirement and like other leafy crops, needs large amounts of water. Monnopa is a variety low in oxalic acid and therefore is less bitter than most spinach. Each plant at maturity weighs about ½ pound.

Strawberry

If you live in the North, you can produce your own strawberries one or two months ahead of the outdoor crop. It takes about 10 to 12 weeks to bring the plants from dormancy to fruiting. They can be potted one per 5-inch pot or four per 12-inch pot in a soil rich in organic matter.

There are basically two types of strawberries, everbearing and single crop. The everbearers produce a few fruit gradually all summer. The June bearers produce a larger crop over a shorter period of time, usually about one to three weeks. There are several small-fruited everbearers which can be grown from seed. These are more like wild strawberries and are called alpines. It takes about three months from seed sowing until the first fruit is ripe.

All of the strawberries should be started in a cool (45° to 50°F.) greenhouse for at least six weeks. At flowering and fruit set they need 60°F. temperatures. Fruit set and fruit shape will be improved by hand-pollination. Use a chicken feather or flick each cluster of flowers with your finger.

I usually remove the first runners that develop to put more energy into the fruit. When about one half of the fruit remains, let runners develop. After all the fruit is picked, the plants can be set out in the garden and the runners pegged down for next year's plants. Each plant should produce 20 to 40 berries.

Tomato

Tomatoes have produced fruit well into winter in solar greenhouses even in northern latitudes. Though tomatoes prefer warm temperatures and high light intensity, they seem to tolerate cooler temperatures than eggplants or peppers. Though growth will be slow and blossoms will drop, fruit that has been set in the early fall will slowly ripen into midwinter in cool houses. There are indeterminate types which continue to grow on and on or determinate types which stop growing after reaching a genetically determined height (usually three feet or less). Tomatoes come in a variety of sizes, shapes, and colors. There are small-fruited, sweet-tasting, miniature, red-fruited types like Sweet 100 and large-fruited, acid-tasting, large, yellow-fruited types like Golden Sunrise. Some are orange or pink when ripe. Small-fruited types are best for slow, winter ripening. Watch for varieties that are followed by V, F, or N. These letters stand for verticillium virus, fusarium wilt, and nematode resistance.

Tomatoes are usually sown in peat pots and transplanted into gallon or larger containers. If the young plants are too tall, plant them deep for support. Roots grow readily out of stem tissue. Tomatoes need at least six hours of sunlight daily. They set fruit best with night temperatures between 60° and 75°F. and day temperatures between 70° and 90°F. My own

Photo 13-15: *Small-fruited tomato, staked. Flagstaff, Arizona.*

observations in Pennsylvania indicate that tomatoes will begin to thrive again around March 21 in a cool greenhouse.

Rain or prolonged humid weather reduces fruit set as will hot, dry weather. In the greenhouse, each flower should be flicked with your finger to help insure pollination.

If large plants have few fruit, you may have used too much nitrogen fertilizer and water. Nitrogen is needed for fast growth when the plants are young but for best fruit development, reduce nitrogen and increase potassium and phosphorus. Low light levels also increase leaf

Photo 13-14: *Climbing tomatoes, trellised. Maxatawny, Pennsylvania.*

Photo 13-16: *Tomato in cylinder. Maxatawny, Pennsylvania.*

area at the expense of fruit.

Leathery scars on the ends of the fruit (blossom end rot) are caused by moisture stress, too much fertilizer, not enough lime (calcium), and hot dry, humid weather. Mulch with straw or peat to reduce soil moisture and temperature fluctuations.

Smokers can transmit a virus to tomatoes on their hands. Milk has been reported to act as a deactivator of the virus. Do not replant tomatoes in the same soil that has been used for tomatoes, potatoes, eggplants, or peppers. They are all susceptible to the same diseases.

The newer dwarf types are particularly suitable as container plants. Many will be comfortable in a six- or eight-inch pot. The smallest is Tiny Tim, maturing at 12 inches, followed in height by Small Fry, Pixie Hybrid, and Patio.

Most standard-sized tomatoes and especially indeterminate varieties will need support and training. A cage can be built from wire or stakes and strings used for support. The side shoots (suckers) are usually removed and the lower leaves are removed after the clusters (trusses) of fruit mature. Each plant will yield 6 to 10 pounds of fruit. Allow one square foot for each miniature plant and up to three square feet for the standards.

In Flagstaff, Dave MacKinnon's late-summer planted, cherry-type tomatoes produced six pounds of fruit between Christmas and mid-January. Ripening stopped for about two weeks, and then fruit began to come in heavily again.

David Kruschke and Karen Funk have grown tomatoes for several seasons in their Wisconsin attached greenhouse. Plants seeded in July will yield fruit through mid-February. Blossoms begin to drop off in November. In early-summer they set large plants back out in the garden. Big Boy, Big Girl and Red Cherry are their recommended varieties.

Near Seattle, Washington, the gardeners at Pragtree Farm report that summer-planted tomatoes ripened into November inside their double-glazed, domed, walk-in cold frame.

Cold-Hardy Salad Greens, Flowers, and Herbs

These are only a few of the most popular vegetables. No matter what your climate, a solar greenhouse will allow you to bring a wider variety of plants than you are now growing into cultivation. Harvests will be longer. A good example of this is David MacKinnon's experience with tomatoes in Flagstaff. The climate there in summer is so hot and dry that most garden crops are difficult to grow. Besides being arid, the season is extremely short due to high altitude. Typically, tomatoes just come into production, then they are nipped by frost. MacKinnon's greenhouse does significantly more than provide plentiful tomatoes through August, September, and into the winter. They will produce fruit abundantly in spring. In summer, the outside temperatures can get too hot for tomatoes, but inside his self-shading greenhouse, the air can be slightly cooler than outside. With less intense light and a more humid environment, the plants are less likely to be stressed.

For food in the dead of winter, you should plan to experiment with varieties that you may not have seen or tasted before. The greenhouse should provide occasional potherb dinners and abundant salads, all extremely rich in vitamins. For example, you might consider planting a lot of parsley for salads. Both parsley and endive will produce copiously in winter, for vitamin-rich

Photo 13-18: *New Zealand spinach cascades from retaining wall. Cape Cod Ark.*

and strong-flavored salads. Corn-salad is mild and will do well with low light. So will dandelion; large-leaved European varieties are available in catalogs. Turnips, like beets and kale, will produce many more willowy and tender leaves inside the greenhouse. All are good in salads. The New Alchemy Institute reports that Malabar spinach grown on stakes has borne potherbs till mid-December. New Zealand spinach grows abundantly for them all winter. It is a trailing plant that will cascade from a high spot. Search the seed catalogs for unfamiliar but cold-hardy crops.

Herbs are another realm of horticulture that

Photo 13-17: *Herbs in rock wall and winter greens. Cape Cod Ark.*

Photo 13-19: *Wintering flowers and herbs over for spring propagation. Epping, New Hampshire.*

Hampshire, can pay for the fuel that heats their home with young herbs started in their attached-pit greenhouse.

Herbs are useful for making teas, for flavoring, for repelling insects, and for medicinal purposes. Several of them, like roquette, parsley, and chervil, are excellent additions to salads. I have found that most of the herbs grow well with a 60°F. night temperature although many are perennial and will tolerate an occasional freeze. They can be grown from seed, cuttings, or by division. There are few herbs that don't propagate readily by cuttings and I find this

Photo 13-20: *Climbing nasturtiums. Cape Cod Ark.*

the greenhouse can open to you. Fresh herbs are only rarely for sale. A wide variety will grow over winter and tolerate light picking. In the North, many herbs will be winter-killed outdoors. You can grow magnificent plants by potting them for the greenhouse around the time of the first frost. These plants prefer the cool temperatures you'll have in the solar greenhouse. Propagating herb cuttings in spring can become a very profitable enterprise almost anywhere there are numbers of other summer gardeners. Joe and Gail White of Epping, New

simpler than trying to grow them from seed.

My favorites are the various mints which I use for tea, thymes for their aromatic smell and pungent taste when used in soups and stuffings, and scented leaf geraniums, whose aromatic oils repel insects.

The annual herbs which are more often grown from seed include anise, basil (Sweet Green or Dark Opal), coriander, and fennel.

Other interesting perennial herbs suitable for the greenhouse include chives, sweet marjoram, sorrel, chervil, tarragon, angelica, lemon balm, lemon verbena, parsley, rosemary, and sage.

Parsley, chives, and thyme can be harvested for fresh seasoning. Rosemary is harvested by clipping the tops when in full bloom. Basil, fennel, mint, sage, sweet marjoram, and savory are harvested at about the time of blooming.

Many kinds of flowers can be grown in cool greenhouses. In the Cape Cod Ark, the New Alchemists have flowering marigolds and climbing nasturtiums through January. Marsha Mackie of McMinnville, Oregon, has had some success growing cut flowers for a local restaurant in winter. Camelia and azalea are among the woody plants which prefer cool temperatures and will bloom in late winter. All sorts of spring bulbs can be forced. A few common flowers that do well in cool conditions are chrysanthemums, sweet peas, primroses, winter-flowering forget-me-nots, pansies, and violets. Growing plants for flowers in winter can be a tricky business for some species, involving day length as well as temperature. Since the aim of this book is to encourage food production, please refer to the Bibliography, especially *Winter Flowers in Greenhouse and Sun-Heated Pit* by Taylor and Gregg for a discussion of greenhouse flowers.

For detailed information about selected greenhouse vegetable varieties, with particular reference to days from sowing or transplanting to maturity outdoors, please refer to Appendix VIII. Varieties have been selected based on general availability.

Chapter Fourteen

Solar Greenhouse Gardening: Regional Reports

To aid the reader in further understanding both the physiology and the psychology of crop production and related activities in the solar-greenhouse biosphere, the following reports from various sections of the country are included. The reports are kept in the first person to retain the flavor and authenticity of the experience.

Crop Production in the Integrated Greenhouse

Wild Rose, Wisconsin
(David Kruschke, Karen Funk)

In January 1975, the first seeds were sown in a ground-level area called "the pit." This area is 3-feet-by-56-feet and 16 inches deep, and is composed of ⅓ topsoil and ⅔ local soil (which consists of a considerable amount of sand). We first tried radishes, lettuce, and onions, which did quite well, except that harvest dates were extended by about one month (i.e., radishes took almost two months to mature). However, they were just as tasty as any garden-grown variety.

In April 1975, the first tomatoes were seeded, after many visitors were curious whether tomatoes could be grown here. There was no problem with their sprouting or seedling life; however, the crop was damaged by aphids (transported in on small pepper plants). We removed all plants and let the sun heat and dry out the growing area for one month. This was effective, as tomatoes seeded in July 1975 were not infested. The use of a "kitchen spray" can be effective in controlling aphids. A recipe for this will follow in the "Garden Pests and Other Problems" section.

October 1975 was the beginning harvest of tomatoes, and the introduction to the growing area of two frogs and two lizards. These were designed to naturally keep the insect population down. They also provided a touch of summer, with their whistling, for the long winter months ahead.

The first year's tomatoes continued to yield fruit until the middle of February 1976. After November, the blossoms aborted, but plants remained intact after pruning. We felt this was partially due to allowing nighttime temperatures in the pit to occasionally fall below 55°F. at night. When insulation panels are put on promptly at sunset, the pit temperature remains above 55°. The other factor for blossoms not setting can be due to not enough available natural daylight, during certain months at this latitude. Once available light is less than 9½ hours a day (as after October 31 and before March 31) blossoms tend to abort. Leafy and root vegetables require less available light, and

Photo 14-1: *Roots in warm soil, vines trailing down to light.*

continue to grow with only seven hours' daylight per day.

The first part of June, or after the danger of frost is gone, we transplant a large number of our tomatoes to the outdoor garden. These are at varying degrees of growth, and some are flowering. The rigors of transplanting do not seem to hurt flowering plants; however, they do not seem to bear much sooner than plants that have not flowered.

The next major change for the indoor garden came in November 1976, with the removal of the barrels, and the replacement with three large planters. These were filled with rock, local soil, and peat moss. Not only did the planters serve as a heat-storage system and had aesthetic value, but

they almost doubled our growing area. Being elevated, and having some bottom heat, certain crops did much better; i.e., tomatoes and herbs. This extra area also allowed us to experiment with many untraditional greenhouse plants. These included: Sweet corn, cucumbers, green and soybeans, and zucchini. Although fun, they weren't that successful. In all cases, seeds sprout very rapidly. Radishes come up in less than 24 hours, and even parsley comes up in 6 days.

A. Tomatoes

Tomatoes have been a long-time favorite in our household, for a variety of reasons. They stay pest free with preventative care, they grow and yield well, have a high nutritional value, are a natural air freshener, and are an economically stable crop. Tomatoes are an important supplemental food to us, as well as being income producing. This is especially true during the winter months, when vine-ripened tomatoes are nonexistent in this area.

The varieties we have grown are: Rutgers (85 day), Earliest (69 day), Red Cherry (72 day), Big Boy and Big Girl (78 day), and Early Girl (54 day). Our favorites have been Big Boy and Girl, for their productivity, large size, and flavor. However, an early variety gives you a better chance for production in winter months. We also grow Red Cherry, or any cherry tomato, that can be used as snacks for visitors or the children.

Compact-growing vegetables that yield well in a small space are well worthwhile. Radishes, lettuce, onions, parsley, and all the herbs are a good choice. This is particularly true for parsley and herbs, as they are never available in fresh form in this area. The available dried herbs are both expensive and lack flavor.

1. *Continued Productivity* Temperature must be kept above 55° at night to enable blossoms to set. We accomplished this in two ways: insulating panels are put on promptly at sunset; and all tomatoes were moved to the elevated planters, where an average temperature of at least 72°F. could be maintained. Available daylight less than 9½ hours a day also inhibits the setting of blossoms. An alternative could be the use of supplemental artificial light. This would mean that artificial light would supplement daylight for 1½ hours a day in November and February, and 2½ hours in December and January. This also would be beneficial on heavily clouded or stormy days. We have not tried this technique as yet, as we have been happy with productivity until mid-February without utilizing lights.

We also use pruning and propagate plants from cuttings to prolong productivity. Some of our plants are more than a year old, and still going strong. This is accomplished by pruning away any dead or unhealthy-looking matter, or cutting back until a compact brush of one or two stems is attained. Some of these cuttings are used as new plants transplanted to a different area. The stems can be cut and placed directly in the soil. This method works extremely well, plus gives you a new plant that is well advanced in growth.

2. *Pollination* This has not been a problem at all, and we have not had to resort to hand-pollination. It appears that disturbance of the plants by air, people, and panels, allow the plants the opportunity to pollinate. Shaking the plant is less tedious, less time consuming and just as effective as hand-pollination with a camel's-hair brush.

3. *Fertilization and Soil pH* Fertilization can become a real problem for the indoor garden, as there is a tendency to overfertilize. This can cause plants to become too large, leafy, spindly, and set poor fruit and decrease the size of the bulb part of root vegetables. This is especially treacherous during the short cloudy days of November, December, and January, when the high nitrate content of the soil with abundant moisture will cause plants to grow soft, spindly, and abort their blossoms. In the past, we have fertilized by side-dressing, with a ratio of 400 pounds/acre, with a 10-10-10 fertilizer or equivalent. This means that in our west planter, which has a growing area of 45.9 ft.^{2} or .00105 acre, we would put on .42 pounds (191 grams) of fertilizer. However, we now feel that it is safer and economically sound to base a fertilization program on direct soil analysis, with a soil test kit, done at two- to four-week intervals. With this method, not only do you know which nutrients are deficient, but you can also calibrate the amount you need to apply, without overdoing it.

The pH of the planters range from 5.5 to 6.5 (acidic to weakly acidic). This was accomplished by the addition of peat moss to the local soil. This is the ideal pH range for growing tomatoes, parsley, and herbs. The lower pit has a pH range of 7.0 to 7.2 (neutral to weakly alkaline). This is more suitable for leafy green and root crops.

4. *Garden Pests and Other Problems* As in any other problem area, prevention of the problem is the best solution. The opportunity for plant diseases is increased in a warm, moist environment. Therefore, we remove all dead matter promptly, and keep growing areas as clean as possible. We only water early on sunny days, so that the foliage can dry, and excess humidity can be vented out. Watering is done

once a week during spring and fall, and twice or more as needed in the summer months.

Close inspection of any plant brought in is imperative. This includes inspection of the leaves for insects or unhealthy foliage, and inspection of the root system for the presence of nematodes (produce knot-like swellings). Nothing is more discouraging than having one unhealthy plant start an epidemic and wipe out months of growing effort.

Even with care, some insects still find their way to the growing areas. We installed frogs and/or toads, and lizards to keep the population down. They seem content to stay in the growing areas.

For aphids, we use a kitchen spray of 1 pint water, ½ teaspoon tabasco, 1 teaspoon garlic powder (do not use garlic salt), ¼ teaspoon cayenne pepper, and a squirt of liquid detergent. Shake well and spray on both infested and non-infested plants. This seems to kill a large portion of them, and keeps aphids off uninfested plants. If mealybugs appear, it's easiest to remove them with a cotton swab dipped in rubbing alcohol. For a large number of them, plants can be sprayed with a mixture of 1 tablespoon rubbing alcohol to 1 pint water. Plants can be sprayed two times a week indoors, and spray must be reapplied after rains outdoors.

B. The Economic Role that Plants Play

It's exeremly difficult to place any price on the availability of year-round fresh fruits and vegetables. This is especially true since we are still inexperienced indoor gardeners and have made mistakes. However, we have sold our excess tomatoes in December and January for $1.00/pound locally. According to the U.S. Department of Agriculture, it's possible to produce 6 to 10 pounds of tomatoes per plant, for a fall/winter crop; and 10 to 20 pounds per plant for a spring crop.

We feel the economic role of a year-round garden is more than just an individual effort. We can be both producer and consumer and eliminate the intermediate steps of shipping, processing, storing, and distribution. If these steps were eliminated by many people, a significant energy savings would result.

The Solar Greenhouse as Season Extender

Clementsville, Nova Scotia
(George and Pamela de Alth)

In general, the solar greenhouse worked very, very well for us. In fact, it lived up to our highest hopes. I will start with some detailed information by talking about the greens.

Through the winter, two plants of kale and about ten of lettuce lived in a more or less steady state. They were transplants out of last summer's garden but they had been planted there late, in August, so that they were small (no more than eight leaves). The greenhouse never froze once during this cold winter so the plants never died; however, they never grew either, as we had very little sun. I live in a part of Nova Scotia that gets low cumulus clouds from the Bay of Fundy when high-pressure systems dominate our region. So even when there is no storm system about, my greenhouse receives little sun. Once the sun started to ride higher in the sky and gave more heat to the plants, they started to grow. The sap in the maple trees and in the greens started to flow at the same time. By mid-April, my wife and I were able to have a salad a day by merely picking the outer leaves of the lettuce. The two plants of kale grew more quickly and we used them for steamed greens. In addition to these holdovers from the previous summer, my wife planted salad greens and radishes in the greenhouse beds on March 10. They started slowly, but by the first of May the beds were a jungle of greens. To sum up, the greenhouse gave us fresh greens two months before we could have had them from an outdoors setup.

We started planting in flats and pots for the garden on March 19. On that date, onions and leeks went in, and on March 28, so did peppers, eggplant, and tomatoes. The greenhouse brought these around beautifully. On April 3, the tomatoes started to break through the surface. Because of the design of my greenhouse, a good part of the heat that came in during the daytime was stored up high near where it connects with the main part of my house. This, and the fact that the greenhouse is open at the bottom to the cool basement of the house, kept temperatures low at night, often below 50°F. The plants grew well and strong; they never were spindly. Having just put the tomatoes out I feel they are well set for bearing fruit; most are about 10 to 12 inches high with flower buds already formed. The peppers have stayed a bit small and we are keeping them in the greenhouse for a bit more indoor growth. The greens and cabbage plants that we started in the greenhouse on April 13 and later transferred to cold frames are strong and healthy and looking good in the garden. During the summer, we hope we can bring early tomatoes and melons and peppers into the greenhouse and then in the fall, we will try to transplant into it so that we can have greens into December. At that point, we will have completed our first yearly cycle with

Photo 14-2: *Illinois compost bin, open.*

this new structure and then we will begin to fine tune our work in it.

Composting in a Solar Greenhouse for CO_2 and Heat

Illinois and Eugene, Oregon
(Dan Knapp)

In the beginning, I started a "fire" in the compost bin in a walk-in cold frame by shoveling in alternate layers of leaves, household garbage, lawn clippings, and horse manure from the county fairgrounds. Al Casella, a physicist who shared my enthusiasm for solar-energy experimentation, lent me a hydrothermograph—a device which measures the convariation of temperature and humidity graphically, giving a continuous 30-day record. After the compost got warm, I set the instrument up in the greenhouse.

The compost heating principle was a source of exercise; every two weeks or so I would turn the steaming pile out onto the ground to aerate it, then mix in some more horse manure to get the heat going again. Doors closed, in a few days the steam would be rising through the pile up the steep north wall and down the south face of the greenhouse to the ground.

Steam from the compost condenses on the plastic and the roof trusswork, dropping down gently to the soil and plants, keeping things moist and green. When the sun came out the rapid heating of the inside air seemed to accelerate the condensation. If the prairie wind was blowing, the plastic would billow, lift and fall, "spanking" the drops of water into a fine, agreeable, continuous mist. All the plants seemed to appreciate the showers every time the sun came out.

The hydrothermograph showed clearly what was happening: the greenhouse was generating its own unique "weather." I operated the hydrothermograph for 30 days only—November 27–December 26, 1974. One compost bin (about 10 cubic feet of material) was already working at the start of the measurement period. A second pile was built during that month; by the time it had built up enough heat to release warmth and clouds of steam into the greenhouse, the first pile had already reached the burnout stage, so only one pile ever worked effectively at one time. Other than the compost and stored ground heat, the main source of energy input was the sun.

A clear and consistent pattern began to emerge as the instrument's pens traced temperature and humidity variations onto the rotating graph. When the sun shone, temperatures shot up from around freezing into the 60° to 90° range. At the same time, the relative humidity dropped from 100 percent to 50-60 percent. As the humidity dropped, it began "raining" inside the greenhouse, because water vapor which had been in the air was driven by the high temperature differential to condense on the cold ceiling and walls and drop to the ground. After sunset,

Photo 14-3: *And closed.*

temperatures returned to the 20s and 30s, the compost returned the humidity to 100 percent and it stopped "raining."

On cloudy days, temperatures generally stayed in the 30° to 40°F. range, and humidity stayed between 90 to 100 percent, so there was little or no rain in the greenhouse on cloudy days.

Frost Protection

The added moisture in the air seemed to give protection against killing frosts. The temperature inside the greenhouse dropped into the 15° to 20°F. range four times during November–December. (Outside temperature was around zero, with winds.) The plants crusted over with white, fuzzy frost from the compost steam, but the day's warmth soon restored their lush green color with no apparent damage.

A possible explanation for this phenomenon takes us into the physics of "phase change." When water changes from gas to liquid to solid, each transition from one state to another is called

Photo 14-4: *The newest Oregon greenhouse: Compost bin, catwalk, growing area.*

roof and walls) also had an insulating effect, and the two things combined meant that no plants died from killing frosts even during a normally severe midwestern winter.

I grew onions, garlic, Bibb lettuce, cornsalad, chervil, cabbage, parsley, and the rooted cuttings from several shrubs in the greenhouse. Others which would probably have done equally well include mustard, turnips, beets, carrots, cress, kale, broccoli, and more.

I let the compost die out in late December, to see what would happen. Slowly, the heat and with it, the source of moisture died away. The increasing cold and dryness slowed the growth of the plants considerably until growth nearly stopped by late February. The outer leaves grew brown as late winter gave way to early spring. As the daytime temperatures rose, many of the plants started growing again, but only to go to seed.

The contrast between the period when the compost was working and when it was not was striking; while the compost was sending steam and gentle warmth into the greenhouse the plants were a brilliant green. When the compost died, the plants began to turn brown, and went into a defensive survival posture.

I searched for an explanation. *Composting,* a book by Clarence Golueke, extended my knowledge of the processes involved. Compost is a mixture of carbohydrates and protein; the ultimate products of the breakdown of this material by bacterial action, besides heat and moisture, are carbon dioxide and atmospheric nitrogen. So the gaseous environment of the compost-heated greenhouse was an unusually rich nutrient medium for the plant's leaves. I theorized that the constant moisture condensing on the roof might carry some of the nitrogen in solution to the plant roots as well.

a "phase change." A burst of extra energy is either taken in or given off as the substance is pushed through the phase-change "window." Heat energy is given off in the phase change from water to ice, and, since there was a continuous resupply of water in the form of steam, heat energy was continuously being released into the plants and soil as the steam condensed and froze.

Rather than freeze the plants, the cold froze the moisture around the plants. The coating of ice (hoarfrost on the plants, solid sheets on the

Compost also helps to warm the greenhouse, exactly how much it is hard to say. But it does release considerable energy into the system. Compost gets hot—I've measured piles that were in the 165° to 175°F. range. Feeding and aeration lowers the temperature considerably but it soon rises again to the maximum, depending on the ingredients. The cycle of rising and falling temperature seems to take about three weeks to run its course, with some small amounts of waste heat being given off even after that point. Not all the interior heat is available at the exterior of the pile, of course—the "waste heat" generated is probably more in the 90° to 110° range, say six inches above the pile.

In any case, the heat is continuously available over a three-week period. In addition, there are some more subtle energy effects that I've just begun to appreciate and understand.

One is that the heat is a vehicle, an "engine" for moving nutrients from the interior of the pile into the greenhouse ecosystem, where they become available to the plants. These nutrients include water, carbon dioxide, and aromatic nitrogen compounds. These are taken in through the leaves and used directly in photosynthesis, or absorbed by the roots of the plants as part of water uptake from the soil. No pipes, nozzles, spray attachments, nor other hardware are necessary.

Another is the latent energy in all the water vapor. In times of extreme cold this can save the plants from freezing, as I have described.

New Directions

My latest structure is shaped like a fan, or a clamshell. Four trapezoids—all different in base and rafter length—radiate outward from an imaginary point. This arrangement opens the greenhouse to face the sun during its entire circuit of the winter sky. Walls that formerly faced east and west now face northeast and northwest, and so become part of the north wall complex. Therefore, they are opaque and insulated. The three north-facing walls act as absorber plates for incoming solar radiation so the structure should be a better solar collector.

The south face of the greenhouse is also considerably larger in this design, so a correspondingly larger volume of sunlight will be admitted. Compost bins are framed in as before. The available ground-level growing space is larger, and I plan to increase growing space still more by adding shelves to the entire north wall complex, including the compost bin, and by hanging plants from the roof.

I was anxious to get the composting system going again, so after a couple of weeks to get a "feel" for the energy retentiveness of the fan-shaped design, I got a load of fresh horse manure/straw and mixed it with a half-decomposed pile of sticks, garden trimmings, weeds, and garbage that I'd been stockpiling near the greenhouse all winter. By April 23 the pile was steaming and scudding clouds of water vapor, CO_2, warmth, and aromatic nitrogen compounds into the greenhouse. The immediate effects of the addition were exhilarating.

I stopped my daily misting of the interior because the compost steam maintained the interior humidity and created the "rains." Plant growth accelerated visibly and dramatically. Leaves that had turned a pure yellow color from being too dry, too cold, or too weak due to infrequent watering inside the house, turned pure green within six to eight days, starting with the veins and working out into the full surface of

Photo 14-5: *Fan-shaped greenhouse with compost. Eugene, Oregon.*

the leaf. The supercharged air was responsible for this, I'm certain. Plants clipped for propagation didn't wilt or even seem to slow in their growth, but developed new roots within a few days. Also, a curious phenomenon: The leaves and stems of certain plants turned a reddish color, and generally colors of all kinds got more intense and definite.

Compost piles are like sourdough starters: they have to be fed every couple of weeks to keep producing gases. I turned the pile and added new material to it on May 3 because it had been slowly cooling and steaming less for a few days. It took a couple of days to heat up again, but this time it's gotten "hotter" than before. I suspect it was too dry the first time. Also, the bacterial flora may have gotten better established throughout the mixture.

It's really fun to take sick or crowded plants from friends and neighbors out into the composting greenhouse, and give them back healthy and growing within a few days. My wife and I are spending more and more time in the greenhouse, with the result that it has rapidly filled up with plants, and many things have already moved out into our raised-bed garden. We're going into production on certain things like sedums and succulents, false sea onions, and tomatoes, and will be selling these soon. I like to watch the plants' initial reaction: for about three days the leaves just expand and turn a deeper green, then growth really gets underway. And, of course, it's a pleasure to anticipate the volumes of pure-compost potting and gardening soil that are being produced at the same time plant growth is being so stimulated.

Conclusion

In some respects, the solar greenhouse can be considered a kind of paradigm where many disciplines and interests intersect: horticulture, architecture, engineering, and so on. For this reason, the solar greenhouse has become an interdisciplinary tool in various sections of the country to help students understand the practical application of ideas.

For example, with the help of the Ecotope Group students at the Canyon Park Junior High School, Bothell, Washington, have constructed a solar greenhouse which will serve as a center of their *Energy, Food, and You* curriculum. Christina Peterson, coordinator of the program, reports that "students learned to recycle valuable materials; three large (40-foot-by-100-foot) greenhouses donated by Chiyoda Chemical Engineering, Inc., were dismantled and portions of these greenhouses were reused in the construction of the solar-heated one."

Solar-greenhouse construction at colleges and schools across the country is becoming a popular way to both "concretize" and enliven the curriculum. The freestanding solar greenhouse at Yavapai Community College, in Prescott, Arizona, was built through the cooperation of people in a number of departments who plan to utilize the greenhouse in courses.

The high school students who constructed an

Photo 1: *Canyon Park Junior High School. Bothell, Washington, D.C.*

active solar greenhouse in the Chelsea Public Schools were sophomores in a special class called "Coordinated Vocational Educational Training."

293

Photo 2: *Yanapai Community College. Prescott, Arizona.*

The students at the Open Living School in Evergreen, Colorado, who built a solar greenhouse (oil-drum storage, beadwall system) are even younger.

Clearly, the solar greenhouse can be a vital educational tool that holds considerable promise in curricula of the future.

Those people who have had the experience of an attached greenhouse on their home customarily declare: "Everyone should have one." Undoubtedly, the attached greenhouse will emerge as a "retrofit" item, possibly satisfying federal requirements as a "solar collector."

On the other hand, the freestanding greenhouse may eventually become an "institution" in cities and other places where people can garden communally. And already there are signs of this development in the Southwest.

Also, there are some indications that the rooftop greenhouse might eventually become part of the urban scene.

The beauty of the solar greenhouse is that it, in some form or other, is applicable to the broad spectrum of American life. And perhaps, unlike with the bomb shelters of the fifties, we'll build positively above ground, site of food and heat.

Appendix I

Automatic Vent Openers Which Do Not Require Electric Power for Operation

Solar Vent

Dalen Products, Inc.
201 Sherlake Drive
Knoxville, TN 37922
> Actuates from 68° to 75°F.; power enough to handle up to 9 pounds of lift weight.

Power Vent

Bayliss Precision Components, Limited
Ashborne, Derbyshire
Great Britain

Heat Motor System

Southern California Greenhouse Manufacturing
3266 North Rosemead Boulevard
Rosemead, CA 91770

Appendix II

Sources for Conductivity and pH Meters

Conductivity and pH meters are available from the following sources:

Conductivity Meters

Hach Chemical Company
Box 907
Ames, IA 50010

Industrial Instruments, Inc.
89 Commerce Road
Cedar Grove, NJ 07009

Lab-Line Instruments, Inc.
Melrose Park, IL 60160

pH Meters

Hach Chemical Company
Box 907
Ames, IA 50010

Markson Science, Inc.
Box 767
Del Mar, CA 92014

Cole-Parmer Instrument Company
7425 North Oak Park Avenue
Chicago, IL 60648

L. G. Nester Company
P.O. Box 666
Millville, NJ 08332

Appendix III

Estimating Greenhouse Heat Loss

Conrad Heeschen

To make a rough estimate of the amount of heat a greenhouse loses, we need to know several things:

1. The area of each different type of surface of the greenhouse,
2. The U-value (see Table 1) for each of these sections,
3. The average inside temperature of the greenhouse (t_i), and
4. The average outside temperature (t_o).

(A) We then list each area as shown below and multiply it by the appropriate U-value to get a heat-loss factor for the surface, $U \times A$. The heat-loss factor tells the number of Btu's of heat lost through that entire surface in one hour for every degree of temperature difference between inside and outside.

(B) We then add up all the different heat-loss factors to get a total heat-loss factor for the entire greenhouse. This is the amount of heat, measured in Btu's, that the greenhouse will lose in one hour for each degree of temperature difference between inside and outside.

(C) To get the actual losses during one hour, we must multiply the total heat-loss factor by this temperature difference.

(D) If you want to calculate the heat losses for the entire day, use the average inside temperature and the average outside temperature. After we find the hourly heat losses, we multiply by 24 hours/day to get the total daily heat loss. This procedure is illustrated in the following example:

Glazing:	
Single Layer of Glass	1.22
Double Layer of Glass	.37
SG, plus Insulated Shutter (R9), 14 Hours/Day—Average U over 24 hours	.57
DG, plus Insulated Shutter (R9), 14 Hours/Day—Average U over 24 hours	.3
Opaque:	
2″ x 4″ Frame Wall Sheathing Both Sides, No Insulation	.26
2″ x 4″ Frame Wall & 3½″ Fiberglass	.07
2″ x 6″ Frame Wall & 5½″-6″ Fiberglass	.04
8″ Concrete, No Insulation	.39
8″ Concrete Block, No Insulation	.31
8″ Concrete & 1″ Foamboard	.13
8 ″Concrete & 2″ Foamboard	.08
8″ Concrete Block & 2″ Foamboard	

For more details and examples of different materials and wall sections see *HUD Handbook No. 49406,* "Miniumum Design Standards for Heat Loss Calculations," available from U.S. Dept. of Housing and Urban Development, 451 Seventh Street SW, DC 20910.

Table 1: *U-Values for Typical Wall Sections*

297

Now we are ready to find the daily heat loss. The product $U \times A$ equals the number of Btu's of heat lost per hour for each degree of difference between inside and outside temperatures. If the average temperature inside (t_i) was 55°F., and the average temperature outside (t_o) was 10° on a particular day, the difference ($\Delta t = t_i - t_o$) would be 45° and the total heat loss per hour, on the average, would be

$$H = U \times A \times (t_i - t_o)$$
$$= 132 \times 45$$
$$H = 5,940 \text{ Btu's per hour for this temperature}$$
$$\text{difference or, } 5,940 \text{ Btu's/hour} \times 24 \text{ hours}$$
$$= 142,560 \text{ Btu's per day}$$

Now suppose the average temperature for this day was 35° instead of 10°; the temperature difference would only be 20° ($55 - 35 = 20$), so

$$H = 132 \times 20$$
$$= 2,640 \text{ Btu per hour, or only } 63,400 \text{ Btu}$$
$$\text{per day.}$$

We also have to make an estimate for the heat lost because of infiltration. Depending on how tightly you build and weather-strip, the losses from infiltration can be anywhere from one-tenth to one half the total heat losses.* Let's assume we have done a fairly good job of building and that these losses will be about one-fourth of the total losses, or ·about 1,500 Btu per hour, if the average outside temperature is 10°. Multiply this times 24 hours

---

* If you ventilate, the losses will be much greater. If you are using fans and know how many cubic feet per hour you are exhausting (Q), you can calculate the heat loss from ventilation with this formula:

$$H_v = .018 \times Q \times (t_i - t_o).$$

and add it to the heat losses from conduction: $1,500 \times 24 = 30,600$ Btu/day

$30,600 + 142,000 = 172,000$ Btu/day heat losses

Just to be on the safe side we will add 10 percent to this:

$172,000 + 17,000 = 189,000$ Btu/day total heat losses

Now we can compare this to the amount of solar radiation the greenhouse received (which we calculated in the last chapter). The total gains on a clear day through the 50° slope of this greenhouse are 213,000 Btu, so we have a surplus of 24,000 Btu's.

In this example we assumed that the greenhouse did not use movable nighttime insulation. If movable insulation were used for 14 hours each night, the average U-value for the glazing would be .3 instead of .57, and the overall heat-loss factor would be 85 instead of 132. This means that the greenhouse would lose only 123,000 Btu instead of 189,000 Btu, and that there would be a surplus of 90,000 Btu's. Of course, if you are going to make use of that surplus you must get it into storage; otherwise, the temperature in the greenhouse would be hotter and you would lose more because of the greater temperature difference between inside and outside.

If we were dealing with an attached greenhouse in these calculations, the surpluses would represent the amount of heat that would be available from the greenhouse during the day to heat the house proper. Of course we would also have to alter the area used in the calculations in order to reflect the fact that one wall is attached to the house.

The U-value tells you the rate of heat flow through a wall, measured in Btu's. The U-value is the number of Btu's that will pass through one square foot of the wall in one hour with one degree difference between temperatures on the inside and outside of the wall. If a wall had a U-value of .1, this would mean that one-tenth Btu would pass through one square foot of wall every hour with one degree temperature difference between the inside and outside. But if the air inside was 70° and outside it was 10°F., the temperature difference would be 60. Then $\frac{1}{10} \times 60$ or 60 Btu's would be lost through one square foot of the wall in an hour. Knowing the size of the entire wall, it is easy to go on and calculate how much is lost per hour through the entire surface.

Appendix IV

How Much Energy Gets into Your Greenhouse

Conrad Heeschen

Suppose you have used the tables to determine the slope of the south-facing glazing which will receive the most solar energy when your greenhouse needs it most. With a little calculation you can use the same table to find out approximately how much energy the greenhouse will actually capture on a clear day.

For example, let us assume we are still at 40° north latitude, at the Maxatawny greenhouse, and that we have chosen a 50° slope for the south side. Now we look in the table for the total daily radiation, "surface daily totals," under the column for 50° for the date we are interested in. We will look at January 21, since we want to find out how much energy we can capture in the coldest time of the year. The total amount of solar energy that strikes one square foot of our greenhouse surface on this day is 1,906 Btu's. Now, how much of this energy actually gets into the greenhouse?

Remember that there are losses each time the sun's rays pass through a layer of glazing and that the losses depend on the angle of incidence (see Chapter Two). The angle of incidence changes as the sun crosses the sky, so it is impractical for us to calculate it for each instant. Instead, if we reduce the value of radiation we get from the table by about 16 percent for one layer of glass and 30 percent for two layers of glass, we will get a rough

estimate of what actually passes through the glazing. Losses from clearer materials would be somewhat lower. Even though this is rough, the results are not too far off calculations I made at hourly intervals.

If our greenhouse has two layers of glass about 1,330 Btu's of solar energy will come through one square foot of the south face. Suppose the area of the south face is 160 square feet, not counting the framing (about what a 12-foot-by-16-foot greenhouse might have) a total of 213,000 Btu's will enter the greenhouse on a clear day from the south face.

Now there are several things you can do with this figure. First you should compare it to the total daily heat losses to see whether you are gaining or losing heat on the average over 24 hours of the day. You can then use the weather charts and data in Chapter Seven to find out how many clear days in a row you will have and see if the greenhouse can accumulate enough extra energy during this period to carry it through the expected number of cloudy days. Finally, you can see how many cloudy days this one day's heat will carry you. Refer to Chapter Five for storage efficiencies.

You can also use the hourly radiation figures in the table to calculate the amount of radiation the greenhouse will gain on a partly cloudy day, or if the greenhouse is shaded during part of the day.

Suppose it stays clear until 1:30 P.M. but then overcast sets in, or the sun moves behind some large trees. Add up the figures in the column under the date and slope you have chosen (i.e., January 21 and 50°) for the hours when the sun shines on your greenhouse:

8 A.M.—	81	Btu/square foot/hour
9 A.M.—	182	
10 A.M.—	249	
11 A.M.—	290	
noon —	303	
1 P.M.—	290	(note that 1 P.M. is the same as 11 A.M. since the sun path is symmetrical about noon)

Daily total = 1,395 Btu/square foot on the outside of the glazing

Now make the correction for the glazing losses:

1,395 Btu/square foot × .70 = 976.5 Btu/square foot;

and multiply by the total surface area,

976.5 Btu/square foot × 160 square foot = 564,900 Btu's.

The greenhouse will gain only 564,000 Btu on this day.

If you have a south-facing kneewall that is glazed you can use the tables to find the amount of energy coming into the greenhouse in the same manner as described above. Use the figures in the column headed 90° instead of the other slopes. If the exact slope of your greenhouse does not appear in the tables, you can interpolate between the next angle higher and lower.

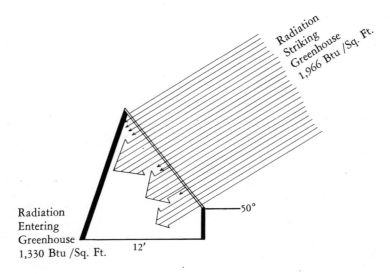

Figure 1: *Computation of greenhouse radiation gains.*

Appendix V

Sun Charts

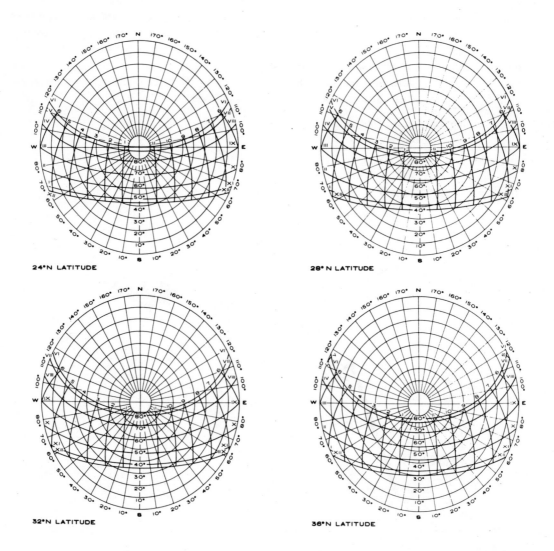

24°N LATITUDE

28°N LATITUDE

32°N LATITUDE

36°N LATITUDE

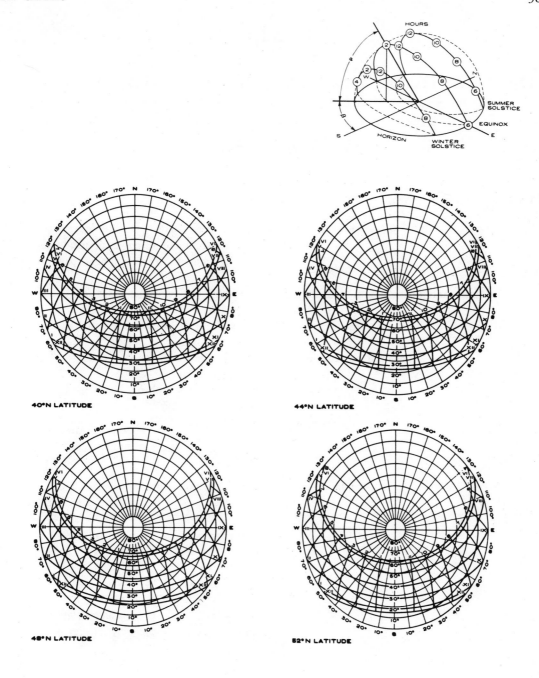

40°N LATITUDE

44°N LATITUDE

48°N LATITUDE

52°N LATITUDE

Appendix VI

Assessment of Commercial Glazing Materials

W. Douglas Davis

Glass:

Solar transmission: Approximately 85% per sheet integrated over the solar spectrum and all angles of incidence. UV cut off < .38 microns; infrared longer than 3.0 microns.

Maximum operating temperature: 500°–550°F. Tempered glass can endure 450°F. differential thermal stress (annealed glass can usually take up to 100°F. differential thermal stress).

Thermal conductance: 1.13 Btu/hour/°F./ft.²

Lifetime: Indefinite if not broken

Weight: ⅛″ 1.63 lbs./ft.²
³⁄₁₆″ 2.51 lbs./ft.² (heavy compared to the plastic
¼″ 3.02 lbs./ft.² cover materials)

Standard sizes: For old-fashioned greenhouses: *   16″ x 18″ & 20″ x 20″
                     18″ x 20″ & 16″ x 24″
storm door size: 34″ x 76″—⅛″ or ³⁄₁₆″
patio door size: 46″ x 76″ & 58″ x 76″—³⁄₁₆″
largest sizes
by thickness: ⅛″ → 34″ x 76″
³⁄₁₆″ → 36″ x 96″
¼″ → 48″ x 120″
standard cases: 34″ x 76″ 1,000 & 1,600 ft.²
(⅛″)

* These four sizes were used a lot in the past for greenhouses.

304

thermopane units: for best price, try to design around the most commonly used 34" x 76" ⅛"-tempered units.

Coefficient of thermal expansion: 4.9×10^{-6} inches/inch/°F. This is much lower than any of the commonly used plastics but still must be accounted for, especially in solar collector fabrication.

Tensile strength: Tempered: 6,400 psi
annealed: 1,600 psi
One-eighth-inch tempered glass will withstand ½-lb. steel ball dropped 10 feet onto a 12" x 12" piece. I have personally observed a 190-lb. man crawl out onto a horizontal frame-mounted 34" x 76" tempered piece of glass and sit in the middle (but he did this very gingerly!)

Note: Annealed glass breaks into razor-sharp shards, tempered shatters into very small rough-edged pieces—*much safer,* when it does break. This is why tempered is required for storm door use.

Refractive index: n = 1.50 (Solar transmittance starts dropping off sharply at 60° angle of incidence.)

Types of glass:

rolled glass   Satisfactory for windows.

float glass   (Floated out on a bath of molten tin!) This glass is of high surface quality and is the most cost-effective glass available for greenhouses and solar-collector covers.

plate glass   This glass is much more expensive than float glass, due to the polishing requirement. Of common glass types, it is of the highest optical quality.

annealed glass   This is your common single- and double-strength window glass which is easily broken upon impact. In manufacture, after the glass is produced, it is reheated enough to soften it, but not so as to deform the product. This process (annealing) relieves strains in the glass which are often present in the glass after it is originally formed.

Watch out for some real bargains in new glass which may have been poorly annealed and would be unusually prone to breakage, often breaking for no apparent reason.

single-strength $\frac{3}{32}''$
double-strength $\frac{1}{8}''$

tempered glass   This glass is treated by a process of reheating and sudden cooling. As a result, the outer surfaces are in a state of compression while the central portion remains in tension, producing a condition which is highly resistant to breakage. Because the central portion remains in tension against the outer compressive force, this glass cannot be cut to a different size after it is tempered. Don't make the mistake of ordering tempered glass and then plan on cutting it into different sizes later.

An additional note on cutting glass: You are much better off (in general) if you can use glass with a factory-cut edge. Poorly scored and cut glass—the type often produced by amateur builders—is prone to breakage due to lessened resistance to thermal stress in the material. The glass often breaks from the edge inward.

Costs: By all means, shop around for your glass. You'll get the best deals if you stick to standard sizes (especially 34″ x 76″ tempered units). Get together with friends building greenhouses and order case lots from the *factory*. I could often get a better price from a smaller shop (in quantity) in Denver than I could from one of the big companies. In Denver, PPG Industries quoted me glass at $.95/ft.² (34″ x 76″ tempered units) while House of Glass could deliver the exact same glass at $.65/ft.² . . . and it was PPG glass! They just didn't have the same overhead, and both were buying from the PPG factory in Dallas. The same glass at the factory in Dallas was $.45/ft.² plus shipping.

The best price I've ever found on 34″ x 76″ insulated Thermopane units was from a place in Denver called Thermoglas.

10 or more	$28.95 each
25 or more	$26.95 each
100 or more	$24.40 each

If you decide to fabricate your own thermopane units, you can get a dessicant-like silica gel to place between the two panes of glass to prevent condensation. This is one trick the thermopane manufacturers use—and they will often try to keep this a secret!

Note: *Natural gas* is the principal fuel used in the manufacture of glass.

Suppliers: Major producers in the United States include:
American-Saint Gobain, Kingsport, Tennessee (ACG)
PPG (Pittsburgh Plate Glass), Pittsburgh, Pennsylvania
Libbey-Owens Ford Glass (LOF), Toledo, Ohio

Building Codes: Check with your building inspector about using overhead glass. Local codes may require tempered or wire glass. The builder should be sure and state to the building official that the overhead glass is for a greenhouse. There are often different rules for these than residences. Similarly, the owner-builder should note that the attached greenhouse should not have to conform to all regulations for additions to homes. I don't think one should use untempered glass overhead in any spaces people will occupy, if there is any chance of it being broken.

Glass Energetics:

Regular Glass   *Tempered Glass*
59.5–100 kwh/m   117–178 kwh/m

$$\frac{59.5 \text{ kwh}}{\text{m}^2} \times \frac{1 \text{ m}^2}{10.7639 \text{ ft.}^2} \times \frac{3,410.08 \text{ Btu}}{1 \text{ kwh}} = 18,850 \text{ Btu/ft.}^2 \text{ glass}$$

(to get Btu/ft. from kwh/m, multiple by 316.807)

In Btu/ft.²:
18,950–31,681 Btu/ft²   37,066.4–56,392 Btu./ft.²

Taking the liberal figures and multiplying by two layers of glass for thermopanes we get:

31,681 × 2   56,392 × 2
= 63,362 Btu/ft.²   = 112,784 Btu/ft.²

                                    manufacturing cost
                                    (energy investment)

Estimated manufacturing energy investment data supplied by Viracon Glass Corporation.

Steve Baer from Zomeworks in Albuquerque (35° north latitude) reports that given the following conditions:

   1,200 Btu/ft. day incident solar radiation—a conservative figure for seven winter months. This
   figure is greater at high latitudes—also much higher when greater reflection is taken into account.

40 degree days/day—average daily temperature of 25°F.
double-glazing 75% transmission
the net gains through a south window would be as follows:

      no insulation at night   **1″ foam polystyrene R 4—4.5
                                                           beadboard night insulation**

             420 Btu/day   580 Btu/day

then: $\dfrac{112,784 \text{ Btu/ft.}}{420 \text{ Btu/day}}$ —for tempered glass $\dfrac{63,362 \text{ Btu/ft.}}{580 \text{ Btu/day}}$ —using regular glass
                                     —no night insulation   —night insulation

   =   268 days   109 days

(number of clear days required at the *above given conditions* to recapture energy investment in the
glass.)

Clear Polycarbonate Sheet

Trade Name: *Lexan®*

Percentage of solar transmission/sheet	$\frac{1}{8}$"	81–89%
	$\frac{3}{16}$"	78%
	$\frac{1}{4}$"	74%

Maximum operating temperature   250°–270°F. (121°–132°C.)

U-value   1.10 for thick material

Length of life   Probably good for plastics in general

Weight   (lbs./ft.²) $\frac{1}{8}$" = .78; $\frac{3}{16}$" = 1.17; $\frac{1}{4}$" = 1.56

Maximum recommended sizes	$\frac{1}{8}$"	24" short dimension
	$\frac{3}{16}$"	36" short dimension
	$\frac{1}{4}$"	48" short dimension

Coefficient of expansion 37.5×10^{-6} in./in./°F.
Thin sheets (4–12 mil) buckle.

Tensile strength   9,500 psi

Costs   Expensive
$\frac{1}{8}$"–$\frac{1}{4}$"   \$2.50–3.00/ft.²—in glass-like thicknesses

Suppliers   Rohm & Haas

Acrylic (Methyl Methacrylate)

Trade Name: *Plexiglas®*

Advantages   Doesn't break on impact or as easily as glass

Disadvantages   Holds onto dust and dirt
scratches when you try to clean it—surface erosion
buckles and cracks if improperly installed
lots of expansion and contraction
expensive

Percent of solar transmission/sheet	⅛″	89%–92%
	³⁄₁₆″	87%
	¼″	85%

Maximum operating temperature   180°–190°F. (82°–93°C.)

U-value   1.09 for .187″ thick. Twenty-one percent better thermal insulation than glass.

Length of life   Good UV stability (resists polymerization). Ten to twenty years but percentage of solar transmission drops drastically with time.

Weight   (lbs./ft.²) ⅛″ = .75; ³⁄₁₆″ = 1.10; ¼″ = 1.50

Coefficient of expansion 41.0×10^{-6} in./in./°F.

Maximum recommended sizes   Same as polycarbonate

Tensile strength   10,500 psi

Costs	⅛″	$1–1.50 ft.²
	³⁄₁₆″	$1.25–2.00 ft.²
	¼″	$1.50–2.50 ft.²

Suppliers   Rohm & Haas. One of world's largest plexiglass producers. They now have a "Rohaglass" plexiglass and polycarbonate double-skin sheet for greenhouses.

Fiberglass Reinforced Plastics

Trade Name: *Filon* & *Lascolite*
(corrugated & flat)

Percentage of solar transmission   86% Tedlar clad
76–78% Filoplated

Maximum operating temperature   Similar to Kalwall®

Lifetime	10–20 years. Use "Tedlar" coated or "Filoplated" (acrylic modified gel coat) for solar application. Standard Filon panels are not recommended for long-term efficiency due to lack of protective surface.
Weight	Corrugated 4–5 oz./ft.^{2} Flat 8–10 oz./ft.^{2}
U-value	.95
Standard sizes	Tedlar, corrugated 51⅜" x 8', 10', 12', 16' Filoplated, corrugated 51⅜" x 8', 10', 12' Flat panels 4' x 8', 12' 36" x 100' rolls
Coefficient of expansion	23 × 10^{-6} in./in./°F.
Tensile strength	10,600 psi

Costs	Tedlar clad
	    $ .55–$ .75/ft.^{2} depending on quantity
	Filoplated
	    $ .44–$ .69/ft.^{2} ″ ″ ″
	4 oz. in rolls
	    $ .66–$ .86/ft.^{2} ″ ″ ″
	8 oz. in rolls
	    $1.00–$1.28/ft.^{2} ″ ″ ″
	10 oz. in rolls
	    $1.29–$1.62/ft.^{2} ″ ″ ″

Suppliers	Vistron Corporation Filon Division 2333 South Van Ness Avenue Hawthorne, CA 90250 Lascolite 3255 East Mira Loma Avenue Anaheim, CA 92806 Lasco Industries 8015 Dixon Drive Florence, KY 41042 Get manufacturers' installation instructions and follow them.

Fiberglass Reinforced Plastics

Trade Name: *Kalwall*®
"Regular" and Seven "Premium" Grades

Percentage of solar transmission	Regular 85–90% Premium 85–88%
Operating temperatures	Kalwall people recommend that collectors using their cover material be vented if stagnation occurs. "Regular" performance is poor at 300°F. "Premium" is better.
U-value	36% better than glass they (manufacturers) claim. (36% less conductance)
Life expectancy	"Regular"—7 years "Premium"—20 years Note—200°F. exposure will produce 10% loss in transmission. Also, suspected significant transmission decrease with time from UV.
Weight	.025" thick .2 lbs./ft.² .040" thick .3 lbs./ft.²
Standard sizes	4' x 10', 4' x 25', 4' x 50', 5' x 50'
Coefficient of expansion	20×10^{-6} in./in./°F. (both grades)
Tensile strength	17,000 psi
Cost	$ .28—$ .46/ft., depending on quantity and grade, plus shipping. Approximately one-month delivery from East Coast to Colorado.
Supplier	Solar Components Division Kalwall Corporation 88 Pine Street P.O. Box 237 Manchester, NH 03103

Write for their catalog (free) and $2.00 for design manual.

Mylar Film Type W Weatherable
Polyester film (1–5 mil)

Solar transmission/sheet	85%
Maximum operating temperature	Rate of degradation double for each 18°F. rise in temperature.
U-value	1.05 Btu/hr./°F./ft.²
Lifetime	4 years (Florida exposure tests)
Weight	Very light
Sizes	Rolls 48″ wide; 12′ long on up
Coefficient of expansion	15×10^{-6} in./in./°F.
Tensile strength	24,000 psi
Costs	$ .08/ft.² and up
Suppliers	DuPont (manufacturer)
Refractive index	1.39
Note	Type W is yellowish due to UV absorbers used to improve stability. Mylar is a polyester film made by DuPont, Inc.
	This material is structurally durable and has a relatively low coefficient of thermal expansion (for a plastic). It is very thin: .0003–.014 inch thick.
	Mylar is almost impossible to "heat-seal", use adhesives.

Solar Polyvinyl Fluoride Film

Trade Name: *Tedlar*®
Type 400 BG 20 TR

Solar transmission	92–94% (4-mil)
Maximum operating temperatures	Service life from −100°F. to 225°F. with short term peaking up to 400°F.
U-value	1.16
Length of life	50% retained tensile strength after 10 years of testing; retains 95% transmission in 5 years.
Weight	.028 lbs./sq. ft.
Sizes	Rolls 26″ & 50″ wide Previously available only in large rolls costing several hundred dollars each. Now available in 50′ & 100′ rolls, 26″ & 50″ width.
Coefficient of expansion	24×10^{-6} in./in./°F.
Tensile strength	13,000 lbs./sq. in. (psi) (4-mil)
Cost	$ .15/ft.²
Suppliers	Du Pont
Note	Tedlar film can be heat-sealed, shrink-wrapped or bonded by adhesives.

Polyethylene—4-mil

Lifetime	¼ year—unstabilized type, Florida tests
Refractive index	1.5
Tensile strength	2,000 psi

Thermal conductivity	1.6 Btu/hr./ft.^{2}/°F.
Thermal coefficient of expansion	300×10^{-6} in./in./°F. 61 times as much as glass.
Note	Polyethylene is especially permeable to CO_2—69 times as much as Tedlar®—perhaps a positive consideration for greenhouses.

Appendix VII

Metric Conversion Chart

WHEN YOU KNOW	MULTIPLY BY	TO FIND
	length	
inches	2.54	centimeters (cm)
feet	30	centimeters (cm)
yards	.9	meters (m)
	area	
square inches	6.5	square centimeters
square feet	.09	square meters
square yards	.8	square meters
	weight	
ounces	28	grams (g)
pounds	.45	kilograms (kg)
	volume	
fluid ounces	30	milliliters (ml)
pints	.47	milliliters (ml)
quarts	.95	liters (l)
gallons	3.8	liters (l)
cubic feet	.03	cubic meters
cubic yards	.76	cubic meters

Appendix VIII
Selected Greenhouse Vegetable Varieties:
Days from Sowing or Transplanting to Maturity Outdoors

Crop Types—Varieties [Days to maturity from sowing (S) or transplant (T)]

Bush Beans (S)
Bushgreen—Tenderpod (50), Tenderette (55), Tendergreen (56), Royalty (51), Limelight (38).
Lima, Broad—Henderson Bush (65), Express (78), Thaxter (74).
Ornamentals—Royalty (51), Burgess Long Bean (70).
Pole—Kentucky Wonder (65), Violet Podded Stringless (63), Romano (70), Blue Lake (60).

Beets (S)
Rugby Queen (55), Detroit Dark Red (58), Burpee's Golden (55), Greentop Bunching (58), Golden Beet (60), Snow White (62).

Carrots (S)
Tiny Sweet (60), Short-n-Sweet (68), Nantes Coreless (68), Juwarot (70), Sucram (70), Little Finger (65), Gold Nugget (71).

Cole Crops (T)
Broccoli—Southern Comet (55), Green Comet (40), Premium Crop F1 (60), White Sprouting (continuous).
Brussel Sprouts—Jade Cross (90), Lindo (80), Focus F1 (95).
Cabbage—Dwarf Morden (60), Savory Ace (78), Green Express F1 (60), Ruby Ball F1 (65), Hispi (60), Starlet (63).
Chinese Cabbage—Burpee Hybrid (75), Michihi (80).
Cauliflower—Super Snowball (60), Snowball 34 (65), Snowcrown (53), Snow King (50), Abuntia (46).
Collards—Vates (85).
Kale—Vates strains (Dwarf Blue Curled or Dwarf Blue Scotch) (55).
Kohlrabi—Primaver White (50), Early White Vienna (55).

Cucumbers (S)
Patio Pik (60), Pot Luck (53), Burpless Green King (58), Burpless Tasty Green (58), Topsy (67), Chinese Long Green (65), Sweet Slice (62), Park's Comanche (50), Burgess Green Ice (48), Cherokee (60), Zeppelin (67).

Eggplants (T)
Morden Midget (65), Black Beauty (73), Classic (76), Burpee Hybrid (70).

Lettuce (S)
Buttercrunch (60), Salad Bowl (45), Oakleaf (42), Ruby (47), Summer Bibb (65), Celtuce (42), Tom Thumb (62), Black Seeded Simpson (45), Slobolt (45), Anita (48).

Onions (S)
Plants—Early Harvest (90), Eclipse (100).
Bunching (Scallions)—White Sweet Spanish (100).
Seed—Early Harvest (90), Autumn Spice (98), White Lisbon (60), Rose Lisbon (63).

Sets—Ebenezer (90), Early Yellow Globe (90), Sturon (120), Stuttgart (110).

Peas (S)
Mighty Midget (60), Dwarf White Sugar (60), Little Marvel (63), Dwarf DeGrace (60), Oregon Sugar Pod (68), Hurst Green Shaft (70).

Peppers (T)
California Wonder (75), Burpee's Fordhook (65), Sweet Canape (60), Gold Topaz (70), Slim Pim (65), Tompa (tomato-pepper) (70), Ace (68), Sweet Banana (72), Bell Boy (70), Park Wonder F1 (65).
Hot—Hungarian Yellow Wax (70), Long Red Cayenne (72), Hot Portugal (75), Large Cherry (69).

Radishes (S)
Spring and Summer—Half Long (24), Yellow Gold (30), Champion (24), Cherry Bell, (24), Icicle (27), Red Prince (25).
Fall and Winter—White Chinese (50), China Rose (52), Summer Cross (45).

Spinach (S)
Bloomsdale (48), Malabar (70), Longstanding Bloomsdale (42), Monnopa (45), Perpetual (50), New Zealand (70).

Swiss Chard (S)
Ruby or Rhubarb (60), Lucullus (60), Fordhook Giant (60), Vintage Green (60).

Tomatoes (T)
Miniature—Tiny Tim (55), Patio (70), Pixie Hybrid (52), Small Fry (65), Sugar Lump (65), Sweet 100 (57), Red Pear (65), Yellow Pear (65), Sub-Arctic Cherry (43), Tumblin Tom (65), Toy Boy (55).
Standard—Big Boy (78), Outdoor Girl (58), Moneymaker (75), Gardener's Delight (65), Supercross (72), Better Boy (70), Cura (70), Early Girl (45), Superfantastic (70), Beefmaster (80), Rutgers (85).

Strawberries (T)
Seasonal—Sparkle (late), Guardian (mid), Earlibelle (early), Pocahontas (early), Apollo (mid), Surecrop (mid), Tioga (mid), Sequoia (early), Earlidawn (early).
Everbearing—Ozark Beauty, Ogallala, Quinault, Fort Laramie.
From Seed—Alexandria (75), Alpine Yellow (80), Tutti Fruiti.

Herbs (S)
Annuals—Anise (75); Basil: Sweet (85), Darl Opal (85), Cress (25-45), Pepper Grass (70), Watercress (70), Summer Savory (60).
Biennials—Caraway (70), Parsley: Perfection (75), Extra Triple Curled (75).
Perennials—Catnip (80), Chives (80), Fennel (90), Horehound (75), Lavender (60), Sweet Marjoram (70), Rosemary (85), Sage (75), Thyme (85), Winter Savory (70).

Bibliography

Abraham, George (Doc) and Katy. *Organic Gardening Under Glass*. Emmaus, PA: Rodale Press, 1975.

————. *Raise Vegetables without a Garden*. Barrington, IL: *Countryside Books,* A. B. Morse, 1974.

Alcott, M. "The Bretons Have a Way with Tunnel-Growing," *Community Grower* 3837 (1969):49-50.

Allen, L. H. Jr., "Shade-Cloth Microclimate of Soybeans," *Agronomy Journal* 61 (no. 1)(1975):175-81.

Allington, P. "Construction of Plastic Tunnels as Developed at the Lea Valley E.H.S.," *Community Grower* 3844 (1969):180-89, 196.

Anderson, Bruce with Riordan, Michael. *The Solar Home Book*. Harrisville, NH: Cheshire Books, 1976.

Anon. "Foam Blanket Gives Strawberries 21° Safety Layer," *Community Grower* 71 (no. 19) (1969):1254.

Anon. "Lettuces Thrive under Plastic Tunnels," *Farmers Weekly* 71 (no. 10)(1969):49.

Anon. "Plastic Covers Speed Crops," *Western Grower and Shipper* 46 (no. 2)(1975):6-7.

Arthurs, Kathryn L., ed. *Greenhouse Gardening*. Menlo Park, CA: Lane Publishing Co., 1976.

ASHRAE Handbook of Fundamentals. New York: American Society of Heating, Refrigerating and Air Conditioning Engineers, 1972.

Baldwin, John L. *Climates of the United States*. Washington: United States Department of Commerce, 1973.

Ball, George J. and staff. *The Ball Red Book*. Chicago: George Ball, 1976.

Bartholic, J. F. "Thin Layer Foam for Plant Freeze Protection." *Proceedings of the 85th Annual Meeting of the Florida State Horticultural Society,* 1973, p. 299-302.

Becker, C. G.; Boyd, J. H. *Solar Radiation Availability on Surfaces in United States as Affected by Season, Orientation, Latitude, Altitude and Cloudiness*. Albuquerque, NM: Technology Applications Center, University of New Mexico, 1957.

Bennet, O. L.; Henderlay, P. R.; and Mathias, E. L. "Effects of North- and South-facing Slopes on Yield of Kentucky Bluegrass with Variable Rate and Time of Nitrogen Application," *Agronomy Journal* 64 (1972):630-35.

Brown, K. W.; and Rosenbur, N. J. "Shelter Effects on Microclimate, Growth and Water Use by Irrigated Sugar Beets in the Great Plains." *Agricultural Meteorology* 9 (1972):241-63.

Cook, Charles, ed. *Vegetable Gardening Know-How*. Charlotte, VT: Garden Way, 1976.

Crawford, Todd V. "Protection from the Cold—Frost Protection with Wind Machines and Heaters," *Meteorological Monographs* 6 (no. 20) (1965):81-87.

Dalrymple, Dana G. *Controlled Environment Agriculture: A Global Review of Greenhouse Food Production.* Washington, DC: Economic Research Service, United States Department of Agriculture, 1973.

DeKorne, J. and E. *The Survival Greenhouse—an Eco-System Approach to Home Food Production.* El Rito, NM: Walden Foundation, 1975.

Deryckx, Woody and Becky. *Two Solar Aquaculture-Greenhouse Systems for Western Washington: A Preliminary Report.* Seattle, WA: Tilth and Ecotope Group, Southfork Press, 1976.

Deutsch, Ronald M. *The Family Guide to Better Food and Better Health.* New York: Meredith, 1973.

Doty, Walter L., ed. *All About Vegetables.* San Francisco: Chevron Chemical Co., 1973.

Eccli, Eugene, ed. *Low-Cost, Energy-Efficient Shelter for the Owner and Builder.* Emmaus, PA: Rodale Press, 1975.

Eldin, F. "Radiation Transmission through Glazings." Presented at Solar Energy Now Conference, 1974, at Phoenix, Arizona.

Fell, Derek. *How to Plant a Vegetable Garden.* Barrington, IL: Countryside Books, A. B. Morse, 1974.

Fisher, R., and Yanda, B. *The Food and Heat Producing Solar Greenhouse.* Santa Fe, NM: John Muir Publications, 1976.

Fisher, Stephen S. *Climatic Atlas of the United States.* Cambridge, MA: Harvard University Press, 1954.

Flanagan, Ted. *Growing Food and Flowers in Containers.* Charlotte, VT: Garden Way, 1973.

Geiger, R. *The Climate Near the Ground.* Cambridge, MA: Harvard University Press, 1965.

Golueke, Clarence G. *Composting: A Study of the Process and Its Principles.* Emmaus, PA: Rodale Press, 1972.

Goold-Adams, Deenagh. *The Cool Greenhouse Today.* London: Faber and Faber, 1969.

Gringorten, Irving I. "A Stochastic Model of the Frequency and Duration of Weather Events." *Journal of Applied Meteorology* 5 (1966):606-24.

Guide to Standard Weather Summaries and Climatic Services. Asheville, NC: Naval Weather Service Environmental Detachment, 1975.

Hix, John. *The Glass House.* London: Phaidon, 1974.

Jensen, Merle, ed. *Proceedings of the Solar Energy Food and Fuel Workshop (April 1976).* Environmental Research Laboratory, University of Arizona, Tucson International Airport, Arizona, 1976.

Johnson, T. E.; Wellesley-Miller, S.; Chahroudi, D.; Brooks, J.; Wagner, S.; Heeschen, C.; and Bryan, D. "Exploring Space Conditioning with Variable Membranes." Report to National Science Foundation (NSF GRANT GI 41306), 1975.

Kobayashi, T., and Sargent, S. L. "A Survey of Breakage-Resistant Materials for Flat-Plate Solar Collector Covers." Presented at the International Solar Energy Society meeting, Denver, Colorado, 1974.

Kramer, Jack. *The Underground Gardener.* New York: Thomas Y. Crowell, 1976.

Krause, W. "New Crops Show Promise in Plastic Tunnels." *Community Grower* 72 (no. 10) (1969): 49.

Lawand, T. A. "Solar Energy Greenhouses: Operating Experiences." Ste. Anne de Bellevue, Quebec: Brace Research Institute, 1976.

Lekie, J.; Masters, G.; Whitehouse, H.; Young, L. *Other Homes and Garbage Designs for Self-Sufficient Living.* San Francisco: Sierra Club, 1975.

Lindlahr, Victor. *You Are What You Eat.* Van Nuys, CA: Newcastle, 1971.

Mastalerz, John W., ed. *Bedding Plants—A Penn State Manual.* University Park, PA: Penn State University Press, 1976.

Minimum Cost Housing Group. *Rooftop Wastelands.* McGill University, Quebec, 1976.

National Climatic Center. *Climatic Atlas of the United States.* Asheville, NC: National Climatic Center, 1969.

Newcomb, Duane. *The Postage Stamp Garden Book: How to Grow All the Food You Can Eat in Very Little Space.* Los Angeles: J. P. Tarcher, 1975.

Parsons, R. A., ed. *Hobby Greenhouses and Other Gardening Structures.* Northeast Regional Agricultural Engineering Service, Ithaca, NY: Cornell University Press, 1976.

Powell, B. H. "Steaming Conditions in Polyethylene Tunnels Ideal for Celery," *Community Grower,* 79 (no. 8) (1973):465.

————. "Tunnel-Grown Peppers Can Match the Exports, but Weather Governs Tomato Returns," *Community Grower,* 4026 (1973):437.

Rodale, Robert. *Basic Book of Organic Gardening.* New York: Ballantine, 1971.

Seeman, J. *Climate Under Glass,* Technical Note 131, Geneva: World Meteorological Organization, 1974.

Siminovich, D. "Foam for the Frost Protection of Crops. Ottawa, Ontario: Department of Agriculture, 1972.

Skelsey, Alice. *Farming in a Flowerpot.* New York: Workman, 1975.

Taylor, Kathryn S., Gregg, Edith W. *Winter Flowers in Greenhouse and Sun-Heated Pit.* New York: Charles Scribner's Sons, 1969.

Winsor, P. A. "Black Polyethylene Tunnels Best for Forcing Timperley Early (Rhubarb)," *Community Grower,* 79 (no. 12) (1973): 724-26.

————. Black Tunnels for Early Rhubarb Show Good Returns," *Community Grower,* 4025 (1973): 405-7.

Yanda, W. F. and Susan. *An Attached Solar Greenhouse.* Santa Fe, New Mexico: The Lightning Tree, 1976.

Contributors

Jim DeKorne, author of *Survival Greenhouse,* has been working with greenhouses since 1973 with a primary interest in producing the maximum amount of food in the minimum amount of space. Convinced that there are ways of getting a tremendous amount of yield in a small area, DeKorne has done extensive experiments with organic hydroponic greenhouses using various low-tech methods of adding CO_2 to fertilize plants. In addition, he runs a workshop using his two wind generators to operate the power tools. In the self-reliant spirit of Thoreau, DeKorne and his family have set up "The Walden Foundation," promoting ecologically sound, yet comfortable, alternate sources of energy for everyday use.

Conrad Heeschen studied Advance Studies in Architecture on the graduate level at M.I.T. where he specialized in Energy Utilization and Conservation. He has been involved in research on passive utilization of solar energy for several years, and has designed and built an award-winning solar water heater. Heeschen is interested in developing regional self-sufficiency in food and energy production in the New England area and is currently constructing a large solar greenhouse on his farm in Maine.

David J. MacKinnon's background is in physics and meteorology which he trained for on both the undergraduate and graduate levels. For the past three years he has been deeply involved in solar energy projects at the Museum of Northern Arizona in Flagstaff. MacKinnon's efforts have been in both theory and practice on solar greenhouses at the Museum and for Rodale Press in Pennsylvania. Currently MacKinnon continues to work on R & D related projects for both the Flagstaff greenhouse and Rodale's greenhouse located in Maxatawny, Pennsylvania.

Leandre Poisson is an inventor and materials expert in Harrisville, New Hampshire. He has been involved with an organization named Solar Survival which encourages solar-living concepts on a small-scale industry basis which are indigenous to particular regions in the country. Poisson has several innovative greenhouses of his own design at his home in Harrisville.

Herb Wade has a history of involvement with solar-energy projects as both a consultant and an administrator. While working as a part-time faculty member at Northern Arizona University, he lectures in Mechanical Engineering with special course emphasis on direct-energy conversion and solar energy. He is also Associate Director of the Arizona Solar Energy Research Commission responsible for technical matters on the solar commercialization plan for the state of Arizona. Wade served as past chairman for the Arizona Solar Energy Association.

John White has been a Professor of Horticulture for the past 19 years at Penn State University where he also received his Ph.D. White works closely with Dr. Robert Aldrich in the Department of Agricultural Engineering on research dealing with energy conservation and solar heat for greenhouses. Although White's primary interest is with flower crops recently he has been working with container vegetables studying the most advantageous methods for plant production.

Index

Index